TWENTY-FIRST-CENTURY
FEMINISMS
IN CHILDREN'S
AND ADOLESCENT
LITERATURE

Children's Literature Association Series

# TWENTY-FIRST-CENTURY FEMINISMS IN CHILDREN'S AND ADOLESCENT LITERATURE

## ROBERTA SEELINGER TRITES

University Press of Mississippi / Jackson

*Children's Literature Association Series*

www.upress.state.ms.us

The University Press of Mississippi is a member of the
Association of American University Presses.

Cover art by Katharine Anne Seelinger, age 19

Portions of Chapter 1 also appear in *Tulsa Studies in Women's Literature*;
portions of Chapter 3 appear in *Children's Literature Association Quarterly*.

First printing 2018
∞

Library of Congress Cataloging-in-Publication Data

Names: Trites, Roberta Seelinger, 1962– author.
Title: Twenty-first-century feminisms in children's and adolescent literature / Roberta
Seelinger Trites.
Description: Jackson : University Press of Mississippi, [2018] | Series: Children's literature
association series | Includes bibliographical references and index. |
Identifiers: LCCN 2017032086 (print) | LCCN 2017042739 (ebook) | ISBN 9781496813817
(epub single) | ISBN 9781496813824 (epub institutional) | ISBN 9781496813831 (pdf single) |
ISBN 9781496813848 (pdf institutional) | ISBN 9781496813800 (hardback)
Subjects: LCSH: Children's stories, American—History and criticism. | Young adult fiction,
American—History and criticism. | Feminism and literature. | Feminism in literature. |
Feminists in literature. | Girls in literature. | Sex role in literature. | BISAC: LITERARY
CRITICISM / Children's Literature. | SOCIAL SCIENCE / Feminism & Feminist Theory. |
SOCIAL SCIENCE / Children's Studies.
Classification: LCC PS374.C454 (ebook) | LCC PS374.C454 T75 2018 (print) | DDC
813/.6099282—dc23
LC record available at https://lccn.loc.gov/2017032086

British Library Cataloging-in-Publication Data available

*I dedicate this book to my children—*
*George, John, and Katie—*
*with gratitude that they've grown up to be*
*the feminists I always hoped they'd be.*

# CONTENTS

# ACKNOWLEDGMENTS

I am fortunate to belong to various communities of academics who have shaped my vision and supported my scholarship. At Illinois State University, Mary Jeanette Moran influenced me to consider a more careful study of feminist ethics of care, while Chris Breu introduced me to material feminism. I am also grateful to the many members of ISU's Department of English who have made me the feminist I am today: Lee Brasseur, Susan Burt, Karen Coats, Ricardo Cortez Cruz, Kass Fleisher, Sarah Hochstetler, Cynthia Huff, Tim Hunt, Hilary Justice, Susan Kalter, Susan Kim, Robert McLaughlin, Sally Parry, Amy Robillard, K. Aaron Smith, and Jan Susina. Several of our graduate students have been instrumental in helping me develop the ideas in this project, most notably Tharini Viswanath, who fine-tooth combed the manuscript, and members of various graduate seminars, including Jenn Coletta, Lauren Gray, Karly Grice, Shannon Harman, Amy Hicks, Wesley Jacques, Agathe Lancrenon, Katy Lewis, Rebecca Lorenzo, Meghann Meeusen, Niall Nance-Carroll, Beth Pearce, Eric Pitman, Scott Pyrz, Shelby Ragan, Erika Romero, Katy Stein, Danielle Sutton, Britni Williams, Elizabeth Williams, and Emily Woster.

The larger community of children's literature scholars in the Children's Literature Association and IRSCL has also given me more inspiration and encouragement than I could ever have hoped for. Margaret Mackey and Mark West have been consistently enthusiastic about this project, and Jackie Horne's insightful commentary has also proven to be enormously helpful. Throughout my career, I have been fortunate to learn from such scholars in these two organizations as Michelle Ann Abate, Hari Adhikari, Marina Balina, Linda Benson, Mike Cadden, Joseph W. Campbell, Ramona Caponegro, Kate Capshaw, Joel Chaston, Beverly Lyon Clark, Amanda Cockrell, Paula Connelly, Sean P. Connors, Sara K. Day, Gregory Eiselein, Liz Gillhouse, Stacy Greathouse, Melody Green, Melanie Goss, Libby Gruner, Marah Gubar, Betsy Hearne, Martha Hixon, Peter Hunt, Billie Jarvis-Freeman, Judith John, Vanessa Joosen, Kara Keeling, Adrienne Kertzer, Kenneth Kidd, Jon Klassen, Lydia Kokkola, Don Latham, Sue Larkin, Greta Little, Kerry Mallan, Beth Marshall, Michelle H. Martin, Muhammad Masud, Jill P. May, Chris McGee, Rose Miller, Jennie Miskec, Mpale Mwansasu-Silkiluwasha,

Joel Myerson, Phil Nel, Maria Nikolajeva, Marilynn Olson, Mia Österlund, Amy Pattee, Lissa Paul, Julie Pfeiffer, Anne K. Phillips, Scott Pollard, Julie Pond, Catherine Ross-Stroud, Susan L. Stewart, Jane Rosen, Teya Rosenberg, Joe Sutliff Sanders, Daniel Shealy, Kate Slater, Melissa Sara Smith, Jackie Stallcup, John Stephens, Lee Talley, Gwen Athene Tarbox, Eric Tribunella, Lynne Vallone, Abbie Ventura, Annette Wannamaker, Jean Webb, Karin Westman, Naomi Wood, and Yoshida Junko. Many of these people have influenced my thinking for more than twenty-five years, so I am grateful to have so many long-term colleagues who are also friends; I am also grateful to the scholars too numerous to name who have taught me at conferences and with their articles.

I am indebted to the many friends in the College of Business who have saved my sanity with kindness and laughter, including Dean Ajay Samant, Terry Noel, Nancy Kerns, Zarah Fatah, the Leadership Team, all the members of MQM, and the generous staff of the COB.

The staff at the University Press of Mississippi has been helpful, efficient, knowledgeable, and—most important to me—*kind*. ChLA is fortunate to be in partnership with them.

Daily doses of friendship have come from people like Pamela Riney-Kehrberg, Susan Burt, Susan L. Stewart, the Witzig family, and Norma Huber. Regular music therapy has been graciously provided by friends like Sally, Bob, Rick, and Djim.

My family, however, deserves a special commendation here. I began writing my first book on feminism, *Waking Sleeping Beauty*, when I was pregnant with my first child, who was born in 1993. His brother followed in 1995, and *Waking Sleeping Beauty*—along with my third child—both arrived almost simultaneously in the spring of 1997. I feel as though I have been revising that book to craft this book for the intervening years, all the while watching these three young people *becoming* feminist adults who make me infinitely proud. And finally, my heart ever belongs to George Major, who is the most supportive spouse, parent, colleague, and friend imaginable and who makes every day a better one for me.

# INTRODUCTION

It has been twenty years since I published *Waking Sleeping Beauty: Feminist Voices in Children's Novels* in 1997. When I told an alumnus of Illinois State University's PhD program that I was writing a companion volume to that book, he joked that I should give it a title like "Twenty-First-Century Feminisms: What the Hell Happened?" His wry comment was an astute observation about the backlash that Feminist Studies has faced in the first part of the twenty-first century. I was hired to be the feminist who "shook things up" in the children's literature program at Illinois State University in 1991, but I never dreamed that in 2017, I would still need to stave off attacks from defensive students about the "feminist agenda." I probably would have despaired had I known that I would still have female students who claim they have never been discriminated against, even though earlier in the semester they have railed about the double-standards their parents set in giving their brothers more freedom and spending money than they had. I never suspected that I would have to face rooms full of students who believe that all feminists are man-haters who "just want to be men," as one of my students put it. During my lectures about feminism, I have spent an inordinate amount of time on trivial issues, such as reassuring my students that no one wants to take away their bras or their razors or their make-up—even though witnessing how the media has reduced feminism to a matter of "policing how people look" should be a red flag to students.

As a corrective, I give my students a true-false quiz, in which I ask ten questions along the lines of "I believe all people should be treated equally under the law" and "I believe some women are smarter than some men and some men are smarter than some women." All ten statements are sensible assertions that most people agree with. Students are shocked—and sometimes angered—when I tell them that if they agreed with six or more of these questions, they have feminist sympathies, and if they agreed to ten, they *are* feminists. Many students don't like being called feminists because of the media distortions they attach to that label. Students, however, sometimes begin to recover from their discomfort when I give them my definition of feminism: feminism is the belief that all people should have equal rights under the law, regardless of race, gender, orientation, religion, ability, social class, ethnicity, or any other factor. It helps considerably that at the August 2014 Video Music Awards, Beyoncé called a feminist "the person who believes in the social, political, and economic equality of the sexes," and in September 2014, Emma Watson—who played Hermione in the Harry Potter movies—spoke to the United Nations, saying, "Feminism, by definition, is the belief that men and women should have equal rights and opportunities." When I show these video clips to my students, they feel reassured that maybe feminism isn't entirely frightening, if both Beyoncé and Hermione self-identify as feminists.

Throughout my career, I have emphasized the positive aspects of feminism, particularly in terms of those concepts that empower girls to have equal rights and opportunities—and voices, choices, and communities that are equal to those of the male characters in literature for the young. Certainly, those values continue to shape this book: I hope to show how authors in the twenty-first century are employing various forms of feminism to break down binaries in complex and creative ways that empower girls regardless of whether they identify with the gender they were assigned at birth. Most of this book thus focuses on positive forms of empowerment. Nevertheless, because of the well-documented backlash against feminism identified by Susan Faludi, there are times that I will demonstrate how a novel's failure to question sexist assumptions weakens its potential as a feminist novel. Although there are some who would disagree with me, I think it is neither strident nor toxic to identify injustice, especially when that injustice is leveled against people who are not yet fully enfranchised because of their age.

## A BRIEF REVIEW OF THE LITERATURE

The earliest feminist critics of children's and adolescent literature in the 1970s and 1980s were influenced by important second-wave feminist theorists, such as Elaine Showalter, Sandra Gilbert and Susan Gubar, and Carolyn Heilbrun. For example, Mary Cadogan and Patricia Craig's *You're a Brick, Angela! The Girls Story from 1839–1975* identified strong girls at work in British children's novels in the tradition in which Showalter and Heilbrun were working. Children's literary critic Anita Moss was another early voice to urge the field towards greater awareness of feminism, as was Perry Nodelman. Mitzi Myers called attention to the powerful roles played by women in authority, especially mothers, in the lives of fictional children throughout eighteenth- and nineteenth-century literature.

Nineteen eighty-seven was a watershed year for feminism in children's literature. Jack Zipes's edited collection *Don't Bet on the Prince: Contemporary Feminist Fairy Tales in North America and England* brought together the strengths of feminism and folklore studies, and Ruth Bottigheimer performed similar—and more extensive—work with the Grimms' fairy tales in *Bad Girls and Bold Boys: The Moral and Social Vision of the Tales*. Perhaps the most influential study published that year was Lissa Paul's "Enigma Variations: What Feminist Theory Knows about Children's Literature." That article inspired many of us to think not only about gender inequality and entrapment, but also to consider how children—especially girls—transcend gendered limitations through such devices as trickery, deceit, and imaginative creativity.

African American feminists rightly criticized much of second wave feminism for its focus on the experiences of white women. Authors such as Alice Walker, bell hooks, Barbara Christian, and Patricia Hill Collins recognized that, too often, white feminists ignore how gender intersects with race; they encouraged feminists to consider the experiences of all women, not just white women. Judith Butler also shifted second-wave feminism into more nuanced understandings of gender as a social construct, especially with her insistence that gender is performed. These intellectual forces influenced the study of children's and adolescent literature in multiple ways, leading critics to think of gender in less binary biological terms and instead grapple with how cultures construct genders via multiple factors, including not only race, but also social factors such as education and imperialism.

For example, in the 1990s, many feminist children's literature critics began to explore ideology and nation-building. Kimberley Reynolds's *Girls Only: Gender and Popular Children's Fiction in Britain, 1880–1910* interrogated the gendered power differentials between boy and girl characters and the ways that publishing practices influenced gender construction among child readers. Claudia Nelson explored tensions between childhood masculinity and femininity in *Boys Will Be Girls: The Feminine Ethic and British Children's Fiction, 1857–1917*. Anna E. Altmann deconstructed important gender roles at work in fantasy literature, while Lynne Vallone also explored gender construction as a wide-scale social force in *Disciplines of Virtue: Girls Culture in the Eighteenth and Nineteenth Centuries*. Beverly Lyon Clark's work on Louisa May Alcott's *Little Men* (1871) was one factor that led her to explore significant gender roles at work in children's school stories more generally in *Regendering the School Story: Sassy Sissies and Tattling Tomboys*. Elizabeth Keyser similarly connected Alcott's early work to later feminist gestures. Foster and Simons's *What Katy Read: Feminist Re-readings of "Classic" Stories for Girls, 1850–1920* also examines transgressive characters at work in girls' fiction, with a focus on early American children's literature. Additionally, Sherrie Inness was one of the many scholars working in cultural studies in the 1990s who identified strong females at work in popular culture, including those in superhero stories and comics. Clark and Higonnet's *Girls, Boys, Books, Toys: Gender in Children's Literature and Culture* employed cultural studies to critique gender and social construction throughout children's culture. Our field is fortunate that many of these scholars who published influential feminist criticism in the 1980s and 1990s have continued writing sophisticated feminist scholarship that has led the field of children's and adolescent literature to be consistently aware of gender and gender construction.

These twentieth-century feminists helped feminism explode as a field of study within children's and adolescent literature by the beginning of the twenty-first century; myriad critical studies since then have continued the work of feminism in children's and adolescent literature and culture. Space prohibits me from mentioning all the extant studies, but most of the feminist studies published during the first decade of the twenty-first century reflect a continued commitment to understanding gender as a social construct. Susan Lehr's *Beauty, Brains, and Brawn: The Construction of Gender in Children's Literature*, for example, makes twentieth-century feminist theory accessible to future teachers of literature; Elizabeth Marshall critiques the prescriptive nature of gender norms, especially as they delimit girlhood within educational settings. Christine Wilkie-Stibbs's *The Feminine Subject in Children's Literature* employs French psychoanalytical feminism to demonstrate how the *féminine* can help us understand the aesthetics of embodiment through speech and writing in children's fiction. Brian Attebery's *Decoding Gender in Science Fiction* examines the interplay of gender issues at work in speculative fiction for adults and young readers, while Victoria Flanagan theorizes about performativity in her interrogation of cross-dressing in children's literature, *Into the Closet: Cross-Dressing and the Gendered Body in Children's Literature and Film*. Additionally, Bradford, Mallan, Stephens, and McCallum's *New World Order in Contemporary Children's Literature* identifies feminism—especially ecofeminism—as a major factor in the creation of new world orders in fiction for the young.

More recent trends demonstrate how children's and adolescent literary critics have begun to examine issues of the material world, such as embodiment, cognition, queerness, motherhood, and material forces at work in narrative structure. Kathryn James's *Death, Gender and Sexuality in Contemporary Adolescent Literature* is one example: she investigates the relationship between death and sexuality in adolescent literature from a feminist perspective, while Holly Blackford's *The Myth of Persephone in Girls' Fantasy Literature* extends feminism to narrative theory in children's literature via the mechanism of transitional objects. Alice Curry connects ecofeminism to children's literature in *Environmental Crisis in Young Adult Fiction*, and Sara K. Day's exploration of feminist reader response theory in *Reading like a Girl* examines the power relationships at work in how narratives position the reader. Derek Thiess's *Embodying Gender and Age in Speculative Fiction* applies feminist complications of gender to issues of age in science fiction, work previously begun and developed far more extensively by Maria Nikolajeva in *Power, Voice, and Subjectivity in Literature for Young Readers*. And Lisa Rowe Fraustino and Karen Coats have collected important feminist essays on motherhood in children's literature in *Mothers in Children's and Young Adult Literature*.

Feminism has also inspired several major studies on masculinity in children's literature, including John Stephens's *Ways of Being Male*, Kenneth Kidd's *Making American Boys*, and Annette Wannamaker's *Boys in Children's Literature and Popular Culture*. Discussions such as these—in other words, those that queer gender, interrogate orientation, and deconstruct traditional thinking about what it means to be a "boy" or a "girl"—have been particularly influential in the twenty-first century, as I will discuss at greater length in Chapter 5. Kerry Mallan's *Gender Dilemmas in Children's Fiction* queers five specific controversies in the field (desire, beauty, the cyber-body, sexual identity, and "the serio-comic dilemma of gender") in ways that invite readers to deconstruct gender in children's literature. Abate and Kidd's *Over the Rainbow* links feminism to queer theory in significant ways, while Lydia Kokkola's *Fictions of Adolescent Carnality* interrogates multiple dimensions of teenaged sexuality, including both the heteronormative and the queer.

Many studies that are not focused directly or solely on gender issues but that reflect feminist values have also been written. Books on specific topics, such as the history of African American children's literature (Michelle Martin's *Brown Gold: Milestones of African American Children's Books* and Rudine Sims Bishop's *Free Within Ourselves: The Development of African American Children's Literature*), childhood and postcolonial otherness (as in Roderick McGillis's *Voices of the Other: Children's Literature and the Postcolonial Context*), and the Victorian "cult of childhood" (Marah Gubar's *Artful Dodgers: Reconceiving the Golden Age of Children's Literature*) contribute richly to the field of literary criticism—and they are all informed by feminism. Other studies similarly influenced by feminism, but not necessarily focused only on gender issues, include Robyn McCallum's *Ideologies of Identity in Adolescent Fiction*, Adrienne Kertzer's *My Mother's Voice: Children, Literature, and the Holocaust*, and Mike Cadden's *Ursula K. Le Guin Beyond Genre*. Several edited collections touch on gender issues in children's and adolescent literature, especially collections about dystopian adolescent fiction, such as Hintz and Ostry's *Utopian and Dystopian Writing for Children and Young Adults*, Dunn and Michaud's *The Hunger Games and Philosophy*, Pharr and Clark's *Of Bread, Blood and the Hunger Games*, Basu, Broad, and Hintz's *Contemporary Dystopian Fiction for Young Adults*, Connors's *Politics of Panem*, and Day, Green-Barteet, and Montz's *Female Rebellions in Young Adult Dystopian Fiction*. The twenty-first century has, therefore, been a remarkably productive time for feminist studies in children's and adolescent literary studies, especially in the ways that feminism has pushed the boundaries of the field into explorations of nuanced readings of gender, sex, and sexuality within cultural contexts.

## TWENTY-FIRST-CENTURY FEMINISMS, THE MATERIAL, AND REPRESENTATION

In *Waking Sleeping Beauty*, I relied heavily on poststructural concepts of the "primacy of discourse" (26). I still believe that most aspects of human life are mediated by language and discourse.[1] But material feminism has argued convincingly that, although bodies are mediated by discourse, they are not *solely* constructed by discourse. We limit our thinking about humanity if we think of bodies as *only* discursive constructs. Undergoing puberty and making the transition from childhood to adulthood is an embodied experience, one usually enmeshed in gender issues. Whether teenagers identify as transgender, cisgender, agender, or gender fluid, biophysical changes in the body make it difficult to separate the lived experience of puberty from gender identification. Moreover, although the concept of "adolescence" is constructed differently in every culture, the physical changes that demarcate the transition from childhood to adulthood happen similarly to human bodies in every culture. For example, although menstruation is a bodily function made discursively taboo through language in many cultures, it is a phenomenon that happens regardless of language: girls who have never been told about menstruation and don't understand what it is neverthe-less experience menarche; women with cognitive differences who have no capacity to employ language menstruate; women in comas still menstruate. Thus, although it seems fair to argue that much of what we know about the material world we understand through a medium—discourse—that affects and influences our perceptions, the physical world and our physical bodies are not constituted by discourse alone.

Childhood Studies is a field that has paid close attention to this distinc-tion: *children* are physically defined entities, as Coats argues in "Keepin' It Plural: Children's Studies in the Academy"; children, especially babies, are physically smaller than adults, for example. But the idea of *childhood* involves the complex network of concepts that influences our ability to understand and interact with those physically constituted *children*. While most scholars acknowledge that *children* are embodied, we also know that our perception of them is influenced by the many discourses that shape the concept of *childhood*. Childhood Studies, it seems to me, has done well to recognize that the material reality of the child is interconnected with the discursive construction of the child.

The central argument of material feminism is to reconnect the physical world with language, "not to privilege the discursive over the material but to understand the material in discursive terms" (Hekman, "Constructing" 88). Susan Hekman demonstrates that, in our strenuous efforts to avoid the toxicity implied by essentialism (the belief that women can be reduced to a physical "essence," such as nurturance or weakness), feminism began in the 1980s to rely heavily on the "linguistic turn" toward poststructural theories that emphasize the discursive and deemphasize the material. "Inspired by . . . postmodern theorists who examined the discursive constitution of social reality, many feminists turned to discourse at the expense of the material" (Hekman, "Constructing" 86–87). Susan Bordo even defines this phenom-enon as being the result of "panic" that is "a possible expression of feminist anxiety over being identified with marginalized and devalued aspects of female identity" (40). The poststructuralist "linguistic turn" that encour-aged us to interrogate gender as a performance of discourse was initially advanced by such theorists as Judith Butler in *Gender Trouble*—although even she raised concerns about "the question of whether the material body is fully constructed" in the preface to a later edition of that book (xvi).

Material feminists have also observed that feminism influenced by the "linguistic turn" is more likely to focus on epistemology—how we know what we know—rather than on metaphysical questions of ontology, that is, questions of being and evaluations of what constitutes reality. Alaimo and Hekman observe, "Whereas the epistemology of modernism is grounded in objective access to a real/natural world, postmodernists argue that the real/material is entirely constituted only in language and has its reality only in language. In their zeal to reject the modernist grounding in the material, postmoderns have turned to the discursive pole as the exclusive source of the constitution of nature, society, and reality" (2). Hekman argues, "Although the solutions offered by these theorists are persuasive, they all entail a redefinition of epistemological concepts—rationality, objectivity, and so forth. They do not move beyond the epistemological sphere to attempt to grapple with the reality that the concepts describe" ("Constructing" 89). The postmodern emphasis on language/discourse encourages us to think in terms of representationality: what is representation? What are the mechanisms of representationality by which we *know*? But this epistemological emphasis often comes at the expense of ontological issues: What is adolescent *being*? How is childhood's *being* different from adulthood's? How does gender identity influence our very *being*?

These questions become especially pertinent in children's and adolescent literature because texts are always and only discursive. While toys are material and books are, too, the narratives and poetry to which children are exposed through picture books, chapter books, nonfiction, poetry, drama, film, television, video games, and multi-media sources, are largely—and sometimes entirely—discursive. Children's literature *is* representational: it can only *represent* the material body. What pertinence, then, does material feminism have to the study of children's literature?

The most obvious answer is *through representations of the material world*. Children's literature may be a largely discursive phenomenon, but it is still heavily invested in exposing children to innumerable aspects of materiality, such as human embodiment, toys and other physical objects, physical spaces and geographies, and the environment. Although my earlier work focused largely on the discursive, it did so with an emphasis on the epistemological at the expense of the ontological. I would like now to examine how those issues interact with the discursive in children's literature as a way not to dismiss my earlier work but to bolster it. Representationality of gender relies on discursivity, but much of that representationality nevertheless engages child readers in ontological questions about how gender intersects with the material world.

## AN EXAMPLE: *A COOL MOONLIGHT*

In *Waking Sleeping Beauty*, I assert that social forces emerge from discourse to make people what they are: "subjectivity is a fluid concept based more on the primacy of language than on the primacy of the individual mind. Poststructural critics define the subject as constructed by language and by the exterior force that language asserts upon the individual (Belsey 46–50). Thus, it is language that makes us who we are" (26). Were I to rely solely on poststructural feminism to analyze a text such as Angela Johnson's *a cool moonlight* (2003), I likely would focus on how discursive issues position the protagonist in terms of agency, objectification, and empowerment (or lack thereof) in her relationships. The narrator, Lila, has a skin condition—xeroderma pigmentosum, or "xp," as she calls it—that makes it impossible for her to be exposed to any ultraviolet light, so she lives her life at night, covered up with clothing and sunscreen, only allowed outdoors after sundown.[2] She is self-conscious about her condition and describes other people being "mean" to her because of her xp (24). She even gathers a series of objects that she hopes will magically help her shift her subject position, giving her enough agency to survive sunlight. She knows that the discourse about her disease affects people's perceptions of her; she is pleased, for example, that one boy in kindergarten got punished for calling her "vampire girl" (24).

My earlier work focused on how discursive constructs can empower a character like Lila to have a voice that enables her to have agency and caring relationships with other people; the key concepts in the type of poststructuralist feminist analysis that I engage in *Waking Sleeping Beauty*, then, are voice, choice, and community. Within her family, Lila has a *voice*, but she is in many ways silenced by her isolation; she can be awake only at night, a situation about which she has very little *choice*. Lila is empowered by her relationships, especially those with her mother and her sister, but her two closest friends—Elizabeth and Alyssa—prove to be more illusory than a source of real *community*. Lila has created Elizabeth and Alyssa herself; they are discursive constructions. Lila has used language to tell herself a story about them to comfort herself and to create for herself a sense of community.

Poststructural feminism also emphasizes epistemology, so were I reading *a cool moonlight* solely through that lens, I would consider Lila's thought processes. For example, Lila is epistemologically aware: although she sometimes questions whether she should believe people or not (6, 7), she talks about her own epistemology, saying that she *knows* through her senses:

"you can be a part of anything in the dark if you have night eyes, ears, and a nose"; she claims to be "good at it" and believes that people are more comfortable in the dark because "they don't have to worry about people looking at them"—that is, objectifying them (89). She understands the discursive relationship between agency and objectification, and from a poststructural feminist perspective, I would emphasize how discourse affects every aspect of Lila's agency.

However, by adding a material feminist lens to the analytic framework, scholars can acknowledge that narratives also ask the (material) child reader to consider what it means to be ontologically embodied. Ontological status in the material world is affected and shaped by discourse, but novels invariably rely on discourse to also represent the material in the way that characters, setting, and actions are depicted. A novel is only—and can only ever be—a representation of the material world, but novels for the young rarely ignore either the material or the related issue of ontological status. Thus, it is significant that Lila *knows* that she is a "moon girl," but she wants a different ontological status: she wants to *be* a superhero, "the sun goddess/moon girl" so that she will "never have to wait for day or night to have power" (117). She knows that it's "not so bad to have just one power" (117), but she nonetheless questions why her ontological status is so different from other people's. She is effectively questioning how the materiality of her own embodiment positions her ontologically because XP cannot be explained away by discursivity.

The key to Lila's self-acceptance therefore comes through a combination of her epistemological growth and ontological acceptance. Although she fears she doesn't "understand a lot," she trusts that her sister does (13). In a gesture that is both literal and figurative, Lila describes how her sister, Monk, routinely covers her with sunscreen: "Monk's hands were soft and *knowing*. they never missed a spot" (17, italics added). Later, Lila says, "my hands are smaller than hers, but i think they know just as much" (20). In connecting epistemology to embodiment—in giving her hands the agency to have knowledge—Lila is refusing the type of Cartesian split that Elizabeth Grosz implores us to recognize as sexist. As long as western philosophers believe "mind" to be a different entity than "body," Grosz argues, ideas of the mind and spirit become elevated to a higher status than issues of embodiment—and, she maintains, since historically women have been associated with the flesh and men with intellect, the Cartesian split between body and mind has created a false dualism that is both inherently sexist and simultaneously partial to privileging such disembodied constructs as rationality and discourse. Lila knows her body is positioned by a culture that marginalizes her for living in the dark, and so she tries to understand what it means that within her culture, she is labeled as having a disability.

"Disability is not entirely reducible to social construction," legal scholar Adrienne Asch insists (13). Lila's body defines her daily life more than discourse does because discourse alone cannot change her health condition. She shops, learns, plays, reads, cooks, and eats on a schedule dictated by her body, a schedule at odds with that of most of the rest of her community. She is something of a peeping Tom, too: she peers through the windows of a neighbor's house and enjoys looking at two ballerinas on a music box in their living room. Probably because of her physical isolation, Lila has mentally constructed two imaginary friends, Elizabeth and Alyssa, whom she imagines will help her fill what she calls a "sun bag" with talismans that will enable her to go out during the daylight hours. By the end of the novel, she grows enough to recognize that she has constructed these friends discursively—but they have been inspired by a material object: the music box on which two ballerinas with wings dance in a perpetual ballet. Lila's friends may be imaginary—or they may be angels who help her accept her mortal condition. Either way, they serve as foils to Lila's embodiment: while it is possible for Elizabeth and Alyssa to exist only in Lila's mind, unlike them, Lila does have a body that she must acknowledge. And she has learned from the experience of playing with them that the relationship between body and discourse matters. The body cannot be ignored.

Ultimately, Lila whirls like the ballerinas on the music box in a circular motion at her night-time birthday party, but she is covered in hundreds of summer fireflies that have magically landed on her. She has accepted that she will never be able to go into the sun: "*it's* there and *i'm* here" (132, italics in the original). But she knows the time for talking about going out into the sun has ended: "it's not important to talk about it all anymore, or tell anyone who doesn't already know. the telling is over" (133). She has privileged discourse in her fantasies about denying her disability, but now she is putting closure on that type of epistemology. She is not defined solely by her body (or its disability or race), but neither is she defined entirely by the social constructions of discourse. Because she is a fictional character, she is a linguistic representation, yes, but as a discursive construct, her representation includes both embodied and discursively constructed materiality. Material feminism thus encourages literary critics to keep discourse in perspective as one among many of the factors that empowers and disempowers people; the environment, technology, animals, embodied cognition, microbes that cause illness, and carbon dioxide levels are among the myriad forces that also shape the human experience.

## MATERIAL FEMINISM AND THE STRUCTURE OF *TWENTY-FIRST-CENTURY FEMINISMS IN CHILDREN'S AND ADOLESCENT LITERATURE*

Material feminists insist that embodiment be considered in terms of both the material *and* the discursive. Although many refer to this intellectual shift as the "material turn," implying that it is turning away from the "linguistic turn," material feminists never ignore the discursive. Susan Hekman writes that material feminism is a "complex theory that incorporates language, materiality, and technology into the equation" ("Constructing" 92); furthermore, "material feminists explore the interaction of culture, history, discourse, technology, biology, and the environment, without privileging any one of these elements" (Alaimo and Hekman 7). As a result, many twenty-first-century feminisms are influenced by an attention to material issues; concerns with embodiment, intersectionality, environmentalism, and the ethics of care all acknowledge the presence of the physical in ways that linguistic-turn feminism largely failed to address.

Material feminism (and the feminisms it has influenced, such as posthuman feminism, for example) has much to offer to the study of children's and adolescent literature, especially given how very embodied both children and adolescents are. My work in material feminism thus strives to demonstrate that youth is a multi-faceted stage of life that involves complex interactions among embodiment, discourse, the environment, technology, and culture. I apply the principles behind material feminism and interrelated manifestations of feminism (such as Critical Race Theory and ecofeminism) to those texts written for the young to demonstrate how shifting cultural perceptions of feminism affect what is happening both in publishing for the young and in the academic study of children's and adolescent literature. The structure of the book moves from examinations of the individual to examinations of the individual in social groups, the individual and the environment, and the individual within relationships. Thus, the first chapter establishes material feminism as a theory that examines the individual in terms of the intra-actions of the material and discourse; subsequent chapters then discuss the individual in terms of social constructions and group identities (Chapter 2); interactions among individuals, the environment, and technology (Chapters 3 and 4); and ultimately individuals and their interactions with other people

(Chapters 5 and 6). The work therefore begins with a specific focus on language, representationality, and the material and moves to an examination of race as a lived material phenomenon *and* a social construction. How embodied individuals interact with the environment is explored through ecofeminism and the dystopic; how people interact with each other involves romance, sexuality, and feminist ethics. The logic of the book thus progresses from a focus on the individual to an examination of the individual in social contexts, environmental contexts, and interpersonal contexts; the narratives I have chosen to analyze are thus grouped together in terms of the relationships between the protagonist and her social, environmental, or interpersonal interactions.

To be more specific, after an opening chapter that explains the philosophical principles on which I base the material feminism of my argument, in Chapter 2, I examine issues of age as they intersect with other forms of oppression, including gender, race, ability, class, and several other factors. In Chapter 3, I demonstrate how ecofeminism helps us extend concerns about oppression and material feminism in terms of how enmeshed the body is with the physical world. In chapter 4, I specifically explore embodiment in terms of the dystopic because of the way that dystopias foreground various aspects of what it means to inhabit a human body. In Chapter 5, I examine how performativity, discourse, and embodiment lead authors who are concerned about gender to queer the binaries of sexuality, orientation, and gender identity. In Chapter 6, I circle back to the philosophy that informs my argument to interrogate the ethics of twenty-first-century feminisms in preadolescent and adolescent literature.

Throughout, I have chosen those narratives for the young that communicate about twenty-first-century feminist issues. As I chose novels to analyze, I started with the basic premise I laid out in *Waking Sleeping Beauty*; I was looking for novels about girl protagonists with some degree of voice, choice, and community. I then looked for novels that explore the material in any one of a number of ways: through embodiment, through the environment, through technology, or through the material nature of caring relationships. All these novels are available in English, and although the majority of them are written by US authors (a bias that stems from my own nationality and from the practicality of how available these books are to me), I have paid close attention to inclusivity in terms of diversity, multiculturalism, ability, gender identity, and sexual orientation. The novels about which I write are mostly targeted to middle-grade or young adult readers. These are ages when many young people are coming to terms with their own embodiment and the sexism in their culture—although YA novels are more likely than middle grade novels to directly explore political issues, sexuality, death, and sexism as a cultural institution. Admittedly, my work focuses on narratives written for children aged nine to eighteen, rather than on either picture books or graphic novels, because of my own lack of visual acuity. I am simply not a skilled critic of graphic narratives. Nor does this book deal with the complexities of gender studies that include constructions of masculinity, largely because of space restrictions. Indeed, the intersection between material feminism and masculinity studies is complicated enough to deserve its own book. The goal of this particular work is to interrogate the ways that material feminism can expand our understanding of materiality, maturation, and gender—especially girlhood—in preadolescent and adolescent narratives.

The fear of materiality is legitimately based in a fear of essentialist binaries of gender; for many theorists, such as Mallan in *Gender Dilemmas* and Kokkola in *Fictions of Adolescent Carnality*, concepts of "queering" become the safety net that keeps us from the totalizing binaries that created rigid gender categories in the first place. But if we queer gender altogether (which neither Mallan nor Kokkola advocates), feminism becomes obsolete. In other words, if we deconstruct concepts of gender so far that they collapse into meaninglessness, we obviate the need for feminism. As it happens, practicality tells us that feminism is *not* obsolete: most of the children in the world are taught from a young age to think of themselves as either male or female, and those who have spent a lifetime thinking of themselves as female eventually become in adulthood statistically more likely to have experienced the physical and material effects of sexism, such as depressed wages, domestic violence, and rape. Transchildren help theorists—and the rest of the world—to rethink problems with gender binaries, but they do not erase the realities of the dominant culture's epistemological tendency to categorize children by sex binaries that are as rigid and ancient as those found between the pairs of animals boarding Noah's Ark.

Additionally, while adulthood and childhood exist as less of a binary than male/female does, children are in point of fact specifically not-adult. Real children are transitioned into adulthood via the construction of gender: based on the appearance of their genitalia at birth, people mature having been assigned a gender that is discursively formulated but based on what Robyn Wiegman calls "the epistemology of the visual" (8). Babies who look like they have penises get assigned into the category of boyhood; babies who look like they have labia get assigned into the category of girlhood—even when their own developing sense of dysphoria leads them to reject these assignments later in their development.

Fictional children, of course, have no material genitalia upon which gender role construction is predicated. My work in the twentieth century focused on *how* authors construct gender discursively, but now I am asking *why* do they do so? Why do authors so frequently use the discursive to represent the materiality of the human body in gender binaries? Why are girl protagonists girls instead of boys? Or trans? Indeed, trans and queered characters are increasingly recognized within the field, as I discuss in Chapter 5, but even when a novel features queered/trans characters, all the background characters are automatically assigned roles in gendered binaries. Feminist theorists from Irigaray in *Speculum of the Other Woman* to Butler in *Gender Trouble* have explored the underlying psychic and social structures that create—indeed, engender—the widespread cultural phenomenon of gendered thinking. My goal is to explore how representations of materiality affect the relationship between gender and empowerment in literature for youth. I will argue that it is not enough to examine epistemological issues of empowerment that involve how girls think of themselves as agents or as strong; we must also examine how the materiality of gender representation allows for ways of being empowered (and disempowered) within the complex interactions that exist among individuals, their environments, their discursive and social constructs, and their material constructs.

TWENTY-FIRST-CENTURY
FEMINISMS
IN CHILDREN'S
AND ADOLESCENT
LITERATURE

## CHAPTER 1

# BECOMING, MATTERING, AND "KNOWING IN BEING" IN FEMINIST NOVELS FOR THE YOUNG

The first time Katniss sees the mockingjay pin that becomes her emblem in the arenas of Suzanne Collins's *The Hunger Games* (2008), it is pinned on the dress of the daughter of the mayor, Madge. Mockingjays are a hybrid bred between mockingbirds and "jabberjays," which are birds genetically altered to spy on the people of Panem, the dystopic country in which Katniss lives. Katniss looks at the pin and thinks "Real gold. Beautifully crafted. It could keep a family in bread for months" (12). As a material artifact, the mockingjay pin is valuable as a commodity—gold—that can be traded for another commodity—bread. After Katniss volunteers to be her district's tribute in the Hunger Games, Madge urgently pins the mockingjay on Katniss's dress, imploring her to wear it in the arena during the games. Now the pin's meaning shifts because Katniss perceives the pin to be a token of friendship: "maybe Madge really has been my friend all along" (38). In the sequel, *Catching Fire* (2009), Katniss acknowledges how her perception of the pin shifts again after she learns that it originally belonged to Madge's aunt, who died as a tribute in the Hunger Games twenty-five years earlier: "it means something completely different now that I know that its former owner was ... a tribute who was murdered in the arena" (*Catching* 196–97). Katniss also thanks Madge, acknowledging that "mockingjays are all the rage in the Capitol, thanks to you" (*Catching* 91). The mockingjay becomes the face of the rebellion because it is an accidental hybrid, one that "the Capitol never intended to exist. ... They hadn't anticipated its will to live" (*Catching* 92). Her designer for the Hunger Games also creates a charcoal-colored dress made of feathers that transforms Katniss herself: "Cinna has turned me into a mockingjay" (*Catching* 252). By the end of *Catching Fire*, the gamemaker of the Hunger Games tells her, "you're the mockingjay. ... While you live, the revolution lives" (386). Katniss's embodiment has merged with the pin itself, permanently destabilizing both her perceptions of the mockingjay emblem and of her own embodied identity.

Ultimately, the pin is a material object, but its meaning shifts depending on how Katniss is perceiving it and whether what matters to her in the moment is gold or friendship or grieving a martyr or rebelling against the Capitol. As a symbol of the rebellion, the materiality of the pin, too, begins to shift: it even shows up imprinted in bread as a "symbol of resistance" (*Catching* 150). The mockingjay pin illustrates beautifully the inherent instability between signifier and signified. As the signified, the pin is gold; it is a replica of a bird; it is decorative jewelry. As a signifier, its meaning shifts from being a status symbol to a token of friendship to a commemoration to a sign of rebellion. The pin shows how *matter* and *meaning* continually interact in a process dependent on perception and cognition. In a similar way, the material body and discursive constructs about it continually interact in processes of meaning-making that are unstable, fluid, and never-ending. The shifting relationship between the matter and meaning of the mockingjay pin invites readers to consider how the material and discourse affect one another, just as readers are invited to consider how material embodiment and discursive gender constructs recur throughout Katniss's many different performances of both masculine roles (as hunter and stalker) and feminine roles (dressed in a fashionable dress for the Capitol and as the object of the media's gaze).[1] As such, the mockingjay pin in the Hunger Games series can help us understand the continual transactions between embodiment as matter and social (or discursive) constructs as they work together to shape how people think about gender, especially during childhood and adolescence.

Katniss's relationship to the mockingjay pin can also help us understand one of the most profound shifts in twenty-first century literature for the young, which involves the confluence of two important social forces: the widespread recognition of the importance of human embodiment in gender theory and the widespread acceptance that discourse matters—that it affects and shapes human perception just as surely as materiality shapes and influences human perception. We cannot think about gender formation during childhood and adolescence without paying attention to discursive constructions that influence our perceptions of gender, but then, we can't think about gender formation without also acknowledging that embodiment is a material phenomenon that affects how we live our lives.

The goal of this volume is thus to address how embodiment and materiality have important effects on feminist interpretations of preadolescent and adolescent narratives. In my previous work, *Waking Sleeping Beauty: Feminist Voices in Children's Novels*, I focused almost exclusively on how discourse constructs girls into femininity. Given that characters in children's and young adult (YA) novels are entirely constructed out of language—that is, given that they are always already discursive constructs—that approach still makes sense to me.

Nevertheless, the "material turn" in feminist theory has inspired me to broaden my understanding of how we can approach issues of gender in extended narratives for young people. Reacting to the poststructural "linguistic turn" that emphasized gender as always and only a social construct, material feminism asks us to consider how the material interacts with discourse to affect gender. For example, whether children and teenagers identify as transgender, cisgender, agender, or gender fluid, they inhabit specific bodies. Those bodies interact with the surrounding environment in ways that have profound effects on those bodies. Material artifacts, too, affect constructions of gender—for example, how social media and smart phones have increased people's access to photo opportunities (such as "selfies"). Cis and trans girls who see their own images reflected back to themselves repeatedly and on multiple platforms may well experience their bodies more self-consciously than girls who have not interacted with the omnipresence of the smartphone as a physical artifact. Because of the confluence of bodies, the environment, technology, and artifacts as material factors of lived experience, Stacy Alaimo and Susan Hekman argue that "matter matter[s]" (5). Following them, I would argue that if we do not pay attention to the material as it affects the construction of gender during preadolescence and adolescence, we are missing a large part of the story.

Before I begin my analysis of twenty-first century feminisms in literature for the young, I would first like to offer a review of the feminist theory from which material feminism has emerged.[2] The following section thus examines how different feminisms have defined being female/woman/girl in various ways: 1) as a physical reality that is defined in opposition to maleness; 2) as a social construct; 3) as a gendered performance; and 4) as a process-of-becoming through which material bodies interact with discourse to enact the lived reality of gender. The section that follows next interrogates how the study of being and the study of knowing create unique opportunities for interrogating the process-of-becoming inherent in the gendered experience of adolescence. In the final section of this chapter, I use these theories to analyze Libba Bray's feminist YA novel *Beauty Queens* (2011), a novel that openly interrogates gender as both material and discursive. This chapter thus provides a background for the relevant theoretical concepts and a blueprint for how various feminisms manifest themselves in twenty-first century literature for young people.

## DISCURSIVE AND MATERIAL BODIES

Katherine Hayles, a scholar of the posthuman, usefully distinguishes the "enacted body" from the "represented body," with the enacted body being "that which is present in the flesh" and the "represented body" being that which is "produced through the verbal and semiotic markers constituting it" (xiii). For the purposes of studying literature, manifestations of both types of bodies matter. Real readers have enacted bodies; no reading trans-action happens without the presence of an enacted body. But stories are filled with represented bodies—bodies constituted semiotically rather than somatically. This study will focus more on the body as represented than as enacted, and yet it is important to ask ourselves how represented bodies affect the bodies of enacted readers. When a young girl experiences a novel such as Patricia McCormick's *Cut* (2000), do the representations of cutting she reads inspire her to cut her enacted body? Or do they inspire her *not* to cut? Or does the story inspire her to have more empathy for those who feel this compulsion? Or does the novel make her roll her eyes because the plot is so maudlin? In any of these scenarios, an enacted body has been af-fected by the represented embodiment in the story. Enacted and represented bodies interact; that interaction affects the enacted body in ways that are manifested materially.

Historically, representations of the female have often seemed to be di-vided between those who define *female* in terms of matter or in terms of discourse. Those who focus more on the matter of the human body as a biological entity often revert to essentialist arguments that imply there is something in the "essence" of being female that is biologically different from the "essence" of being male; poststructuralists who follow Derrida and Fou-cault focus instead on sex and gender as "social construction"—as concepts that exist more as a function of representation than of matter.[3] For example, in a 1988 *Signs* article, Linda Alcoff distinguishes "cultural feminists" from "poststructuralist feminists," arguing that cultural feminists, such as Adri-enne Rich and Mary Daly, reify essentialist positions by opposing "female" or "feminine" traits in opposition to "male" or "masculine" traits based on the assumption that sex is a determinant and biologically-discernible di-chotomy. Poststructuralists, on the other hand, deconstruct the concept of "woman" to argue that as a "category 'woman' is a fiction and that feminist efforts must be directed toward dismantling this fiction" (Alcoff 417). Alcoff raises concerns about gender as entirely discursive when she asks: "If gender is simply a social construct, the need and even the possibility of a feminist politics becomes immediately problematic. What can we demand in the name of women if 'women' do not exist and demands in their name simply reinforce the myth that they do? How can we speak out against sexism as detrimental to the interests of women if the category is a fiction?" (420).

With *Gender Trouble*, Judith Butler tries to address the inherently unstable position of defining gender as *only* a discursive construct by interpreting gender through concepts of social construction:

> If one "is" a woman, that is surely not all one is; the term fails to be exhaustive, not because a pregendered "person" transcends the specific paraphernalia of its gender, but because gender is not always constituted coherently or consistently in different historical contexts, and because gender intersects with racial, class, ethnic, sexual, and regional modalities of discursively constituted identities. As a result, it becomes impossible to separate out "gender" from the political and cultural intersections in which it is invariably produced and maintained. (4–5)

Butler is specifically deconstructing the concept of "woman" within feminism as a political enterprise by interrogating how (in)effective it is to use the terms of the oppressor—in this case, the term "woman"—to try to enact an emancipatory political force. She develops her solution to this problem by interpreting gender as a matter of *performativity*: people perform gender; it is neither a biologically stable nor a discursive status. As one philosopher describes Butler's position: "gender is a doing"; it is a process of reiterated interactions with social norms; gender is not a static entity (Barad, *Meeting* 57). The point seems particularly germane to a study of preadolescence and adolescence, since it is during the second decade of life that many people become more self-conscious about needing to perform—or reject the performance of—socially prescribed gender roles.

In *Bodies That Matter*, Butler further interrogates gender as a function of both representationality and materiality. She writes:

> The category of "sex" is, from the start, normative; it is what Foucault has called a "regulatory ideal." In this sense, then, "sex" not only functions as a norm, but is part of a regulatory practice that produces the bodies it governs, that is, whose regulatory force is made clear as a kind of productive power, the power to produce—demarcate, circulate, differentiate—the bodies it controls. Thus, "sex" is a regulatory ideal whose materialization is compelled. (1)

The Foucauldian theories from *History of Sexuality* that Butler cites here invoke Plato: the concept of "sex" as a "regulatory ideal" echoes the notion of a "Platonic ideal," in which a concept is somehow divorced from the material that corresponds to the ideal. In Butler's theory, the ideal regulates the material through the idea of performativity: performativity is the "reiterative and citational practice by which discourse produces the effects that name it"; "the regulatory norms of 'sex' work in a performative fashion to constitute the materiality of bodies and, more specifically, to materialize the body's sex, to materialize sexual difference in the service of the consolidation of the heterosexual impulse" (*Bodies* 2). It is important to note that Butler does not deny the existence of the enacted body; rather, she argues that it cannot exist divorced from the "regulatory ideal" comprised by our discursive understandings of what "sex" is.

Butler objects to those who interpret her work as being entirely a function of the "linguistic turn," saying, "the point has never been that 'everything is discursively constructed'; that point . . . belongs to a kind of discursive monism or linguisticism" (*Bodies* 8).[4] Butler instead proposes "a return to the notion of matter, not as site or surface, but as *a process of materialization that stabilizes over time to produce the effect of boundary, fixity, and surface we call matter*" (*Bodies* 9, italics in the original); "Thus, the question is no longer, How is gender constituted as and through a certain interpretation of sex? . . . but rather, through what regulatory norms is sex itself materialized?" (*Bodies* 10). She perceives social construction as a "temporal process which operates through the reiteration of norms" (*Bodies* 10), and she gives as a famous example the obstetrician's utterance, "It's a girl," to demonstrate how gender indeterminacy ("it") is replaced by discursive performativity: we are pronounced a gender—such as, "a girl"—from the first moments of our lives (*Bodies* 7). For Butler, performativity determines gender through a process by which the linguistic determines the interpretation of the material.

The philosopher Karen Barad critiques Judith Butler for underplaying the material, although Barad is careful to ensure that readers understand that she is not accusing Butler of any form of idealism or monism or "erasure of 'real flesh and blood bodies'" ("Getting Real" 91). Rather, she is concerned that Butler's concept of performativity does not take into account the primacy of the material because the material can exist prior to and independently of discourse: "Isn't some *fixed* sense of the substantive character of materiality required to think about how materiality constrains processes?" ("Getting Real" 91, italics in the original). According to Barad, the most useful understanding of performativity involves how the concept allows us to think about the discursive power by which language influences our perceptions: performativity is "a contestation of the excessive power granted to language to determine what is real" (*Meeting* 133).

In order to talk about the relationship between the material and the medium through which it is represented, Barad relies on the work of physicist Niels Bohr, who critiqued Newtonian scientific notions of objective observation. Bohr believed that "*theoretical concepts are defined by the circumstances required for their measurement*"; in other words, "there is no unambiguous way to differentiate between the 'object' and the 'agencies of observation'" (Barad, "Getting Real" 94–95, italics in the original). Barad interprets Bohr's position thusly: "*we are a part of that nature we seek to understand*" (*Meeting* 26, italics in the original). She considers his "intertwining of the conceptual and physical dimensions of measurement processes" to be "central to his epistemological framework" (*Meeting* 196), and she critiques Butler for "limit[ing] . . . an account of the materialization of human bodies, or more accurately, . . . the construction of the surface of the human body (which most certainly is not all there is to human bodies)" ("Getting" 107). Butler, for example, fails to take into consideration the chemical and physical properties that make brains responsive to regulatory ideals such as "sex" in the first place. She does not consider the materiality of the embodied brain in her account of performativity—nor does she acknowledge the biochemical properties that trigger puberty and its attendant issues of gender identification.

Barad demonstrates the impossibility of an entirely linguistic or non-material phenomenon; the material mediates the discursive, and the discursive mediates the material. She insists that "the relationship between the material and the discursive is one of mutual entailment. Neither is articulated/articuable in the absence of the other; matter and meaning are mutually articulated" ("Posthumanist" 140). As Susan Hekman puts it, "instead of assuming, as do the social constructionists, that language creates social reality, [material feminists] assume instead that language, bodies, technologies, and other elements interact to create" discourse, that is, the flows of the semiotic, material, and social through which meaning is enacted ("Constructing" 114).

At the heart of what Hekman, Barad, and Butler are considering is the question of representationally: in what ways does discourse alter, affect, or distort our understanding of the material?

> Representationalism is the belief in the ontological distinction between
> representations and that which they purport to represent. . . . That is, there

> are assumed to be two distinct and independent kinds of entities—rep-resentations and entities to be represented. The system of representation is sometimes explicitly theorized in terms of a tripartite arrangement. For example, in addition to knowledge (i.e., representations), on the one hand, and the known (i.e., that which is purportedly represented), on the other, the existence of a knower (i.e., someone who does the represent-ing) is sometimes made explicit. When this happens, it becomes clear that representations are presumed to serve a mediating function between independently existing entities. (Barad, *Meeting* 46–47)

Barad's work points in the direction of cognitive theory: the "knower" to whom she refers must experience cognitive activity in order to perceive the "known" and subsequently interpret meaning as "knowledge." *Perception* is the complex cognitive activity at work here.[5] The material feminists who follow Barad privilege the process of knowledge construction over either the phenomenon of the knower's experiences or the physical reality of objects themselves. Representation, in this view, is an ongoing and iterative process.

The question of representation is of interest to feminists because of the ways discourse represents (and alters and distorts) the female/feminine: "representation is the normative function of a language which is said either to reveal or to distort what is assumed to be true about the category of women" (Butler, *Gender* 2). As Simone de Beauvoir might have it, "woman" is the "second sex," a representational construct defined by men inherently as that which is not-man. Alcoff defines the problem this way:

> Man has said that woman can be defined, delineated, captured—under-stood, explained, and diagnosed—to a level of determination never ac-corded to man himself, who is conceived as a rational animal with free will. Where man's behavior is underdetermined, free to construct its own future along the course of its rational choice, woman's nature has overde-termined her behavior, the limits of her intellectual endeavors, and the inevitabilities of her emotional journey through life. (406)

I should add that nowhere is the "emotional journey through life" more fraught with gendered stereotypes than during adolescence. These words "woman" and "girl" are consequently representations of a lived materiality.

When Barad talks about representationality, she points to the "ontological gap" between word and thing, such as the gap between the word "woman" and the enacted adult, female body ("Posthumanist" 123). Barad proposes that the ontological gaps between the material and meaning provide us with a way to think about what she terms "*intra-activity*"; that is, she proposes that we consider the mutually implicating processes of how perceptions of phenomena shape our understanding of the material, which in turn affects how we use discourse. The discursive meaning Katniss attributes to the mockingjay pin, whether she thinks of it as a commodity or friendship-token or emblem of rebellion, affects her perception of the material object in a process that continually redefines both Katniss's discourse and her perception of the pin as a material object. Barad would consider this continual process to be a matter of intra-activity, of the transaction between matter and meaning. As Barad defines it, "The neologism 'intra-action' *signifies the mutual constitution of entangled agencies*" (*Meeting* 33, italics in the original). Meaning does not reside purely in the discursive, nor does it reside in matter itself, but rather in how the perceiver continuously connects them intra-actively. Barad offers further clarification of intra-activity when she says: "Discursive practices and material phenomena do not stand in relationship of externality to each other; rather *the material and the discursive are mutually implicated in the dynamics of intra-activity*. The relationship between the material and the discursive is one of mutual entailment" (*Meeting*152, italics in the original). She believes that "phenomena" (rather than "things") are the basis of that which we know and that "the primary semantic units are not 'words' but material-discursive practices through which boundaries are constituted" ("Posthumanist" 135).

Barad thus argues that "matter and meaning are not separate elements. They are inextricably fused together, and no event, no matter how energetic, can tear them asunder" (*Meeting* 3). She refers to the intra-activity between the material and discourse as *mattering*:

> matter does not refer to a fixed substance; rather, *matter is substance in its intra-active becoming—not a thing but a doing, a congealing of agency. Matter is a stabilizing and destabilizing process of intraactivity* [sic]. Phenomena—the smallest material units (relational "atoms")—come to matter through this process of ongoing intractivity [sic]. "Matter" does not refer to an inherent, fixed property of abstract, independently existing objects; rather, *"matter" refers to phenomena in their ongoing materialization*. (*Meeting* 151, italics in the original)

As Barad puts it, "*Matter(ing) is a dynamic articulation/configuration of the world*. In other words, materiality is discursive . . . just as discursive practices are always already material" (*Meeting* 151, italics in the original).⁶ Thus, the process by which Katniss continually reinterprets the mockingjay pin is an example of *mattering*. Indeed, Katniss's sense of self, her relationships with other people and the Capitol, her performance of gender, and her growth to maturity all affect her agency, and these processes are all what Barad would call "dynamic articulations" through which she "(re)configures her own world" (Barad, *Meeting* 151). These are processes of *mattering*—although the mockingjay pin provides the most easily identified instantiation of *mattering* in the series.

This all matters to the study of how feminisms work in YA literature because Barad positions agency itself as a process of "mattering": "Agency is not an attribute but the ongoing reconfigurings of the world"—by which Barad means that matter and discourse (which can also be read as "matter and meaning") interact constantly in the perceptual process of meaning-making (*Meeting* 141). Barad considers work that acknowledges the agency of the material and of discourse as interactive processes to be "agential realism" because our agency is engaged by our own perceptions of the transaction between matter and meaning (*Meeting* 34); alternatively, Nancy Tuana refers to this theory as "interactionism" ("Viscous" 192). Thus, if phenomena interact, they affect one another; we can talk easily about "interactions" between people or between people and the environment. "Intra-activity," however, is the specific way that we can acknowledge the process by which the material and discourse affect, shape, influence, and inform one another, since the very act of perception is an ongoing agential process that affects the nature of that which is perceived. This becomes especially clear when we think about gender and how children are socialized into discourse about gender that affects their understanding of their material bodies and eventually their performances of gender during and after puberty.

Barad's work is important to a material feminist reading of adolescent literature because, via the mechanism of intra-actionism, she emphasizes the primacy of process and *becoming* to agency. Gendered bodies are not simply material objects; they are constantly redefined as agents through the discursive processes of mattering: "*Matter comes to matter* through the iterative intra-activity of the world in its becoming" (Barad, *Meeting* 152, italics in the original). To elaborate, Gilles Deleuze theorizes *becoming* not as being a process of growth alone, but as the process of desire by which the one *becoming* seeks to "find the zone of proximity, indiscernibility, or indifferentiation"—that is, a merging of proximal zones "unforeseen and nonpreexistent, singularized out of a population rather than determined in a form" (1). Intra-activity is thus implicated in *becoming* in the sense that "one can institute a zone of proximity with anything" (Deleuze 2). Following Deleuze, Rosi Braidotti insists that "the subject is a process, made of constant shifts and negotiations between different levels of power and desire. . . . What sustains the entire process of becoming-subject is the will to know, the desire to say, the desire to speak; it is a founding, primary, vital, necessary and therefore original desire to become" (22). *Becoming* is a matter of interrogating form through a desire to be something else; "becoming is always 'between' or 'among': a woman between women, or an animal among others" (Deleuze 2). *Mattering*, as the intra-activity between concept and that which is being conceptualized, and *becoming*, as the ongoing process by which identities shift and merge, can work together to help us understand how teenaged girls (both trans and cis) are continually reimplicated in gendered tensions between the material and the discursive.

This division between word and thing is another Western dichotomy that implies a false separation between the real and discourse: reality is, of course, implicated in shaping discourse, and discourse is in turn implicated in shaping reality. As Butler puts it, "language and materiality are not opposed, for language both is and refers to that which is material, and what is material never fully escapes from the process by which it signified. But if language is not opposed to materiality, neither can materiality be summarily collapsed into an identity with language" (*Bodies* 68). Butler observes, for example, that the printed word has a material existence; it functions via a mechanical reproduction that involves ink and paper or via electronic transmission and physically composed computers. Similarly, materiality and discourse are inseparably intertwined in creating and sustaining gendered bodies, whether we are talking about preadolescent and adolescent cis and trans girls in the twenty-first century or Katniss's gendered embodiment and agency in Panem.

## ONTOLOGY/EPISTEMOLOGY

Intra-activity emphasizes the importance of ontology. Ontology is the study of the nature of being: what it means to exist, what being is, what constitutes reality. Susan Hekman observes that feminists have been wary of ontological metaphysics because of modernist implications about reality that assume "a fixed reality about which we seek absolute knowledge" ("Constructing" 109). She prefers the "new ontology," which posits that "knowledge is always mediated by concepts and, in many cases, technology as well" ("Constructing" 109).

Ontological issues matter in literature for the young for several reasons. The first is one we all know because of Hamlet's adolescent musings: "To be or not to be." During adolescence, many teenagers gain for the first time the cognitive skills to question their being and their life's meaning. Second, for those cultures in which adolescence is an identified stage of life, adolescence itself is an ontological status; it is a unique period of existence in which being is typified by transition, change, and impermanence.[7] Third, many of the pubertal issues of gender and sexuality that evolve during adolescence are also ontological: what does it mean to *be* (cis)female? or (trans)female? or (cis/trans)male? what does it mean to *be* asexual or bisexual or pansexual or demisexual or lesbian or gay or heterosexual? How does the relationship between one's gender identity and one's sexual orientation influence one's sense of being? Ultimately issues of agency that are so important to feminism are enacted as ontological *mattering*: the subject is enacted by agency, the material, and discourse; being and action are thus ontologically inseparable.

Hekman describes "social ontology" as the branch of feminism that investigates the ontological power of social construction: although all societies are different, they do all contain individuals who are grouped together in various configurations that maximize the larger group's survival. "Teenagers" serve as an example of a social category; the subject position of a teenager is generally regarded as unique but also as sharing similarities to and differences from the subject position of the child and the adult. Hekman considers "the subject" to be the most prominently studied aspect of social ontology in the twenty-first century: "What it means to be a subject . . . is central to the character of any society; defining the individual is a fundamental element of social organization. The definition of a subject in any given society provides individuals with the possibility of an identity" ("Constructing" 113). We become subjects through social interaction; we define our individual identities within that social context. "Having a viable identity, being accepted by my society as a subject, is necessary to social existence. Without it I am, quite literally, no one" ("Constructing" 113). Hekman usefully defines *identity* in these terms: "each of us possesses a coherent, core self that allows us to function as mature adults in a social world and provides us with an individual identity. But we need not assume that this core self is essential, disembodied, or abstract. . . . Rather, it is itself socially constituted in the early years of childhood" (*Private* 5).[8] As Coats puts it:

"In postmodern culture, identity is no longer conceived as something one achieves through looking inwards for the eternal, unchanging truth of oneself, but instead emerges at the nexus of a set of discourses—of race, gender, ethnicity, class, and so on—that one uses with degrees of submissiveness or subversion to fashion a provisional performance of the self" ("Identity" 112). But as Hekman notes, the linguistic turn has deemphasized the idea of identity as the suspicious residue of essentialism. She nevertheless observes that even Judith Butler has come to admit that we "appear to require" identity; Hekman believes that we need "a core sense of self in order to function in the social world" ("Constructing" 115).

Although the linguistic turn has rightly made us suspicious of identity as a stable, fixed, and incontrovertible element of the human psyche, a feminist social ontology celebrates the internal creation of a sense of self, one that is predicated on one's own ontology and one that rejects rigid social scripts. Hekman writes, "What we need is a core sense of self in order to function in the social world. Just as importantly, we need a way to theorize about that identity" ("Constructing" 115). Identities can be rejected; people can reject the "social script," but each individual's "body/language connection" is wrapped up in their sense of being ("Constructing" 115). If subjectivity then is the ontological status granted by our agency interacting with our social context, then identity is how we define ourselves within that context. Preadolescent and adolescent literature is rife with issues of subjectivity and identity, as I noted in *Waking Sleeping Beauty* (26). While I still reject inherent and fixed notions of a stable and inherent identity, I now believe that the concept of identity serves as a useful way for people to define how they position themselves in relationship to other people: I have a sense of my identity in terms of being a woman, a feminist, a parent, an American, etc., largely because I am comparing my identity to those social groups with whom I share various affinities and contrasting myself to those with whom I do not.

Susan Hekman, together with Stacy Alaimo, notes that poststructuralists have been far more comfortable with epistemology—the study of knowing and how we know what we know—than of ontology because of the postmodern argument that "the real/material is entirely constituted by language" and our knowledge-based perceptions of language (Alaimo and Hekman 2). The epistemological is another indisputably central aspect of preadolescent and adolescent literature: characters learn, they think about what they know, they interrogate their own and others' knowledge, and they often doubt what they know. The philosopher Elizabeth Anderson argues that epistemology is a significant function of feminism: "Feminist epistemology is about the ways gender influences what we take to be knowledge" (188); feminist epistemology "investigates the influence of *socially constructed conceptions and norms of gender and gender-specific interests and experiences on the production of knowledge*" (190, italics in the original).[9] Alcoff advocates for a new "social epistemology" that, as well as concerning itself with traditional issues of epistemology, is also "self-conscious about the interconnections between knowledge, power, and desire" (2). Foucault famously interrogated the connection between knowledge and power (*Discipline* 27–28).[10] How is knowledge motivated by desire? How do the distinctions between self-knowledge and knowledge of others empower us? And how is our knowledge of gender both empowering and disempowering?

Twenty-first century depictions of feminism in novels for the young are thus integrally linked to issues of both the epistemological and the ontological. One example is the game that Peeta and Katniss play with a soldier in *Mockingjay* (2010); they call the game "Real and Not Real," and they play it to help Peeta overcome the hallucinogenics that have so addled his brain that he can no longer tell the difference between his hallucinations and reality (272). Katniss narrates this passage in the first person:

> "Most of the people from [District] Twelve were killed in the fire."
>
> "Real. Less than nine hundred of you made it to [District] Thirteen alive."
>
> "The fire was my fault."
>
> "Not real. President Snow destroyed Twelve the way he did Thirteen, to send a message to the rebels."
>
> This [game] seems like a good idea until I realize that I'll be the only one who can confirm or deny most of what weighs on him. (272)

The passage demonstrates the importance of Peeta's understanding of ontology: if he cannot distinguish reality from hallucinations, he cannot learn to trust Katniss again. And he bases his ability to trust almost entirely on *knowing* what is real: he must have an epistemological awareness of material phenomena in order to appreciate and accept reality. Katniss, on the other hand, has an insight about epistemological awareness that she is being given too much power over Peeta if she is the only person who can affirm his knowledge. She knows that her own being—and his—depends on him being and knowing independently from her being and knowing; she cannot be the sole person to define or determine his reality.

Feminist literature for the young is often informed by this relationship between being and knowing. Barad proposes the use of a term she refers to as "onto-epistem-ology—the study of practices of knowing in being" ("Posthumanist" 147). While the term "onto-epistem-ology" may be more jargonistic than is strictly speaking necessary for my purposes, the issues of "knowing in being" that Barad explores are nevertheless important to this form of analysis. The relationship between knowing and being is an inherently material question: perceptions interact with the material to affect both what we know and how we exist. Moreover, how we *know* ourselves to *be* gendered—as children, teenagers, or adults—involves the intersections of epistemology and ontology. Thus, material feminism offers the concept of "knowing in being" as a material approach to epistemology that simultaneously critiques poststructural theories of epistemology and complicates gender as an intra-activity of the material and the discursive.

## BEAUTY QUEENS: MATTERING, BECOMING, AND "KNOWING IN BEING"

Bridgitte Barclay uses material feminism to interpret the satiric qualities of Libba Bray's *Beauty Queens* in its functioning as a dystopia: "When read through the framework of material feminism, the young adult dystopian *Beauty Queens* offers an honest discourse about multiple removals from power and satirizes dominant culture's norms to show the power of becoming, of indeterminacy, and of hybridity" (141). Barclay is right that material feminism offers intriguing ways to open up this novel's satire of material culture, but she equates "*becoming*" with the term "transforming," missing the Deleuzian element of desire that Braidotti emphasizes (and that Bray depicts in her novel).[11] In *Beauty Queens* desire takes many forms, including in its influences on sexuality, consumerism, relationship formation, and identity formation. My goal then is to demonstrate that complicating the concepts of *becoming, mattering,* and "knowing in being" can help provide a material feminist reading of any children's or YA novel, but especially a YA novel like *Beauty Queens* that surfaces the tensions between objects, perception-as-knowing, and intra-activity.

*Beauty Queens* is a novel about fourteen contestants whose plane has crashed on a deserted island en route to the Miss Teen Dream pageant; the group demonstrates some level of diversity in terms of race, physical ability, gender identification, social class, and implied religious heritage. *Beauty Queens* addresses "knowing in being" early in the novel, in a conceit by which "The Corporation," a firm that runs most of the country, directly addresses the reader:

> This story is brought to you by The Corporation: Because Your Life Can Always Be Better™. We at The Corporation would like you to enjoy this story, but please be vigilant while reading. If you should happen to notice anything suspicious in the coming pages, do alert the proper authorities. Remember, it could be anything at all—a subversive phrase, an improper thought or feeling let out of its genie bottle of repression, an idea that challenges the status quo, the suggestions that life may not be what it appears to be and that all you've taken for granted (malls, shopping, the relentless pursuit of an elusive happiness, prescription drug ads, those annoying perfume samples in magazines that make your eyes water, the way anchormen and women shift easily from the jovial laughter of a story about a dog that hula-hoops to a grave report on a bus crash that has left five teenagers dead) may be no more consequential than the tattered hem of a dream, leaving you with a bottomless, free-fall feeling. (1–2)

This four-sentence paragraph hails the reader in Althusserrian terms by situating the represented reader's "knowing in being" as belonging to a consumeristic American teenager who likely identifies as "feminine," given the reference to the perfume ad in the magazine.[12] This is a represented/ implied reader whose ontological status is defined by the material: by malls, shopping, prescription drugs, perfume, television, buses, hula-hooping dogs juxtaposed with the bodies of dead teenagers. The represented teen-reader is also enacted epistemologically by the material activity of consuming through shopping, pill-taking, and media consumption. In The Corporation's construction of the reader, she learns through shopping; thus, consumer desire shapes her "knowing in being" and determines the direction her *becoming* will take. Bray, however, acknowledges the enacted reader's agency by depending on the reader to understand the irony at work here: the text expects readers to *know* that their *being* and their agency are not determined solely by consumer desire.[13] Bray trusts real readers to be enacted in their own agency through the process of reading and decoding the irony of these words.

Bray also plays with ontological status when she notes that "what you've taken for granted . . . may be no more consequential than the tattered hem of a dream, leaving you with a bottomless, free-fall feeling" (1–2). In that passage, three metaphors interact to demonstrate the illusory nature of reality. The narration acknowledges that the reality the implied/represented reader takes for granted may not be a matter of consequence, and indeed might only be—first—the frayed edge of—second—a dream—and thinking about the shallow nature of consumer-oriented life may cause any teenager to feel as if s/he is—third—falling endlessly. These metaphors invite readers to question the relationship between being and how we know what is real; moreover, the metaphors also emphasize indeterminacy and instability.[14] Within this construction, the fictive Corporation posits desire for material goods and consumption as the only possible way to make meaning in an unstable world. Against that propaganda, Bray proffers another and different way of *being* in the world: she is inviting readers to enact their agency by being more self-aware, more conscious of corporate manipulation of desire, and more concerned with how identities merge and shift. Her invitation is thus a call for readers to grow more aware of the processes of *becoming* and the ways that consumer desires manipulate their identity formation(s). Bray's irony is also wrapped in epistemological awareness: in order to exist meaningfully, the real/enacted reader must question all knowledge.

Bray emphasizes the importance of both *becoming* and performance throughout *Beauty Queens*. Everything about a beauty pageant is performance, of course: the girls frequently talk about their continual dieting and hair-grooming; with the pageant circuit also comes "teeth bleaching. . . . Eyebrow shaping. Tanning booths. Bikini waxes. Lipo" (72), and for at least one of the girls, hormone therapy. After the crash, the surviving contestants elect one of the white beauty queens, Miss Texas (Taylor), to serve as their leader on the island; she urges them to practice their routines daily so that they will still be able to perform well at the pageant after they are rescued. Taylor fines the other girls if she thinks they have not behaved with appropriate femininity—and indeed, performing femininity is all Taylor knows how to do. Her "knowing in being" shifts dramatically when she learns that The Corporation does not plan to rescue them. All her life, Taylor has believed that "if you did everything right, they had to love you," but on the island, she learns that performing femininity in the socially prescribed ways is not enough to make her loved (204). That truth causes her to become mentally unbalanced, and in ways more extreme than the other girls, she quits performing femininity. Her embodied materiality shifts: "Her normal smooth blond hair was a matted tangle. She'd camouflaged her face and arms with dirt like a soldier in a war movie. The white dress she'd taken the care to wash every day was ragged" (216). She becomes something of a jungle commando who ultimately saves the other girls—and she develops a new desire as she learns that "I love myself. They make it so hard for us to love ourselves" (352). This desire affects her *becoming.* Of all the girls, she alone elects to stay on the island, where she will no longer need to perform gender in ways that The Corporation would approve. In her new *becoming,* she rejects consumer desire and the performativity it engages. Taylor's decision makes clear that readers *can* reject certain types of gendered performativity in a gesture that deconstructs the very nature of performativity itself.

Bray, however, does more than deconstruct gender performativity. Throughout her book, she emphasizes the importance of *mattering,* that is, the importance of perceptual processes as the continuously re-forming intra-action between lived materiality and discourse. As they think about their own bodies, as they regard their own bodies, and as they use changing discourses to describe their bodies and their relationships, these girls experience the intra-activity of *mattering* and they do so in relationships with each other that are increasingly cooperative and communal. Their identities are *not* stable; their bodies are *not* fixed entities, and the discourse they employ liberates them to think about the materiality of their embodiment as a process rather than as static and immutable. As long as "beauty" equals only one thing to each of these contestants, they are content to participate in never-ending competitions with each other in which they devalue their own agency. On the other hand, once they experience a kaleidoscope of perceptions because of multiple challenges on the island—monsoons, floods, dehydration, snakes, hallucinogenic plants—they are more open to the idea that beauty (like most abstract concepts) has more than one definition. They gain appreciation for their agency as a phenomenon in process, open to the potential of *becoming.* Their identities merge with the environment, with each other, with their idealized former selves, and with the lived reality of their wilder new embodiment. And the first step in liberating themselves from their patriarchal and monolithic thinking has been predicated on their desire to begin working cooperatively, rather than competitively.

Two concepts in the novel thus exemplify the ongoing process of *mattering:* 1) the girls' changing perceptions of community as sisterhood and 2) beauty. For another one of the white beauty queens, Adina, the discourse and the relationships implied in the word *sister* motivate her to change her relationship with the other contestants, especially as they all learn to think differently about *beauty* as both a concept and a material effect of their embodiment. Adina at one point criticizes the girls for the single-mindedness of their competitiveness: "We are supposed to be sisters. Sisters who love

and trust one another, who work together until it's clear that there is a favorite sister chosen to be the best and wear a pretty crown. So let's cut the
crap" (220). Adina is teaching the other girls to desire cooperation so that
their *becoming* can shift.

In another example, Shanti realizes she is trapped in quicksand and begs
her fiercest competitor, Nicole, who is African American, to help her: "You
won't help a sister out?" (190). Nicole, angry that Shanti has been performing
as an ethnic Indian national (rather than performing as the second-gener-
ation girl from southern California she actually is), refuses to help Shanti:
"On, no. You did *not* just play that. . . . You are not my sister. You are a total
fake and a liar" (190). These two girls help the novel problematize how and
why whiteness undergirds most beauty standards in the US But once Shanti
admits she has been performing an ethnic role for a reason (because she desires having "an edge" as a girl of color in the competition), Nicole agrees to
help her—and also ends up trapped in the quicksand (190). They then hold
hands "for one last, sisters-in-non-white-dominant-culture-solidarity hand
clasp" before they finally free themselves (193). Later, chased by Corporation
agents who have infiltrated the island, Shanti and Nicole again hold hands,
refusing to abandon one another; "Not without you," Nicole tells Shanti,
just before a powerful wind disperses the agents (346). The two girls have
shifted the meaning of the word *sister* because of the materiality of their
proximal entrapment; in joining hands, they demonstrate their desire to
work cooperatively, so they are temporarily linked as physical beings, and
they thus *become* metaphorical sisters.

Yet another white beauty queen learns to prize her own willingness to
learn in terms of her *becoming* because she is worried that, someday, beauty
won't be enough to make her happy. She tells the Corporation agent who
has been taunting her: "Maybe I'm not the smartest person in the world, . . .
but at least I keep trying. I keep learning" (356). For this character, knowing
in being impels the forward momentum of her *becoming*; her desire stems
from wanting to know and learn even more than she wants to be considered
beautiful. Perceptions have affected these girls' knowing in being, which
in turn affects their understanding of the discursive and the desires that
motivate their *becoming*, so their perceptions of beauty and of sisterhood
shift as significantly as their agential *becomings* do.

Furthermore, the island also offers the type of posthumanist challenge
to agency that material feminists, such as Barad and Tuana, advance. Tuana
affirms "the urgency of embracing an ontology that rematerializes the social
and takes seriously the agency of the natural"; the concept of *mattering*

insists that the material has agency, particularly in its recognition that the material intra-acts to influence and shape the discursive ("Viscous" 188). And indeed, on the beauty queens' island, the environment itself has agency. Clouds gather ominously in the sky: "an army of angry clouds massed along the horizon, awaiting further instruction" (18). A tidal wave floods the girls' encampment: "the wave hit full force, upending girls like bowling pins, the fast-moving current carrying them down, out, under" (53). The ground itself also has volition: "The earth beneath them gave way suddenly, and the girls were swept down the mountainside in a spiral of mud and sequins and screams" (55). When they eat a hallucinogenic plant, one girl can see "the edges of the jungle unfolding, showing her more and more, like one of those accordion birthday cards" (78). Later, when the island's wind rescues Nicole and Shanti from the agents who are chasing them, the text explains: "A wind soft as a warm breath blew across their faces. It left them and turned fierce, stripping leaves from trees and pulling the dirt from ancient earthen walls. Like an angry fist, it pushed the black shirts . . . forcing them back into the jungle. . . . The wind howled with such force that Shanti and Nicole could almost hear something human in its cries" (346). The girls hear something *almost* human: the wind is not actually human but it nonetheless has agency. Agency does not belong solely to humans on this island. As one of the girls thinks: "things were different out here in the jungle" (138).

Once the beauty queens experience shifting perceptions because of the agency they recognize in the natural world, they gain appreciation for their own agency as a phenomenon in process, open to the potential of *becoming*. Their experiences on the island create in them desires they've never before experienced—not only sexual desires, but also more basic desires (such as the increased desire for safety, food, and fresh water) and also for more psychosocial desires (such as companionship and self-approval). These desires lead to a blending of *becomings* as their identities merge with the environment, with each other, with their idealized former selves, and with the lived reality of their wilder new embodiments.

In one of the book's most pivotal chapters, the girls recognize that they have been happier as castaways than they were as pageant contestants. Mary Lou, a white contestant from Nebraska, says, "Maybe girls *need* an island to find themselves. Maybe they need a place where no one's watching them so they can be who they really are" (177, italics in the original). Adina responds to Mary Lou saying "maybe," as she "*gazed* out at the expanse of unknowable ocean" (177, italics added). The ocean is as inscrutable as the inner-lives of these teenagers who have spent their whole lives being the object of other people's gazes. Bray's use of the term *gaze* reinforces how the male gaze has objectified the girls, stripping them of their agency and reducing them only to their bodies. Moreover, Bray is demonstrating how dependent on the gaze performativity is: without an audience to perform for, performativity no longer *matters*.

Bray immediately replaces the concept of performativity with the idea of *becoming* in the next paragraphs:

> There was something about the island that made the girls forget who they had been. All those rules and shalt nots. They were no longer waiting for some arbitrary grade. They were no longer performing. Waiting. Hoping.
> They were becoming.
> They were. (177)

Bray links the process of *becoming* with ontological status: "They were becoming" quickly becomes "they were" (177). The passage is as dramatic of a demonstration of the feminist potential of intra-activity as any I have yet found in adolescent literature. Everything these girls perceive changes them, just as their perceptions change what they are observing. The beauty queens experience changed materiality in their new living conditions, including experiencing the materiality of their bodies differently. Their *becoming* is intertwined with their perceptions and *mattering*, but their discourse with one another allows them to process differently who they are, how they are living, what they know, and what they like and don't like about themselves.

Several of the girls experience major transformations in their own process of *becoming*. Mary Lou, Miss Nebraska, rejects the rigid sexual inhibitions her mother and Midwestern culture have placed on her, recognizing that she is a "wild girl who likes sex and adventure" (299) and that the only shame in her sexuality is "allowing yourself to be shamed. To let the world shape your desire and love into a cudgel with which to drive you back into a cave of fear" (265). She has been taught to think of gender as a performance: "when it came to love, the message for girls seemed to be this: Don't. Don't go after what you want. Wait. Wait to be chosen, as if only in the eye of another could one truly find value. The message was confusing and infuriating. It was a shell game with no actual pea under the rapidly moving cups" (125). She has watched other girls at school, learning how to act demure, shy, and "giggly" (161). She has learned "to be afraid of her own body" (161), but on the island, she enjoys the sexual desire she feels when running naked in the moonlight: "how good it felt to command her body in this way. How erotic the thrill of it! Like a caged beast finally allowed to hunt.... But somewhere deep down, she loved the sheer heady freedom of it. In this state, she was not afraid of the jungle, but part of it" (167). Mary Lou has merged with the jungle; she has become "part of it." This, then, is her *becoming*, and it is directly linked to erotic desire. Mary Lou's understanding of her own being has changed both because of the materiality of existing within the jungle and because that material experience allows her to employ a different discourse in her self-talk about her own sexuality. She has embraced the intra-activity between the physicality of her sexuality and her discursively-dependent self-talk to achieve a new level of self-acceptance.

Petra, Miss Rhode Island, has long ago come to terms with herself as a transgendered white teenaged girl, but she is also able to become more open and less self-loathing about having male genitalia. (In one particularly comic scene, she pees standing up over someone with a jelly fish sting to alleviate the toxins of the sting—and she feels great pride after having done so.) Two of the more conservative girls also come to accept Petra as a legitimate Miss Teen Dream contestant because she is—as they originally fear—neither breaking the rules nor an aberration "against nature and God" (99). Petra responds to this last allegation, saying, "Maybe you should ask God and nature why they put a girl inside a boy's body?" (99). She also asks the contestants to consider an ontologically complex question: "What makes a girl a girl? What makes a guy a guy?" (107). Just asking these questions liberates the pageant contestants to think of femaleness differently. Perhaps more than any other character in the novel, Petra foregrounds the ongoing intra-activity of embodiment as matter and gender as a discursive meaning.[15] Both Petra and Mary Lou are experiencing the vibrating tension between discourse and the material. What *does* make a girl a girl? Genitalia, hormones, and outward appearance—which are bio-material phenomena? Internal feelings, sexuality, and self-knowledge—which are based in the chemistry of the brain and the endocrine system but are also defined by discourse? Performativity—which Butler defines more discursively than materially? Or also the potential for *becoming* and the intra-actions among all of these things?

Barad's position that the material has agency and that meaning occurs through process can be illustrated with at least two additional examples of nonhuman agency at work in *Beauty Queens*. One involves a snake, the other a manufactured beauty product. In the first example, Miss Illinois drops a spear "which stuck fast in a fat tree root" (62). Miss Illinois and the girl who is watching her, Miss Michigan, assume that the tree has no agency. But everything on this island seems to have some sort of agency, some sort of transformative power. And so, it is not particularly surprising when the tree root starts moving: "the giant, gnarled tree seemed to uncoil, and Jennifer saw that it was not a mass of roots looped about the trunk but a freakishly big snake" (62). The snake swallows Sosie (Miss Illinois), and Jennifer (Miss Michigan) helps Sosie to free herself. The two eventually have a romantic attachment: Jennifer is a white lesbian; Sosie is white, hearing-impaired, and bi-questioning. When Sosie is inside the snake, Jennifer performs the role of rescuing savior by driving a spear through the snake's head. From inside the snake, Sosie places "what looked like a smallish white tub between the snake's back teeth," which allows Sosie to slide on the snake's saliva out of its jaw—just before the snake explodes (64). The snake "had probably once been a glorious creature," but Jennifer and Sosie can see that it has been ill: "Its long body was covered in disgusting sores and tumors. Its scales were mostly gone. The few that remained were an iridescent greenish blue that dazzled. . . . Jen was reminded of the old, tough-as-algebra barflies in her neighborhood, the ones with the long, permed hair who still clung to the leopard-print dresses they'd put on thirty years ago and refused to retire" (66). Sosie pities the dead snake; Jennifer tells her, "That poor thing tried to eat us," which makes Sosie correct herself: "Poor bitch" (66).

The snake demonstrates intra-activity as process, as both performance and *mattering*. As the "known"—that is, as matter—the snake is first known (or perceived) as a tree root and only secondarily is the knower able to perceive the known as "snake" and arrive at the knowledge, the discursive meaning, that the snake is "dangerous." The snake is motivated by a desire that is quite literally a *becoming*: when the snake eats Sosie, they temporarily merge and become one. Furthermore, the snake has once been "glorious"; then it has been ill, and now it is dead. The girls first perceive it as a tree root, then as a life-threatening menace, and then as a woman past her prime; their perceptions have undergone a series of cognitive transformations, just as the snake's desire has also led to its changed state of being. Sosie has been outside of the snake; then she is inside of it; then she is outside it again. She has been instrumental in blowing the snake up so that the girls become "coated in snake insides" (64); that is, the inside of the snake is now the girls' outer covering. Libba Bray is demonstrating here the instability of meaning and perception; perceptions shift, meanings change, and discourse alone cannot account for the entirety of any phenomenon. Even when Jen and Sosie think of the material object using the wrong words—"tree root"— the snake is still a snake. It is not defined solely by discourse. And yet in its death, as Jen compares the snake to a worn-out barfly, discourse changes her perception of the snake. So does her conversation with Sosie: the snake is not a "poor thing"; it is a "poor bitch." Meaning resides in the intra-activity between matter and discourse; here matter redefines discourse, just as discourse redefines matter. And readers are exposed to processes of *mattering* that demonstrate the agential potential of both discourse and object.

It turns out that Sosie has blown the snake up with a container of "Lady 'Stache Off," a beauty product marketed by The Corporation for its "triple beauty action": it is a moisturizer, a tanning product, and an exfoliant. Conveniently enough, it can also be used as a toilet sanitizer (35). The product's slogan is this: "Lady 'Stache off. Because there's nothing wrong with you . . . that can't be fixed" (37, ellipses in the original). Bray's ability to demonstrate the agency of materiality is evident in the product's multivariate uses: this inanimate compound removes hair, moisturizes, changes the skin's color, and even sanitizes. All of these processes involve changing the surface of another material object, whether it is a human body or a toilet. As a symbol, Lady 'Stache Off thus demonstrates that beauty is superficial—only skin-deep. But the product's agential realism becomes even more—and literally—unstable when the Corporation realizes that "if you change one compound in Lady 'Stache Off, it becomes highly unstable. All it needs is a charge of some kind and you've got incredible shock-and-awe capabilities" (91). This is how Sosie has exploded the snake: from inside the snake's body, she has used what is intended as a product for external use in its transformed state as an explosive, blowing apart the snake as a signifying menace and enacting her own agency in the process. Indeed, Lady 'Stache Off becomes central to the rest of the plot in that it is a weapon that The Corporation intends to sell to the corrupt dictator with whom it is making an illegal arms deal. Ladybird Hope, the girls' role model as a former Miss Teen Dream and a member of the Corporation's Board of Directors, proves to be the evil mastermind behind a plot to kill off both the corrupt dictator and all the surviving beauty queens. Eventually, the girls expose Ladybird and save themselves from the mass murder she has planned. They are freed, in part, because multiple cases of Lady 'Stache Off blow up The Corporation's compound. The Corporation proves to be its own worst enemy.

With the text's parodic multi-modality, Bray allows space for readers to question how their agency has been manipulated by consumer desire and corporate greed. For example, after Mary Lou decides to embrace her sexuality, the text includes "A WORD FROM YOUR SPONSOR":

The Corporation would like to apologize for the preceding pages. Of course, it's not all right for girls to behave this way. Sexuality is not meant to be this way—an honest, consensual expression in which a girl might take an active role when she feels good and ready and not one minute before. No. Sexual desire is meant to sell soap. And cars. And beer. And religion. (178)

This passage is clearly part of Bray's overt feminist agenda—but it is also part of the playful irony that positions the text to interact with readers via their "knowing in being." Moreover, the text interrupts itself frequently with "words from your sponsor" or "fun facts" about each of the surviving Miss Teen Dream contestants or commercials for various Corporation products, such as "New Maxi-Pad Pets. Accessories for your period. Brought to you by The Corporation: In your homes and in your pants" (318). These interstitial narrative ruptures allow Bray to mock corporate American depictions of compulsory femininity; the satire also affords space in which readers can reflect on how their consumer desires have the potential to negatively affect their own *becoming*. Most of all, these parodic commercials emphasize the intra-activity between the material and discourse. Menstruation, for example, is a material phenomenon—and although maxi-pads shaped like animals are, as of this writing, only a figment of Bray's imagination—the Maxi-Pad Pets demonstrate the idea of a material object changing discourse about menstruation. They "come in twelve different pet-pal shapes so you can change your mood as often as you change your pad!" (316); different girls are depicted as wearing a "sexy lynx" or "a cute, cuddly puppy" or "a playful platypus" or "a happy hamster" (317). "Who's got a tiger in her trousers?" one girl asks in the mock commercial (317). The Corporation's clear purpose in developing the Maxi-Pad Pets is to change how girls think about menstruation by making their product desirable. As one of the commercial's girls says about her friend who looks "haggard" because "it's that time of month": "I guess somebody doesn't know how much fun having your period can be with new Maxi-Pad Pets—the revolutionary new fashion maxi pad that makes you feel like you've got a special friend in your pants" (316). Bray's satire works effectively because the goal of making menstruation "fun" is so ludicrous. Indeed, most of the narrative disruptions in *Beauty Queens* rely on the playful—that is, the ludic—as a form of interaction. This form of play is an interactive game: readers are being invited to destabilize meaning. Especially significant here is the destabilization of femininity as a material product of manipulated consumer desire.

Libba Bray is not afraid of her own feminist agenda, nor does she try to hide it. By the end of the novel, Miss Mississippi is able to proclaim, "I've learned that feminism is for everybody and there's nothing wrong with taking up space in the world, even if you have to fight for it a little bit" (335). She and the other girls have vowed to quit apologizing and saying "sorry" so frequently; even more powerfully, Miss Mississippi says, "I've learned that I don't really care if you like these answers or not, because they're the best most honest ones I've got, and I just don't feel like I can cheat myself enough to give you what you want me to say" (336). Given that earlier in the novel, she has asked, "Do you think my new feminism makes me look fat?," the character seems to have come a long way (251).

In an interview with cultural critic Amy Gentry, Bray admits that her social critique is motivated by her anger at misogyny: "I thought, why is there so much misogyny? I mean I know that misogyny is always with us, but why is there so *much* misogyny? Why are we so hard on ourselves?" (Gentry, italics in the original). Bray openly acknowledges that her intent in *Beauty Queens* is to teach girls to deconstruct the rhetoric that surrounds them:

> Just pay attention to the rhetoric. Pay attention to the messages. Because if you can't deconstruct the rhetoric. . . . if you don't know how to think critically, if you can hear a message like "Well, we really want to protect women" and understand that "protect" really means "oppress." . . . What is the fear, what is the threat that it seems to pose for these people? Because unless you can trace it back, you can't really start trying to root it out at the source. You can't really try to fight. But when push comes to shove about somebody trying to take your rights away. . . . You just have to say Oh hell no, you are not taking my rights. (Gentry)

Bray insists that she wants girls to experience "the whole Roy G. Biv of female experience" (Gentry); her characters problematize and defend the pleasure of make-overs (Bray 153), even while they learn to build huts, desalinate water, fish, hunt, fortify their settlement, and defend themselves against predators, both human and animal. These girls are strong, smart, resourceful, sexual, *and* beautiful. Bray is just one among a generation of novelists who is aware of feminism as a multiply-constructed set of ideologies that involve people who advocate for equality, regardless of gender or gender-identification. Bray's sensitivity to rhetoric undoubtedly positions her to be the type of novelist who can explore the intra-actions among the material and the discursive; as a result, she writes about gender, identity, and self-knowledge not only in terms of performativity but also in terms of *mattering, becoming*, and in terms of "knowing in being." *Beauty Queens*, in particular, is a novel that surfaces the significance to gender studies of the intra-actions among the material and discourse as functions that affect and effect the ontological and epistemological positioning of girls in twenty-first century North American culture.

## CONCLUSION

Material feminism has much to offer the study of feminisms in twenty-first century children's and adolescent literature. While poststructural discourse-oriented feminism allowed critics to ignore material reality, especially embodiment, material feminism insists on the centrality of the material in human lives. Material feminism also offers a corrective to the fear that discussions of identity can become reductive or essentialist, especially given the ways that discourse-oriented feminism privileges epistemology over ontology, while material feminism insists on the necessary interrelationship of the subject's epistemology and ontology. Moreover, material feminism invites us to interrogate the mutually implicating relationships that exist in the dynamics between discourse and the material world. Material feminism calls us to consider how the material world affects discourses about girls in terms of the body, the environment, technology, physical artifacts, and the natural world. In this formulation, identity is not a purely discursive function; it is formed in part via interactions with the material. Furthermore, philosophical interrogations of representationality force us to consider the ontological gap between that which is enacted and its representation; that ontological gap creates the intra-activity of "'things'-in-phenomena," as Barad puts it ("Posthumanist" 135). *Mattering* is thus the process by which the material and the discursive intra-act to define one another; *becoming* is the desire-driven process of merging that demonstrates the relationship between performativity and our intra-active emergence as a phenomenon of ongoing being. Without *mattering*, we would have no *becoming* because our *becoming* depends upon the intra-activity between discourse and material phenomena. *Becoming* is inherent within adolescence itself, given the way that maturation requires change based on merging identities and performativity. What material feminism therefore offers to literature for the young is a way for scholars to think about how material phenomena affect performances of gender while the young grow to maturity; what children's and adolescent literature offers material feminism is the opportunity for us to concentrate on a stage of life that is largely implicated in processes of *becoming.*

## CHAPTER 2

# INTERSECTIONALITIES AND MULTIPLICITIES
*Race and Materiality in Literature for the Young*

In 1989, a legal scholar named Kimberlé Crenshaw wrote in the *University of Chicago Legal Forum* about the problem with privileging one form of oppression over another. She observed the tendency in legal cases for one form of oppression to matter more than another—which effectively "erases," in her terms, the experience of black women (140).

> Black women are sometimes excluded from feminist theory and antiracist policy discourse because both are predicated on a discrete set of experiences that often does not accurately reflect the interaction of race and gender. . . . Because the intersectional experience is greater than the sum of racism and sexism, any analysis that does not take intersectionality into account cannot sufficiently address the particular manner in which Black women are subordinated. (141)

Crenshaw is thus credited with coining the term "intersectionality," which refers to the practice of recognizing that forms of oppression intersect; in other words, when we consider intersectionality, we are acknowledging how terms of oppression intersect to increase the factors involved in oppression. Patricia Hill Collins adopts the term in *Black Feminist Thought* to argue that "For African American women, the knowledge gained at the intersecting oppressions of race, class, and gender provides the stimulus for crafting and passing on the subjugated knowledge of Black Women's critical social theory" (8). Collins asserts that when oppressions are evaluated hierarchically, the range of discrimination and social powerlessness of people who live with multiple forms of oppressions are ignored. Intersectionality thus acknowledges "particular forms of intersecting oppressions, for example, intersections of race and gender, or of sexuality and nation" (Collins 18).

The ideas behind intersectionality are particularly useful in children's and adolescent literature because all childhood experience is always already intersectional, based as the genre is on the relative social powerlessness of people who are not adults. That is, childhood and adolescence are one aspect of identity politics that involves subjects who have less political and economic power than the adults who define laws and social norms. Some of that powerlessness involves embodiment, too: children are typically smaller than adults; adolescents typically undergo the embodied transformation of puberty. Maria Nikolajeva provides a name for this particular form of alterity based on a parallel she makes with the idea of queering heteronormativity. When legal and moral codes are based on heterosexuality, then norms are heteronormative. By extension since all nations accord more social and legal power to adults than children, Nikolajeva asserts that we should also be thinking in terms of age-based norms. "*Aeto-*" is the Latin prefix for "age," so Nikolajeva has coined the term "*aetonormativity*" to refer to age-based norms that position adults as more powerful than the young (8). Nikolajeva argues that especially in the study of youth literature, alterity studies—that is, studies of difference, such as race studies, disability studies, or queer theory—should also include an awareness of age as a form of otherness.

Moreover, as a form of intersectionality, all children's literature that involves multiculturalism, diversity, ability, or difference demonstrates how aetonormativity interacts with other forms of oppression. Taken together, intersectionality and aetonormativity help us consider the unique forms of oppression that occur in the matrix of age and other forms of difference. Since this book is concerned with matters of gender, for example, we can use intersectionality to think about the intersections of oppression that occur when characters are black girls—or differently-abled girls or lesbian adolescents or when their subject positions involve any form of alterity that interacts with age to create multiple sites of oppression.

Michael Hames-García is a material feminist who complicates intersectionality in his work *Identity Complex*, arguing that it is an "established tradition" that has helped scholars perform the important work of identifying "'intersections' of oppression or of identities," but he worries that the study of intersectionality does not go far enough in influencing "core assumptions about identity, history, experience, or knowledge unless women of color constitute the immediate object of inquiry" (xii). The theoretical work of intersectionality is, he believes, hugely important to "women-of-color feminism," but it has not done enough for peoples with identities outside of these intersections, such as gay men, people with disabilities, and working-class straight white men (xii, xiii). The very fact that aetonormativity has emerged as an independent study of alterity validates his point: few scholars of intersectionality account for how age increases the factors of oppression when race and gender and social class intersect. Hames-García thus argues in favor of a theory he calls *multiplicity*, which is built on the shoulders of intersectionality; he wants to "account for how social identities take shape through processes of racial and gender formation, mutually constituting one another" and "to analyze the necessary social interdependence of identities" (xi). Hames-García is aware that oppression affects both oppressor and oppressed, and that the matrices of oppression influence identity: "Although the obscuring of multiplicity that accompanies oppression affects everyone to some degree—not only those who face direct oppression—the consequences of this obscuring take different forms for the oppressed than for those with relatively more privilege" (7). But he is not discounting oppression as a factor when he writes about multiplicity. Rather, he wishes for us to acknowledge "the mutual constitution and overlapping of simultaneously experienced and politically significant categories such as ability, citizenship, class, ethnicity, gender, race, religion, and sexuality" (13). He does not believe that separate identities come to intersect in a linear fashion; in his case, he does not believe that his identity as a Mexican American intersects neatly with his identity as a gay man: "Rather than existing as essentially separate axes that sometimes intersect, social identities blend, constantly and differently, expanding one another and mutually constituting one another's meanings" (13).

It is important to note that Hames-García's work commits him "to the idea that a theory-independent social reality exists outside of our individual subjective belief about it" and that "theories of the social world can help us to understand that reality because they remain to some extent answerable to it" (16). In other words, Hames-García is influenced by the work of Karen Barad and philosophers like her to focus on "the *lived experiences* that give substance to class, disability, gender, race, sexuality, and so on" (10). Because Hames-García so elegantly quotes Barad's work, I will use his words here: "Barad suggests that an adequate social theory of bodies needs to account for '*how the body's materiality*—for example, its anatomy and physiology—*and other material forces actively matter to the processes of materialization*'" (Barad, "Posthumanist" 324; qtd. in Hamas-García 58, italics in the original). Hames-García, for example, cannot think of the physical forms of discrimination he has experienced solely in terms of discursive social constructions. He asks, "How can I understand my ease at hailing a taxicab in New York City or Washington, D.C., in the face of countless stories from black friends about having to walk forty blocks without having one stop for them?" (60). Multiplicity is both a discursive and an embodied experience. Thus, whether we think about race in terms of how other terms of oppression intersect with it, or whether we think of identity in terms of many multiplicities, material feminists insist that social identity can only be understood in terms of the material conditions and experiences of an individual's life.

For example, the Black Lives Matter movement that emerged following protests of police brutality in Ferguson, Missouri, in 2014 points to clear evidence that race, age, and gender are mutually implicated in this country. Treyvon Martin was seventeen when his neighbor in Florida shot and killed him in 2012. Michael Brown was eighteen when a police officer shot and killed him in Ferguson 2014. Tamir Rice was twelve when police shot and killed him in Cleveland in 2014. Paul O'Neal was eighteen when police shot and killed him in Chicago in July of 2016. Carnell Snell was also eighteen when police shot and killed him in Los Angeles in October 2016. All of these adolescents were male; all were African American. All were killed by men considerably older than they were. Racism is a pervasive and pernicious social evil, and the Black Lives Matter movement does important work in raising consciousness about systematic black oppression in the US, especially violence perpetrated against black male youth. One function children's books can play in addressing this evil is to indoctrinate children ideologically in ways that reject the prejudices of earlier eras.

Social movements such as Black Lives Matter have also helped raise awareness of implicit racism in the field of children's literature, as when the editors of major review journals in children's literature began openly questioning racial assumptions at work in children's books. Vicky Smith of *Kirkus Reviews* critiques the "shockingly disproportionate" number of books written by and about white people; in 2016 that reviewing journal adopted a practice of identifying the race of all characters as a corrective that foregrounds white privilege. Roger Sutton of *Horn Book*, however, expresses concern about "labelling a character with an ethnicity that the book itself does not corroborate"; he prefers that readers be allowed to interpret characters the way they want, rather than having an adult place the child characters into racial categories. Both views have merit, so in this work, when I introduce a character for whom race—including whiteness—is ideologically significant, I will identify that character's race. But when race is not ideologically significant to the analysis I am performing, I will not include a racial label. *Beauty Queens*, for example, openly interrogates whiteness as the construct on which cultural definitions of beauty too often rely; Shanti's and Nicole's stories foreground Bray's cultural critique of whiteness as the "default" race in the United States. Throughout the rest of this volume, I will therefore identify the race of characters when multiplicities and aetonormativity combine as factors that affect any girl's ability to function as a feminist.

Specifically, in this chapter, I analyze five narratives that I have selected because they foreground ideologically the multiplicities involved in being a person of color, young, and female. Christopher Paul Curtis's novel *The Mighty Miss Malone* (2012) is a novel with a traditionally linear plot that interrogates the material hardships of a family trying to survive the trauma of the Great Depression. Pam Muñoz Ryan's *Becoming Naomi Léon* (2004) examines how multiplicity and identity formation are implicated in processes of *becoming*. *Claudette Colvin: Twice Toward Justice* (2009) by Phillip Hoose is a nonfiction text for preteens and adolescents about a girl whose efforts to integrate the Montgomery bus system preceded Rosa Parks's. Jacqueline Woodson's National Book Award winning *Brown Girl Dreaming* (2014) is a memoir written in poems—a hybrid work that describes lyrically one young person's growing awareness of identity politics. Sherri L. Smith's novel *Flygirl* (2008) complicates intersectionality and multiplicity in a YA novel about the ethics of passing. Intersectionality, multiplicity, and aetonormativity work together with the material in these five texts to demonstrate how twenty-first century feminist authors destabilize such binaries as those inherent in the false dichotomies of race (white/non-white), gender (male/female), and age (young/old).

## INTERSECTIONALITY AND *THE MIGHTY MISS MALONE*

Christopher Paul Curtis's *The Mighty Miss Malone* can be usefully studied in terms of intersectionality and aetonormativity, especially because Curtis teases his protagonist's identity into strands that are sometimes discrete. For Deza Malone—the Mighty Miss Malone of the novel's title—intersectionality includes the quadruple oppressions of gender, race, social class, and childhood. Set in Gary, Indiana, during the Great Depression of the 1930s, Curtis's story focuses on a young, self-confident girl whose family is supportive and loving. But everything falls apart when Deza's father experiences a traumatic accident, so he can no longer hold a job. The material conditions of his family's lifestyle change dramatically because of their shift in social class. Initially, Deza is depicted as performing ultra-femininity, with a mother who shares her material attraction to pretty dresses, well-groomed hair, and respectable shoes. Deza also performs the role of "good girl": she is a perfectionist and extraordinarily concerned about her grades and about being the smartest girl in the room.

Deza's self-confidence is important to the story; although she experiences oppression, she refuses to think of herself as a victim. For example, when Deza has to write a school essay about her family—its strengths, weaknesses, and each individual's pet peeves—she initially cannot think about a single annoying trait she might have until she asks her best friend, who tells her that other people find it annoying that she acts like a know-it-all. Deza then writes about herself, "*My most endearing trait, and being as modest I am I had to ask my brother Jimmie for this, is that I have the heart of a champion, am steady as a rock and can be counted on to do what is required. Jimmie also said I am the smartest kid he has ever met, but my all-encompassing and pervasive humility prevents me from putting that on this list*" (12, italics in the original). Deza's self-confidence alternates between being charming and being annoying, but it is her most effective tool for dealing with the disempowerment caused by her intersectionalities.

While Deza's father is still employed, she lives in Gary, where she has an African American teacher who respects her intellect enough to tell her to quit performing the gendered role of "smart girl" and start performing as a leader. The teacher acknowledges Deza's intersectionality in terms of race, class, and age: "I believe . . . that if we lose you, we've lost this country. If we can't get *you* to your true path, it's the failure of everyone from President Roosevelt right down to me" (38). The teacher understands that the triad of race, gender, and class could ultimately work together to disempower Deza despite her extraordinary intelligence. The teacher's use of the word "we" in her formulation "if we lose you" is a commentary on her own generation's ability (or inability) to inspire a new generation of black leaders; she knows full well that poverty exacerbates the conditions of oppression for Deza as an African American, as a child, and as a female.

Deza loves to read and is self-aware about the implications of reading as an African American female in a racist society. When she reads words in novels about some girl's "pale, luminescent skin" or "her flowing mane of golden hair" or "her lovely cornflower-blue eyes," the girl tells herself, "No, Deza, none of these books are about you" (233). She believes she has four choices when she reads words that are psychically violent to her performance of gender and her experience of race: "one, I could pretend I had blond hair and blue eyes. But that didn't feel right. Two, I could start reading the novels like they were history books, just a bunch of facts put together. . . .

Three, I could change a word or two here or there and keep enjoying them by pretending they *were* about me, or four, I could stop reading altogether. ... [But] I couldn't stop reading if I wanted to" (233–34, italics in the original). She decides to treat racially gendered discourses as "buggy oatmeal," which might have "a few bad things in them," but that can be tolerated "if you plugged your nose or sifted [the bugs] out" (234). Eventually, however, she does find herself almost unable to perform that type of gendered and racialized reading when her new white English teacher in Michigan presents her with overwhelmingly racist and sexist books. She decides that some novels are "just too terrible to pretend that they [are] anything but stinkers" (234).

At one point, Deza experiences the insensitivity of a racist white librarian. Her parents teach her that she must use the knowledge of other people's racism to create a Standpoint for herself from which she can critique that racism. Having emerged from Critical Race Theory, Marxism, and intersectionality, Standpoint Theory teaches us that "there are some perspectives on society from which, however well intentioned one may be, the real relations of humans with each other and with the natural world are not visible" (Hartsock 117). Per this theory, those who occupy an oppressed standpoint are more likely to be able to critique what is wrong with a culture than those who are in power in the dominant culture. So, for example, after Deza talks to the racist white librarian, she asks her parents, "What does it mean when someone says you're a credit to your race?"; her father tells her that it means she is being given a "warning about whoever it is who's saying" those words (83)—that is, Deza should anticipate that any person saying such words is racist. Deza's father wants her to be aware of the oppressive threat of racism, but he also wants her to critique that racism. He is making her aware of how her Standpoint in her culture can help her critique the intersectionalities of oppression in which she lives and how that Standpoint can help her respond to—and even destabilize—the fixed identity-categories into which middle-class white people want to put her. Indeed, the entire novel uses Deza's Standpoints to critique not only the oppressions of race, gender, class, and childhood in the Depression, but also that same matrix of oppressions as they have affected children during the Great Recession. Published in 2012, the novel is a commentary on how children—particularly underprivileged children of color—were disproportionately affected by the harsh economic conditions of the post-2008 Great Recession.

Materiality and economic conditions, for example, become demonstrably linked through health issues that involve material embodiment. Deza's family is so poor that they can't afford to take her to the dentist. Her teeth become the material symbol of her decaying social order, including her ability to perform gender. She feels "red and white pain" in her back teeth (66). Her own father says, "I've found I can't breathe out of my nose when I'm near Deza because of the smell of her teeth. How sick is that? How pathetic am I that I can't even breathe normally around my own child?" (129). Deza's father describes her teeth in what serves as a metaphor for the Depression-era social decay: he says that his "sassy, smart, beautiful charming little girl . . . is slowly rotting away on the inside" (129). He eventually abandons his family. After Deza hops the rails and rides with her mother and brother to Flint, Michigan, Deza talks about having "toughened up" (200, 233) and her mother says she is glad to have Deza "to lean on" (225). Deza becomes less concerned about high grades and perfectionism once she has lived in a Hooverville shack. "It wasn't long before we stopped looking fresh," she says in a grim acknowledgment of how performing certain types of femininity requires middle-class conditions (201).

Deza's father, and eventually her brother, disappear, seeking a way to support the family during tragically difficult times. Both acknowledge that their desire to work is tied to their ability to perform masculinity for their family. Deza's father describes his inability to get a job as making him feel subhuman; he wants "to feel like a human being and not some animal in a zoo waiting for a handout" (128). He clearly believes it is his job to provide for his family—and eventually, his family learns that his despair has driven him, literally, insane. Later, Deza's brother, Jimmie, also abandons the family when he pursues a career as a singer in order to help their finances. His rationale is that "a man[']s got to do what a man[']s got to do" (220). Because they are males, they have the freedom to leave their family and seek work elsewhere. But Deza, because she is a female and young, must stay with her mother. The intersections of childhood and gender make it impossible for her to help her family financially.

Deza slowly finds herself losing the ability—and the desire—to care about performing femininity—although she and her mother still value education. Her mother tells her, "I love the fact that you're so much smarter than I am. Took him a while to catch on, but you're smarter than your father, too" (216). By the time Deza finds her brother singing in a nightclub in Detroit, she is suffering from such rotten teeth that the odor and the pain are almost unbearable. Eventually, with his singing career, her brother helps the family regain its financial footing and pays to have Deza's teeth fixed. An older friend in Flint has also given her books by W. E. B. DuBois and Nella

Larsen that are obviously intended correctives to the steady diet of books about performing white femininity that she has been exposed to in Flint. She becomes a self-sufficient but also a nurturing member of her family. She has learned that "traditional" femininity is a role she no longer wants to perform because it is performed most easily by white females with the financial resources to perform it. And she has learned to care more about helping her family than about performing gender in a stereotypical way. Christopher Paul Curtis thus uses Deza Malone to interrogate and desta-bilize identity-categories in the United States, demonstrating in the process both that material conditions affect identity and that age is an undeniable intersectional category.

## MULTIPLICITY AND *BECOMING NAOMI LÉON*

Issues involving race and intersectionality are complicated by the relation-ship between discursive and material understandings of how race can be de-fined. Ron Mallon outlines three competing views of race: *racialism*, which is the essentialized (and racist) view that race is entirely a biological mat-ter; *racial skepticism*, which is the belief that race does not exist at all, and *social constructionism*, which "seek[s] to develop an account on which race does exist but is a socially constructed kind of thing" (534). Hames-García participates in this latter endeavor when he argues that "race, like most so-cial concepts . . . means many different things and is not reducible to neat, orderly categories" (46). He asserts that *race* can function in at least three ways: "(1) race has a material-economic reality in the immediate effects and legacies of racism. (2) race has a social and psychological reality as an exist-ing system of beliefs and attitudes with material effects. . . . (3) race exists in a physical or biological form, as bodily matter" (55). He acknowledges that "if one thinks of race as merely shorthand to reference the effects of racial classification and racism, then it is hard to deny its reality (although some might)" (55); he also considers race to be tremendously important to "understanding, explaining, and addressing the effects of contemporary and historical racism" (56). He then asks us to consider the implications of the materiality of race, including considerations of problematic biological implications, demonstrating how much racialism rests on false assumption about an "easy separability of biology and culture" (57).

Nevertheless, Hames-García acknowledges the material reality of living in a culture that defines race visually: "an important dimension of what race is and how it functions results from the interaction of social practices and beliefs about race with visible human difference. . . . While such outward differences as skin color, hair texture, or eye shape may hold little or no meaning for our biological functioning as organisms or for our innate capacities, they can prove crucial, in Western societies at least, for our social functioning" (58). Hames-García then links his argument back to Barad's ideas about intra-activity, especially in the ways that the act of observation changes the nature of what is being observed for the observer: "Unless we accept the causal role of matter in the formation of racial meanings and phenomena, our theories of society will prove incapable of explaining how and why people experience race as they do" (59–60). He cites as an example 1980s data about how "very light" African Americans earned 80% of what white people earned, while "very black" African Americans earned 53% (60). Although race is discursively defined, racism has a material aftermath that is undeniable. Thus, like Barad, Hames-García asks us to think about the interplay between observer and observed and how that intra-activity affects the relationship between discourse and the material. Significantly, he questions the divide between biology and culture as yet another false binary that becomes destablized in the study of material feminism.

Writing about race in children's literature offers the advantage that it is entirely a discursive matter: children's and YA novels are constructed out of words and other types of sign systems (as in graphic narratives). But authors use discourse to describe the material effects of racism—which is often underscored by multiplicities of race and gender and age. Pam Muñoz Ryan's *Becoming Naomi León* emphasizes discursivity as she interrogates how the multiplicities of gender, race, social class, and age interact; she also adds another dimension of multiplicity to the narrative: disability. Most of all, she focuses on the material and the intra-activity involved in perceiving it.

By playing with the unique nature of collective nouns, Ryan foregrounds from the beginning of the novel how the nature of social groups is discursively situated. The novel thus emphasizes the importance of group affiliation in the constitution of social identity. Each chapter is named with a collective noun that invites readers to interact with the meaning-making of these discursive choices: why is it a "*schizophrenia* of hawks" or an "*exaltation* of starlings"? More important, the collective nouns foreshadow the symbolic events of each chapter. In the former of those two chapters, the children confront that it is their mother's alcoholism that makes her seem schizophrenic to them; in the latter, the animals they carve for a Noah's Ark in a Mexican competition earns them the admiration of a large local crowd. That carving has included birds, and it has resulted in the carvers' own exaltation. As a result of this happiness, the children feel embraced by the people of their father's hometown; they feel at home with the half of their cultural heritage that is Mexican. In the final chapter, Naomi can acknowledge that, while little has changed externally in her life, everything has changed for her internally because she has lived through a series of events and come to perceive her life differently. "On the outside of things, nothing much had changed. . . . On the inside though, I was different" (244). She has been a desiring being, one who desires a stable sense of home. Her desire leads to her *becoming* throughout this novel, intra-acting with the material world in ways that affect her agency and enable her to merge identities to become a stronger and more vocal young woman.

Her full name is Naomi Soledad León Outlaw, and she lives with her Anglo-American great-grandmother ("Gram") and her younger brother, Owen, in a trailer on the edge of an avocado grove in California. Naomi knows that her Anglo-American mother was once married to her father, Santiago León, a native of Mexico. Naomi is self-conscious about her mixed racial heritage. She is trying to grow out her curly hair, so:

> Gram had taken to calling me "brown shaggy dog" because of my wild mop and my predisposition to brown-ness (eyes, hair, and skin). I took after the Mexican side of the family, or so I'd been told, and even though Owen was my full-blooded brother, he took after the Oklahoma lot. He did have brown eyes like me, but with fair skin and blond hair in a bowl haircut. . . . Due to my coloring, Owen called me the center of a peanut butter sandwich between two pieces of white bread, meaning him and Gram. (11)

Boys at school make fun of her for her surname, "Outlaw," which she has taken from her grandmother's Oklahoma side of the family. She experiences even more marginalization because she has an invisible disability: selective mutism. Although she is an avid writer and list-maker, she prefers not to talk, and indeed sometimes cannot speak, especially in group situations.

Naomi learns that she and her brother have been abandoned at least twice by their mother: once as very young children during a hurricane in Mexico and later when she left them with her own grandmother, Gram, who blames her for Naomi's selective mutism: "Naomi went to a counselor for two years. She had selective mutism—that's what it's called—from insecurities and Lord knows what other trauma during her young life. That's what the counselor told us, and Naomi still doesn't talk much" (23–24). These passages demonstrate Hames-García's point well: it is as impossible to separate Naomi's invisible disability from her age as it is to separate her race from her social class.

Naomi's mother has renamed herself "Skyla," and she threatens to separate Naomi from her brother and Gram so that Naomi can move to Las Vegas with Skyla and Clive, her boyfriend, to babysit Clive's daughter. Skyla threatens Naomi by implying that physical harm will come to Gram if Naomi doesn't follow Skyla's bidding; Skyla also slaps Naomi and tells her, "There's more where that came from" (120). Skyla mocks Naomi for her silence and for the softness of her speaking voice when she does talk. The girl's disability also takes on symbolic value: Naomi is silenced by her mother, but as she learns more about her Mexican heritage and her father, she gains a stronger voice and learns how to almost roar like a lion. (And, indeed, the symbolism of the lion is reinforced multiple times, since *león* is Spanish for lion.)

Initially, Naomi does not have enough of a voice to take a Standpoint from which to critique the multiple forms of oppression she experiences, although that changes after she journeys to Oaxaca, Mexico, with Gram, her brother, and some family friends to meet her father and his family. Naomi joins with a group in Oaxaca in the annual radish-carving festival that precedes Christmas—and she is given the task of carving the lion that tops the tree they have made of many carved animals, evoking a Noah's Ark. Carving provides the material metaphor for learning about her internal sense of self. Early in the novel, she says that when she is about to carve something, "I imagine what's inside and take away what I don't need" (14); later, her father tells her: "Each piece has a personality. Sometimes you can look at the wood and see exactly what might be. The promise reveals itself early. Other times you must let your imagination dictate what you will find. . . . You must carve so that what is inside can become what it is meant to be" (219–20). By the end of the novel, she thinks about how her father *"had taught me that you must carve what your imagination dictates so that what is inside can become what it is meant to be. In the end, the figure will reveal itself for what it really is"* (245, italics in the original). Certainly, she has known from the beginning how to imagine what she will carve, but the intra-activity of perceiving the uncarved object, which then changes how she perceives it so much that she enacts it into being, initiates a process she recognizes as integral to her identity-formation, especially in the way that her father validates her perception that she must take action in order to *become.* "*I might have begun with a whisper, but it had been strong enough to make a self-prophecy come true*" (246, italics in the original). Although the book can be critiqued from a feminist viewpoint—Naomi must be validated by the patriarchy before she discovers her voice and her mother, moreover, is wicked—Naomi does learn about the process of her own *becoming* from the lived materiality of carving and uncovering her own artistic expression. She merges her identity with the wood, desiring the object inherent in the wood to emerge. Her perceptions change the wood, and the wood-carvings' evolution changes her.

Most significantly, the focus in the novel is on the literal importance of a girl's voice. Naomi's voice becomes the medium through which she can make her identity known, and it is her material body that produces that voice. After she returns from Oaxaca, she roars her Standpoint during a custody hearing. Naomi tells the judge the truth about her mother's abandonment and abuse. Naomi is also articulate about the importance of having an extended family, learning about her Mexican heritage, and living with her Gram, despite the woman's lack of wealth. In Naomi's strongest moment, she shows the value of having one's material needs met both physically and emotionally.

Naomi's Standpoint also allows her to criticize her mother's ablism. Although Naomi has an invisible disability, her brother's is visible. He has been medically designated an "FLK," that is, a "funny looking kid," which is a legitimate medical term that describes the boy's lopsided physical stature and facial features. Naomi is the one to tell the judge at the custody hearing that her mother rejects Owen because of his disability. Skyla has articulated the most direct ablism in the text when she tells her son's doctors, who value Owen's creativity and intellect: "This kid's a Blem. He's crooked and he can't talk right, and you're telling me nothing more can be done to make him right. Well, that's no bargain in my book!" (115). In imagery that echoes the carving of the Noah's Ark in Mexico, Naomi stands before the judge at her custody hearing and thinks "Be brave, Naomi Léon. . . . A sensation came over me, as if someone had unlatched a gate that freed a herd of lunging wild animals" (235). She tells the judge about how she loves her life with Gram, about how Skyla has abandoned her and her brother with Gram, about how Skyla only wants custody of Naomi so that the girl can babysit Clive's daughter: "I told about my carvings . . . and Owen being an FLK and how Skyla didn't want him anymore because she thought he was a Blem" (237). Her mother accuses her of lying, but Naomi looks right at the judge and says with great strength, "I am not lying" (237).

By the end of the novel, Naomi's school librarian asks if he can put her carvings on display in the library. The carvings are the material representation of Naomi's new-found self-confidence: as art and as artifacts, they help her speak for herself. Naomi may live in poverty and she may live with a disability and as part of a racialized minority, but the novel emphasizes the multiplicities of her identity in terms of race, gender, age, and ability. Although she is a girl with a disability, she learns that she can use her voice to critique those who would discriminate against her because of the multiplicities she experiences.

## MATERIAL POLITICS AND *CLAUDETTE COLVIN: TWICE TOWARD JUSTICE*

Phillip Hoose's *Claudette Colvin: Twice Toward Justice* tackles directly the material effects of racism. Part biography and part social documentary, this work of nonfiction relies on a variety of visual artifacts (photographs, newspaper articles, court documents) to support the telling of a story about how one teenaged African American girl attempted to integrate the Montgomery bus system. The book also emphasizes the material repercussions of racism—both in the ways that Claudette is physically handled by the police and by the ways that everyone participating in the Montgomery bus boycott is physically affected. During the Montgomery bus boycott:

> Thousands of black workers, including many who were elderly and some who were disabled, set out from home in the predawn darkness and walked miles each day. Some preferred to walk to show their support for the boycott rather than accept a ride even from the MIA [Montgomery Improvement Association]. . . . Family members made enormous sacrifices and sometimes hobbled home with barely enough energy to eat supper. And family chores like shopping had to continue. That meant more steps. The foot-weary warriors told their stories at the mass meetings, inspiring and encouraging one another to keep walking. (75–76)

The material conditions of racism were exacerbated by the material conditions of boycotting the buses. Through physical artifacts and descriptions of embodiment, readers are steeped in the material realities of what it means to live in a racist culture.

In March, 1955, teenaged Claudette Colvin refused to give up her seat to a white woman on a Montgomery bus. The bus driver stopped the bus and eventually called the police, who then alleged that they had to drag Colvin off the bus, kicking and screaming. Colvin maintains that she was defending her constitutional rights to sit where she had—and indeed, she was within her rights as granted to her by Montgomery civil statutes (Hoose 34). Although she was only fifteen years old, she was taken to the adult jail by police officers who yelled at her, emphasizing her intersectionality by calling her names such as "Thing" and "nigger bitch" and "Whore" (36). During her trial, she was found guilty of violating segregation laws, disturbing the peace, and assaulting the arresting officers (who had, in point of fact, assaulted her). An appeals judge later dropped the first two charges, but upheld the assault charge.

Tensions in Montgomery continued to rise about the unfairness of the city's racism, particularly on the buses. The city's African American leaders wanted someone to be a spokesperson for a bus boycott, but Claudette was deemed to be too young, too "uncontrollable" and "feisty" (52). Her embodiment and materiality affected her ability to interact with the movement's leaders: she had quit straightening her hair and had begun wearing it in braided pigtails, which shocked the more conventional members of the black community (55). When Rosa Parks was arrested on a bus in December 1955, the material contrast to Colvin could not have been more vivid. Parks was middle-class, married, light-skinned, with straightened hair, and she had had two weeks of training on "interracial relations at the Highlander Folk School in Tennessee" (61).

Colvin acknowledges that black leaders discounted her because she was young and because she was angry and grieving the death of her sister; moreover, she was also empowered to the point of rage by an African American history class she took at her high school. The Civil Rights leaders needed to weigh many factors as they made their decision, but aetonormativity was also at work when they chose soft-spoken, light-skinned, and mature Rosa Parks to be the face of the boycott, rather than a working-class, angry teenager like Colvin.

The aetonormativity of Colvin's story intersects poignantly with gender in another particularly vivid way: Colvin became an unwed mother in 1956. She was sixteen years old at the time. This factor, more than any other, led Civil Rights leaders to ignore her experience, her willingness to help the boycott, and the legal injustices she had faced. She says, "It bothered me to be shunned, but I was an unwed pregnant girl and I knew how people were" (79). She was "glad an adult had finally stood up to the system," but she "felt left out" (67). Civil Rights leaders wanted a woman to be the boycott's spokesperson because more women than men rode the bus—and because they wanted to protect men and their jobs (83). The intersection of being female and black was significant—but not if that female was a teenager and pregnant. Thus, the crippling intersectionality of identity politics left Claudette Colvin all but invisible to history. The intersection of being a teenager in an adult's role (as an expectant mother) was probably the greatest factor in making it impossible for aetonormative Montgomery leaders to acknowledge her potential leadership.

Nikolajeva employs Mikhail Bakhtin's concept of the carnivalesque—that is, the idea of Carnival as a temporarily empowering rejection of social rules—to show how aetonormativity is often undermined in children's fiction (10). Child characters can be temporarily empowered by the carnivalesque through playfulness, zaniness, nonsense, role reversals with adults, and/or exuberance, but this temporary empowerment often proves to be something of a steam-letting valve by which adults in children's fiction ultimately regain control. For example, children may float on the ceiling, laughing with Mary Poppins, but she always brings them back to earth with an authoritarian hand. The carnivalesque is thus a notable feature of literature for the young, but it is markedly absent in *Claudette Colvin: Twice Toward Justice*. At no point was Claudette temporarily empowered by the joy or freedom of youth—precisely because she was black, female, poor, and young. This lack of carnivalesque could be a function of the narrative's status as nonfiction; Hoose depicts accurately the harsh conditions Colvin experienced at the time. The absence of carnivalesque, however, might also demonstrate a certain racial coding that accompanies releases of social power: social norms may well dictate an underlying (white) fear of empowering children of color through the carnivalesque. Certainly, for Colvin, there was to be no experience except the unrelenting authority of adults, both black and white. The multiplicities of race, gender (including pregnancy), and age are particularly material and particularly compelling in Colvin's narrative.

Eventually, Claudette Colvin was given a second chance to achieve justice when the young lawyer Fred Gray approached her about being a plaintiff in the court case *Browder v. Gayle*. This trial involved five women who had all been arrested for violating segregation codes on the Montgomery buses. Like Claudette, these plaintiffs were chosen because of their gender and race, but she was the youngest of the group. Despite the popular historical understanding that Rosa Parks and the bus boycott led to the desegregation of the buses, *Browder v. Gayle* actually effected the dramatic change in Montgomery's racist culture. In November of 1956, the Supreme Court upheld the District court case, declaring bus segregation unconstitutional, and the boycott ended in December, 1956.

Throughout *Claudette Colvin: Twice Toward Justice*, Colvin provides perspective on her experiences, making her Standpoint particularly clear: "we black students constantly put ourselves down. If you were dark-complexioned they'd call you 'nappy-headed.' Not 'nappy-haired.' Nappy-headed. And the 'N' word—we were saying it to each other, to *ourselves*. . . . For some reason we seemed to hate ourselves" (22). A significant teacher, however, taught Claudette in an African American history class to take pride in herself, in her history, and in being African American. "She taught us to love whatever color we were," Colvin says (28). And so, "little by little, I began to form a mission for myself. I was going to be like Harriet Tubman and go North to liberate my people" (28). It is crucial to Colvin's story that even before she was arrested, she was educated, discursively aware, and aware of the identity politics that were robbing her of her agency. No simple victim, she was invoking her Constitutional Rights as she got arrested. Most important, she recognized that youth needed to be involved in changing racial discrimination: "I was tired of adults complaining about how badly they were treated and not doing anything about it" (29). From intersecting Standpoints of marginalization, Colvin could both critique her culture and vow to change it. Her youth and the aetonormative forces working against her were thus central to the multiplicity of intersectionalities that positioned her as an early catalyst of the Montgomery bus boycott.

## LANGUAGE/DISCOURSE AND *BROWN GIRL DREAMING*

Jacqueline Woodson's *Brown Girl Dreaming* is a collection of poems that work together to create the memoir of another historically-situated figure, one who lived through the later years of the Civil Rights era: the author herself, Jacqueline Woodson. The first poem describes her birth in "Columbus, Ohio / USA—/ a country caught / between Black and White" (1). The next poem identifies many historical figures whose Standpoint the narrator knows she shares: she is a brown girl critiquing white oppression. That poem describes a fluidity of subject positions that emphasizes multiplicity:

she doesn't know whether she will be like male leaders Malcolm X, Martin Luther King, James Baldwin, or like female leaders Rosa Parks, or Ruby Bridges, but she knows that her hands will be *"ready / to change the world"* (5, italics in the original)—because her world *needs* to be changed. For example, when the narrator's family journeys home to South Carolina, the children are shocked by signs on the bus that tell them "COLOREDS TO THE BACK!"—but their mother whispers to them, *"We're as good as anybody"* (31, italics in the original). The narrative Standpoint is clear.

Multiplicity in this memoir also includes social class: the patriarch of the extended family is the foreman at a printing press, clearly respected by the white men who work for him—but these men nevertheless refer to him by his first name rather than calling him "Mr. Irby" because they unquestioningly follow southern mores that infantilize black men (53). His wife works as a housemaid and admonishes her grandchildren *"Don't any of you ever do daywork . . . / I'm doing it now so you don't have to"* (56, italics in the original). Jacqueline's family lives in a single-family dwelling, and the children are well enough fed and groomed that neighbor children envy them. They are not allowed to play with children their mother considers to be their social inferiors, and *Winnie-the-Pooh* is standard bedtime reading. Yet despite the solid working-class structure of this family, racism acts oppressively enough that they know they have not achieved the American Dream. Their grandmother tells them that protest marches have happened in Greenville for more than a generation, but equality has not been achieved: *"We all have the same dream, my grandmother says. / To live equal in a country that's supposed to be / the land of the free"* (89, italics in the original). Their grandfather tells them that *"brown people have to fight. . . . / gently. Walk toward a thing slowly,"* but they must also *"be ready to die, . . . / for what is right. / Be ready to die, . . . / for everything you believe in"* (73, italics in the original).

Gender intersects with religion in this memoir, too: Jacqueline and her sisters have a strict regimen of hair care and daily life that is dominated by their conservative and evangelical church. Monday and Tuesday are "Bible study"; Wednesday is laundry; Thursday is "Ministry School"; Saturday is evangelizing, and Sunday is church day. But on Friday, "we're free as anything" (119); on this day they ride bikes with their brother, exempt from the gendering required of their faith. The gender divide is underscored by their grandfather's refusal to join his wife at the Kingdom Hall because he "doesn't believe in a God / that won't let him smoke / or have a cold beer on a Friday night" (122). In their religion, "The Sunday sermons are given by men. / Women aren't allowed to get onstage like this, / standing alone to tell God's story" (179). Young Jacqueline doesn't understand why this should be, but she understands that Eve is blamed for the fall of mankind.

Language is the stuff of which discourse is made, and so language is itself a primary source of specific intersectionalities of race and age in this text. Jacqueline's brother gets whipped with a switch for saying "ain't" and "ma'am" (68, 69); his mother clearly does not like the discursive implications of how those words position her son if he speaks them. "The list of what not to say / goes on and on" (69); later in childhood, they are not allowed to use slang or listen to music that contains the word "funk" (262). Jacqueline's mother wants her children to respect themselves and knows well that internalized language leads to the type of discursive self-talk by which people denigrate themselves—but their cousins have trouble understanding them. "*Y'all go too fast*, they say. / *And the words get all pushed together*" (75, italics in the original). Unsurprisingly, Jacqueline's first sense of herself as empowered differently than her siblings comes to her through literacy, writing, and the creation of story. She is most happy when she is reading and writing: "Letters becoming words, words gathering meaning, / becoming / thoughts outside my head"; she loves signing her name to these stories, claiming them with her unique sense of identity (156). In addition, the first time she reads a picture book with illustrations of a black child, John Steptoe's *Stevie* (1970), the self-recognition empowers her, even though she is too old to be reading picture books. But she understands that if anyone had told her she was too old to read picture books, perhaps she never could "have believed / that someone who looked like me / could be in the pages of the book / that someone who looked like me" had written (228). Although her mother and teachers sometimes pressure her aetonormatively to read at a higher grade-level, extending to herself the comforts of childhood reading helps her envision her future as a time when she will no longer be a child but will still be black and female.

Woodson clearly acknowledges the material multiplicity of intersections among race, gender, and age in a poem called "afros." The narrator wishes for an Afro like her uncle's and her mother's, but her mother says: "*This is the difference between / being a grown-up and being a child*" (259). Jacqueline sticks her tongue out at her mother behind her back, and her sister tells her: "*And that's the difference / between being a child and being a grown-up*" (259). The Afro, with its personalized expression of racial pride, is acceptable for adults but not children, in the eyes of Jacqueline's mother. The oppressions that position Jacqueline are also apparent in the narrator's disbelief that she is a writer until a teacher tells her she is. That teacher self-identifies as a feminist who believes in equal rights: "Like Blacks, Ms. Vivo, too, is part of a revolution. . . . / But right now that revolution is so far away from me. / This moment . . . is my teacher saying, / *You're a writer*" (311, italics in the original). Every wish the child narrator makes is "*To be a writer*" (313, italics in the original). Creating stories, playing with language, immersing herself in the discourse of narrative, every imaginative act creates new worlds for her that can "gather into one world / called You / where You decide / what each world / and each story / and each ending will finally be" (320). Only through literacy and the creation of literature can Woodson begin to comprehend her identity—her "You"—and the multiplicities that have empowered and disempowered her—sometimes simultaneously. Discourse is thus central to her identity.

Nevertheless, the material also pervades Jacqueline's youth, in her stories of starched hair ribbons and hair scorching under the heat of a straightening iron, in her stories of strong smells that emanate from the food her grandmother and best friend's mother make, in her stories of the material artifacts of play—bicycles, swings, record-players, and books. Perhaps the most powerful commentary on the relationship between the material and the discursive involves how Woodson's little brother becomes disabled from eating lead paint; the lead poisoning causes severe delays in the boy's physical and mental development. The social injustice is shocking: the preschooler has been eating the peeling lead paint in their New York apartment because he likes the way it melts on his tongue. He is hospitalized and never regains his original cognitive growth trajectory; he has been disabled by the material living conditions of his family. This preventable disability is a tragic result of an oppressive multiplicity that involves social class, age, and race. And it would be impossible to argue that his material experience is defined entirely by discourse.

## MULTIPLICITY AND INTRA-ACTIVITY IN *FLYGIRL*

Historical settings offer writers such as Jacqueline Woodson, Phillip Hoose, and Christopher Paul Curtis the opportunity to emphasize how racial discrimination creates a specific type of intersectionality that those being oppressed could not ignore. Sherri L. Smith similarly avails herself of a historical setting when she problematizes the military's attitudes towards race and gender during World War II. Smith's *Flygirl* is a novel about Ida Mae Jones, a young woman who joins the Women Airforce Service Pilots (WASP) during World War II. The WASP did not accept African Americans when it was formed, so Ida Mae—who is black—decides to pass as white in order to pursue her dreams of flying. Ida Mae has inherited from her father very light skin and "good hair" (7)—and the irony of a young woman of color passing as a White Anglo Saxon Protestant to join the WASP is evident throughout the novel. The ambiguity that lies in the usage of the term "WASP" is problematized several times. For example, Ida Mae is first motivated to join the Airforce Service because of Thomas, her enlisted brother, who for a while is missing in action. The dual meaning of the term emerges at one point when Ida Mae thinks the words, "like me becoming a WASP when I couldn't save Thomas" (198). Later when she fights with her mother about passing so she can be in the military, Ida says, "I thought you finally understood why I wanted to be a WASP" (211). And a white friend who does not know she is passing tells her, "You were born to be a WASP" (253). In all of these cases, "WASP" refers directly to the Airforce Service; nevertheless, Ida Mae can't be a WASP pilot if she does not pass as a white Anglo-Saxon. The irony is an inherent structure that results from the injustice of the military's discriminatory regulations. Smith does not shy away from interrogating the ethics of passing; readers must evaluate for themselves whether it is justifiable to reject one's family heritage if an oppressive and discriminatory system refuses to acknowledge one's potential for *becoming*.

Ida Mae's Standpoint from which she can critique American racism is established early in the novel. Ida Mae cleans houses in New Orleans so she can save money to go to Chicago to earn a pilot's license. She knows how to fly because her father taught her in his small plane before he died, but the nearest testing center in Tuskegee, Alabama, will not grant her a license because she is a woman. As a pilot, she faces discrimination because of both her gender and her race. She eventually alters her father's pilot's license to enlist in the WASP, and she proves herself to be one of the most competent pilots in her company. Nevertheless, she lives in constant fear of being discovered, and she is at times alienated from her family and her best friend, Jolene, at home in New Orleans.

Ida Mae's friendship with Jolene foregrounds the multiplicity of Ida's subject positions. Early in the novel, Jolene teases Ida for wanting to fly when she is a girl—and when her family can't really afford for her to: "You've got the flying bug . . . but some days I think it's more trouble than it's worth. More money than it's worth, too" (2). When Ida says she wants to join the military, Jolene tells her that the role of a woman during war is a material job, protecting the home front: "Men do the fighting, Ida Mae. Women take care of the home. You can be proud of that. It's enough. Too much, sometimes, but it's more than enough" (26). The two girls even discuss their intersectionality in terms of multiplicity; Ida Mae asks her best friend a pivotal question:

> "If you're colored, you get the short end of the stick. If you're a woman, you get the short end of the stick. So what do we get for being colored *and* women?"
> Jolene sighs. "Beat hard with both ends of a short stick." (33)

Ida does not even know how to think of her own identity: "What am I first, I wonder, a woman or colored?" (48). Ida Mae eventually loses her friendship with Jolene because Jolene cannot accept Ida's passing—or the fact that because she is passing, the military doesn't know who her family is. "You are a colored girl, no matter how high yellow you look or how white you act. The army don't even know who your family is. If something happens to you, you think they'll write a letter to some colored folks so we can collect the body?" (206–7). Ida Mae then accuses Jolene of being jealous of both Ida's accomplishments and the fact she can pass: "You can't take it away from me, Jolene. Even if you're jealous. Even if your skin's so dark all you'll ever be is a housemaid" (207). Ida Mae's intra-racial racism is cruel, so race and gender and social class and age (as immaturity) are all implicated in the way this friendship ends. Because Ida Mae can transgress gender and race lines, she can improve her social class—and she makes the mistake of rubbing that in Jolene's face.

Social class is also a factor several other times in the novel, as for example, when one of Ida's new friends in WASP training cannot make a bed because she's never done so before. Her maid once told her "a proper lady didn't have to make her own bed" (78). Ida Mae retorts, "More likely she was afraid she'd lose her job if you knew how easy it was" (78). Ida thinks to herself, "Lily's the kind of girl I'd be cleaning up after in New Orleans" (78)—and throughout the novel, Lily's insensitivity to issues of social class is a recurring motif. Their friend Patsy works carnivals and is frequently amused by Lily's innocence. Lily, however, is Jewish, so religion is also foregrounded as another aspect of multiplicity when one of their bunk mates makes a particularly derogatory remark about Ida Mae and her two new friends in the bunk: "'Carnies and hicks and Jews, oh my!' She smirks, imitating Dorothy's little chant from *The Wizard of Oz*" (76). The three girls become friends because they refuse to let the multiplicity of social class and gender and religion affect them negatively.

Ida Mae is also supremely aware of her youth as a disempowering aspect of her subjectivity, which she makes clear in the beginning of the novel. She fell in love with flying as an eleven-year-old because being in the airplane with her father made her feel: "like a giant, like I was tall as the sky" (31). Flying is, for Ida, both literally and metaphorically, a way to transcend the disempowerment of being marginalized. Although at the beginning of the novel, she thinks that "the dreams of one little colored girl don't matter to a world at war. But they matter to me" (18); by the time she decides to enlist, she realizes, "I'm not a little girl anymore" (55). Her grandfather agrees: "you're not a baby anymore. An adult has to make adult decisions" (62). She is not yet twenty years old—but after serving in the military for a while, she thinks, "I didn't feel like a kid anymore. Something about the training, maybe, or all of the hours in the air, but in the past two years, it feels like I've gotten twice as old as I was when I showed up" for training (219). Ida Mae's identity shifts like a kaleidoscope in the multiplicity that blurs but does not erase racial lines, gender lines, and age.

Through this exploration of multiplicity, *Flygirl* also interrogates performativity as an aspect of *becoming*: Ida Mae cannot pass as a white woman without a desire to perform a new role—and the more she performs the role, the more she realizes her identity has merged with it and evolved into something else. When she first applies to join the WASP, she realizes that she needs to impress the woman at the recruiting office: "show her *who* I am, not what I am. I am Ida Mae Jones of Slidell, Louisiana. Even if I'm playing at being white, even if I paint myself blue, I am still the child of my parents, still that little girl who loves her brother and loves to fly" (47, italics in the original). The term "playing" signals her awareness of her performativity; the idea of passing as performativity is reinforced by her reference to "this charade of mine" (264). She also, however, begins to think of her identity in terms of *being*, "I wouldn't need to be colored if I didn't want to be" (53)— and she can explain her love of flying to her mother in terms that allow the erasure of race altogether: "This is what daddy used to fly for. The chance to be everything other than the color of my skin. . . . So what if they think I'm white? Let them see what they want to see. I'm still me" (55). The unstated ethical dilemma Ida Mae explores involves whether her identity is—or is not—dependent on her race as both a material and discursive construct.

Ida Mae's performativity as she passes initiates an intra-active *becoming*: her perception of herself shifts repeatedly as she thinks of her embodiment alternating between the terms "white" and "colored." For example, when she's with her fellow pilots, who nickname her "Jonesy," she thinks of her interiority as the most important factor in defining who she is: "they don't know everything about Ida Mae Jones. But they know Jonesy, and that's who I really am" (105). But when she attends a dance near the Texas army base where she's been training, she thinks: "I'm a white girl tonight. I'm a WASP," although she knows this is a role she's performing (128). She knows it's "all but illegal" for a white man to dance with her, but she thinks to herself: "You're white now, Ida" (133). Again conflating the performativity of race with thoughts about her own ontology, she thinks: "I'm only pretending to be white. . . . As light as I am, no matter what I do, I'm still that little colored child" (139). Then an African American man in the small Texas town where she is stationed tells her he knows she's passing. He uses the language of action—of "doing"—not the language she uses of passing as "playing" a role:

> "Child, you gonna get yourself killed, or worse, *doing* what you're *doing*."
> I looked at him in surprise and I know that he sees me for what I am—a colored girl *playing* at being white. (150, italics added)

After this incident, she recognizes that "even New Orleans won't be the same for me anymore. I'll only feel safe in the sky"—which is the only way she's found to transcend racist social constructions (154). Ida knows that when the war ends, "so does my reason for passing. Like Cinderella after midnight, I go back to being colored. And *that* Ida Mae Jones, the real Ida Mae Jones, could never go to Lily's wedding as anything other than a serving maid" (179, italics in the original). Although Ida claims that the "real Ida Mae Jones" is African American, when she returns home to visit, she thinks: "I don't even know if I'm colored or white anymore. Ida Mae Jones or Jonesy. I want to be both of them" (215). She realizes that she'll never be able to live in Louisiana in the same way again, recognizing that "life isn't black and white. It's black *or* white. Anything else is just a mess" (266). Ida Mae seems to be acknowledging that race is such a powerful and pervasive construct that it *is* integral to the core of her self-identity. The very words "white" and "black" have affected her self-perception and rendered her unwilling to live forever with the ambiguity of passing. Her *becoming* has involved a series of intra-active shifts in her self-perception that depend on the discourse in which she participates; how she perceives her embodiment depends on the language she is using at the time. Her discursive choices and her embodiment have intra-actively shifted who she is. Because of the discomfort of this *becoming*, by the end of the war she is willing to racialize herself as African American. Trying to be at times black and at times white—which is "just a mess"—would deprive her of her family and heritage, which is a choice she is unwilling to make permanently.

The only way Ida knows how to erase race is to think in terms of her military service, which is also intertwined with the multiplicity of her gender:

> I don't feel Negro any more than I feel white. I'm just me. Ida Mae Jones, and I'm blue. Santiago blue. Take away the uniform, and I really am nothing at all. Take away the wings and I'm someone else's. Someone's maid, someone's daughter, someone's sister, and maybe even someone's wife one day. But I can't have one life without giving up the other. I can fly . . . or be with my family and never fly again. It's not fair. (267)

The text does not resolve whether race is a performance or an ontological reality—or both. But the text complicates beautifully what it means to take on a new role, to merge with a new identity, in a process of *becoming*. Ida Mae is, indeed, no longer the "little colored girl," as she once thought of herself; she is a professional pilot—perhaps despite and perhaps because of both her gender and race (18). And for the purposes of a feminist reading, it is significant that Ida Mae acknowledges that her gender demotes her to a secondary status in a world that defines women in terms of embodied relationships: as maid, daughter, sister, wife—never as autonomous or self-defined or *pilot*. Several of her fellow WASP admit that they joined the WASP because of a man—a father, a brother, an ex-fiancé—who either told these women they could or could not fly. These WASPs are flying to prove that they can. But one woman pinpoints the root problem with this type of thinking: "Aha! *Cherchez l'homme!*" (258). Another replies, "Isn't it funny, ladies, how there's always a man at the bottom of everything we do? Why, I bet men do all kinds of things that don't involve women"; "Like fight wars," one of them says (258). Ida Mae thinks grimly, "Men are not the only soldiers in this fight. Whether they like it or not, whether the army wants it or not, we're WASP. And we're helping to end this war" (258). Ida Mae clearly sees that gender discrimination is an unworkable long-term model for the military, even while she simultaneously does not know how to resolve the injustices and illogic of systemic racism built on false social constructions that binarize race.

Ida Mae's *becoming* raises a host of ethical questions that interrogate both race as a social construct and the ethics of passing in a culture so rigidly immersed in race as a social construct. The first time Ida passes, in the military recruiter's office, she thinks about her mother and "how she'd just die inside if she knew I was playing white" (45). Ida Mae's own family demonstrates that race is not a binary; her father's people have systematically married people lighter than they are, and he was "destined to marry a white woman, to be a *passé blanc* and give his family a better lot in life" (53). But he falls in love with Ida Mae's mother and aligns himself with her African American family. Ida's mother slaps her when she finds out Ida has been passing at the recruiting office: "One look and I can tell what you've been doing. Playing at that same mess as your daddy's people. Do you think white folks don't know? Do you think they can't tell what you are? A high yellow putting on airs and a borrowed hat.... You are part of *this* family. All the clothes in the world can't change that" (50–51, italics in the original). Her mother warns her that if "you cross that line, you cannot cross back just as you please" (56)—which proves to be the case. Ida's brother goes MIA, so her mother journeys to Texas to tell her the news, but the woman has to pose as the family's maid in order to allay suspicions about Ida's race. Echoing Huck Finn's moral decision, Ida thinks: "I will go to hell for this, I think. I should go to hell. My mother's face looks back at me in the dark, my own mother who let me treat her like a servant just so she could talk to me" (165). She begins to think that her decision-making has been "selfish. Selfish, stupid, and dangerous" (167). Evaluating her own dishonesty, she acknowledges that "everything I'm doing is based on a lie" (216) and that "lies breed lies" (267). Ida Mae has been placed in an ethically impossible situation because of the corruption of the world around her. The racist social constructs that prohibit African American women from joining the WASP make it impossible for her to fly *and* be honest. She does, however, decide to rectify at least one aspect of her own dishonesty when she writes a letter to the white man who is romantically interested in her to tell him that she is African American. The novel ends before the reader knows whether he will be able to overcome the culture's racism and remain romantically involved with her, but the reader knows Ida has learned to be honest with herself and comfortable with who she is: a pilot, female, and African American.

## CONCLUSION

Concepts of intersectionality, multiplicity, and Standpoint enable us to think in multi-variate terms about race, gender, age, and a variety of other factors (such as social class, religion, and ability). Critical Race Theory thus provides critics with the tools for considering gender and race as mutually implicating, rather than as isolated factors; Nikolajeva's concept of aetonormativity helps us factor age into the matrix to complicate even further the power issues involved in thinking about feminism as a tool for evaluating multicultural texts for children and adolescents.

Moreover, material feminism influences us to think about race in both discursive and material terms. Although race is a cultural construction, it nevertheless has material impact on people's lives. The narratives under discussion in this chapter demonstrate the materiality of race intersecting with gender, with age, with social class; the protagonists in all five narratives experience a multiplicity of race and gender that manifests itself in the physical world. Ida Mae Jones loves to fly an airplane, at first because it makes her tower over the earth, feeling like a "giant"—not a kid, but later because she understands that race is immaterial to the experience of a pilot flying solo (Smith, *Flygirl* 31). The physical experience of flying thus motivates her to subvert contemporary social constructions of race and gender. Claudette Colvin, Jacqueline Woodson, and Deza Malone all demonstrate the mutually implicated nature of race, gender, and social class. They struggle to maintain specific beauty standards in the face of poverty: Claudette and Jacqueline, for instance, write about their hair care, while Deza's teeth symbolize the multiplicity of gender, race, age, and class in her life. Finally, Naomi Léon discovers that she has an inner-lion's voice after she whittles a material lion out of wood. Her voice and what she has carved are connected not only through the work of her hands but also through a word: her surname. Her self-perception changes through both discursive and physical experiences.

The intra-action between Naomi and the lion is complex: she becomes lion in both word—her name—and deed. She has desired to change who she is; she has desired to have a voice, and she learns to roar like one to defend herself and her brother. Her desire to change motivates her to explore new identities, especially when she is in Mexico. The novel emphasizes her *becoming* even in its title. Jacqueline Woodson's desire, on the other hand, is to become a writer; that desire motivates her experimentations with language and with creating stories. Signing her name to her stories may well be among the earliest of her authorial actions as she physically lays claim to what she has written with her signature. She even thinks in terms of *becoming* when she describes writing: "Letters *becoming* words, words gathering meaning, / *becoming* / thoughts outside my head" (156, italics added). As for Claudette Colvin, the day she first reads about the Montgomery bus boycott, she is "at home, trying to get ready in my mind for all the changes to come—changes in my body, *becoming* a mother, not going to Booker T. Washington, moving away from my family," when a friend brings her a flyer about the boycott (60, italics added). It is a physical artifact—and her name is misspelled on the leaflet: "Claudette Colbert" (61). That same day, she has mixed feelings when she realizes Rosa Parks has been arrested, but she knows that Rosa is "strong and adults won't listen to me anyway. One thing was for sure: no matter how I felt or what I thought, I wasn't going to get my chance" (61). Claudette became many things, but perhaps the most important of her *becomings* was her desire to make a difference. That resolve motivated her to participate in the court case that eventually ended the bus boycott. Because of her determination, she was able to protest the illegality of segregation.

How girls and young women use language and how they interact with their environment affect how they perceive themselves in an ongoing process of intra-activity that affects their *becoming*. Because social constructions of race are so historically rooted in tensions between discourse and embodiment, we can best understand feminism in a multicultural context when we acknowledge that the material and the discursive are reciprocally perpetuating phenomena.

## CHAPTER 3

# ECOFEMINISM, THE MATERIAL, AND GENRE

According to Ynestra King, ecofeminism is the recognition that industrialism's "opposition to nature . . . reinforces the subjugation of women"; that "life is an interconnected web, not a hierarchy"; that balanced ecosystems "must maintain diversity"; and that in order to survive, our species must understand nature, including our own embodiments as beings in nature (King 19–20). In other words, ecofeminism is "the position that there are important connections between how one treats women, people of color, and the underclass on one hand and how one treats the nonhuman natural environment on the other" (Warren xi). Greta Gaard and Patrick Murphy claim that "ecofeminism is not a single master theory and its practitioners have different articulations of their social practice," but they also point to how this type of social activism requires a revolutionary rethinking in our epistemologies about nature (2). They cite the influence of Irene Diamond and Gloria Feman Orenstein, who argue that "once the critique of such dualities as culture and nature, reason and emotion, human and animal has been posed, ecofeminism seeks to reweave new stories that acknowledge and value the biological and cultural diversity that sustains all life" (xi).

Ecofeminism and material feminism are interrelated, especially in the way that ecofeminism insists on the agency of the natural world. Nancy Tuana, a philosopher whose interest in epistemology has led her to think in terms of ecofeminism, notes that both Donna Haraway's and Karen Barad's work stems from rejections of the false binary between nature and culture ("Viscous" 191, 210n). Tuana uses the devastating 2005 Hurricane Katrina to demonstrate how problematic it is to believe in a dichotomy between nature and culture: "Look at Katrina. Katrina is a natural phenomenon that is what it is in part because of human social structures and practices"; the "natural concatenation of phenomena" created the devastation that it did because of its interactions with human structures ("Viscous" 192). Indeed, the deadly flooding that occurred in the Ninth Ward only happened because of man-made structures:

Does it make sense to say that the warmer water or Katrina's power were socially produced, rendering Katrina a non-natural phenomenon? No, but the problem is with the question. We cannot sift through and separate what is "natural" from what is "human-induced." . . . These "natural phenomena" are the result of human activities such as fossil fuel combustion and deforestation. But these activities themselves are fueled by social beliefs and structures. ("Viscous" 193)

Tuana thinks about the way that nature and culture shape, create, control, and influence one another in terms of "interactionism," to "[acknowledge] the robust porosity between phenomena that destabilizes any effort to finalize a nature/culture divide" ("Viscous" 192); "interactionism" differs from "intra-activity" in that "interactionism" is a phenomenon that occurs regardless of whether a human subject's perceptions and observations are involved. Tuana also uses the metaphor of "viscous porosity" to describe the "rich interactions between beings through which subjects are constituted out of relationality" ("Viscous" 188). She is particularly concerned that scholars take responsibility for the epistemic categories they use; that is, she insists that we question and acknowledge that the very process of categorizing a phenomenon changes our perceptions of it ("Viscous" 192). By way of an example, Haraway problematizes the basic epistemic categories of "subject" and "object," arguing that we are "no longer able to sustain the fictions of being either *subjects* or *objects*" because being a subject and being an object are mutually implicated ("Otherworldly" 158).

Children's literary critic Alice Curry values the material turn ecofeminism represents; she believes that ecofeminism serves as one corrective to the linguistic turn, which "dematerialises the planet and leaves no access to the earth except via language" (20). Moreover, she argues that inserting children and young adults as a "third" factor in the relationship between women and nature enriches our understanding of ecofeminism. She writes: "my focus on the young adult enables me to examine the interplay of global forces that position young adults on the cusp of social and political responsibility and interpellated by the ethics and epistemologies of the feminist present" (7). Like Tuana and Haraway, Curry is interested in phenomena as interactions, which she demonstrates with her use of the word "interplay" (7). Clare Bradford, Kerry Mallan, John Stephens, and Robyn McCallum also note that ecofeminism involves "a critical method and an ethical discourse" that "emphasi[zes] . . . intersubjective relations with others" (83–84). Children's and adolescent literature, they argue, is "constrained by the intrinsic commitment to maturation narratives," so ecofeminist narratives for the young will necessarily be anthropocentric; they also recognize the reformist ideological tendencies of ecofeminism novels (Bradford, *et al.*, 91). They write, "The moral and political orientation of personal development becomes intensified when linked to actions informed by ecocritical perceptions, that is, by perceptions that nature, the environment, earth itself, are endangered and in need of appropriate management" (Bradford, *et al.*, 91). Ecofeminist literature for the young is thus uniquely positioned as a mechanism by which to explore the intersubjective and interactionist relationships people develop by interacting with the environment as they mature.

Curry is particularly interested in those narratives by which the young are implicated in shifting understandings of their relationship with the earth:

> What is of most relevance is not the validity of a historical connection between women and nature, but the ways in which such a connection has been perceived, abused, and exploited under the auspices of gender difference. . . . It is this shift from ontological to representational thinking in ecofeminist theorising that I bring to bear on an analysis of young adult subject positioning within the novels under consideration. (4)

Curry focuses on post-disaster and post-apocalyptic novels as potentially "counter-hegemonic" (194), valuing the way that speculative fictions such as M. T. Anderson's *Feed* (2002) and Scott Westerfeld's *Uglies* (2005) offer teens a way to think about the earth and embodiment: "Acknowledgement of the earth as a material entity ties the earth to other 'bodies' and particularly the female body" (194).

I agree with Curry and Bradford, *et al.*, that twenty-first century ecofeminist YA novels are often very self-conscious about the relationship between the environment and the individual; along with emphasizing interactions among nature, culture, and the human body, they frequently depict the intra-activity through which human perception leads the material and discourse to shape one another. Whether YA ecofeminism is classified as speculative fiction or realism, those novels that interrogate environmentalism also tend to interrogate the false duality between discourse and the material. They also invariably demonstrate a young woman gaining an increased knowledge of herself as embodied in the world. This pattern can be found in a wide range of genres, including historical realism, such as Karen Hesse's *Out of the Dust* (1997) and Jacqueline Kelly's *The Evolution of Calpurnia Tate* (2009); contemporary realism, such as Angela Johnson's *Heaven* (1998); magic realism, such as Jewell Parker Rhodes's *Ninth Ward* (2010) and Margaret Mahy's *Kaitangata Twitch* (2005), and dystopic fictions, such as Collins's *The Hunger Games* (2008)—which I discuss in the next chapter. These novels all focus clearly on ideological critiques that link environmental awareness to the lived materiality of maturing girls. Donna Haraway provides a useful ecotheoretical framework for thinking about these novels when she insists that we pay attention to "the urgency of embracing that ontology that rematerializes the social and takes seriously the agency of the natural" ("Otherworldly" 188). These ecofeminist children's and adolescent novels provide a solid platform for this exact type of work in the ways that they demonstrate an ontology that "takes . . . the agency of the natural" as seriously as they take the agency of teenaged protagonists.

It seems worth mentioning that I believe genre distinctions allow us to acknowledge both the expectations young readers bring about literary conventions to a certain genre and the ways that authors can mold or bend those conventions to affect a narrative's ideology. In this chapter and the next, I divide feminist novels into sections that are loosely classified in terms of "realism" (especially focusing on historical and contemporary realism in this chapter) and "speculative fiction" (with explorations of magic realism in this chapter and speculative fictions, such as dystopia and apocalyptic fiction, in the next).

## ECOFEMINISM AND HISTORICAL REALISM

John Stephens refers to fantasy as a "metaphoric mode" (*Language* 287). David Gooderham develops this idea when he argues that "fantasy is a metaphorical mode" (173); that is, all speculative fictions, such as adventure fantasies and science fiction and dystopias, operate by creating an imagined world that operates as a metaphor—or parable—for the world from which the author is writing. But if speculative fictions serve as a metaphor for the contemporary world, realism serves as a form of metonymy—that is, as a reflection of how the world has operated or is operating. John Stephens offers this comparison/contrast of fantastic texts and realism: "The central observations I have made about the modes of fantasy and realism may be summed up as follows. The two discourses encode their concerns with the theme of language and power in quite different ways, in that fantasy is a metaphoric mode, whereas realism is a metonymic mode" (*Language* 287).

As a literary trope, metaphor functions by way of contrast, while metonymy functions by comparison. Love and roses, for example, are very dissimilar, so the metaphor "love is a rose" is contrasting two unlike things. But since metonymy substitutes an associated feature for the idea itself, metonymy is working by juxtaposing comparative ideas: "the press" was nicknamed "the press" when journalists still relied on printing presses. Ecofeminist realism in YA literature, whether it is set in the past or the present, offers a metonymic reflection on patriarchal exploitations of the environment, women, children, and people of color in a mimetic mode that reflects the author's perceptions about the lived realities of a given era.

Karen Hesse's *Out of the Dust* is one of the earliest YA novels that appears to be self-consciously ecofeminist. The novel reflects themes prevalent in much twentieth-century YA feminism in that Billie Joe, the protagonist, must find her voice, must learn how to make her own choices, and must build female community. Indeed, she does all of these things because of the cooperative and supportive relationship she has had with her mother before the woman died. But Hesse's novel points in the direction of twenty-first century ecofeminism in the ways that Billie Joe's embodiment is—as Margaret Mackey might say—"earthed" (507). Billie Joe's embodiment, indeed, her very existence, is affected by the vast agency nature wields in this novel; the destructive forces of the Dustbowl provide overwhelming evidence of nature's agency.

In the first poem of this verse novel, Billie Joe's actual birth is tied to crops and the seasons, to the ground, and to the dust (or at least its absence): "As summer wheat came ripe, / so did I, / born at home on the kitchen floor. / Ma crouched, / barefoot, bare bottomed / over the swept boards, / because that's where Daddy said it would be best" (3). This pregnancy has "ripened" as the wheat has; Billie's mother stoops down to deliver her baby on the ground. Dust has been swept away for the birth, but the whole scene is controlled by the patriarchal presence who dominates the landscape but is not part of it: Billie Joe's father. He wants a son, but what he gets instead is a daughter who can drive a tractor, a "long-legged girl / with a wide mouth," a "red-headed, freckle-faced, narrow-hipped girl" who loves apples and "playing fierce piano" (3).

The novel is set during the Great Depression of the 1930s, and it identifies rabbits as one factor in the devastation of the earth. They eat crops promiscuously, just like they breed—and local farmers have a contest in which they compete to see who can kill the most rabbits. Their destruction demonstrates the interactionism of the animal, human, and land. One character says, "if we keep / plowing under the stuff they ought to be eating, / what are they supposed to do?" (6). Moreover, as an image of fertility, the rabbit is tied to the way the earth is exploited in Dustbowl Oklahoma as surely as women's bodies are exploited. As it happens, Billie Joe's mother dies in childbirth shortly after she has been burned in a horrible kitchen fire. Thinking she is lifting a bucket of water to the stove, the pregnant woman lifts a pail of kerosene that her husband has foolishly left by the stove, which starts a fire. She runs outside to call for her husband, but returns in the same moment that Billie Joe flings the dangerous bucket of kerosene out of the door and accidentally all over her mother, who is then engulfed in a ball of fire. She dies, and so does her newborn son. Billie Joe knows that everyone blames her for throwing the kerosene on her mother, but she also knows it was her father who left the toxic, man-distilled chemical product where it did not belong.

Women articulate the knowledge about the relationship between the land, the environment and people in this novel. For example, Billie Joe's mother understands better than her husband that they need to diversify their crops, and she has planted two apple trees "that she and they might bring forth fruit / into our home, / together" (43). Billie Joe's teacher, Miss Freeland, outlines for them the "thousand steps" it took for the Dustbowl to happen, including overplanting, overgrazing, and the destruction of the sod. President Roosevelt tells the people living in the Dustbowl to "plant trees," but another female, Billie Joe, recognizes the effect of man's exploitation of the earth and knows that trees won't fix the problem: "Trees have never been at home here. / They're just not meant to be here. / Maybe none of us are meant to be here. / only the prairie grass / and the hawks" (75). When the town's original landholder dies, Billie Joe reads in the newspaper that when he "first came / he could see only grass, / grass and wild horses and wolves roaming," but he has sold land to farmers who bust up the sod. Billie Joe wonders, "Will they sow wheat on his grave, / where the buffalo / once grazed?" (108). Only after Billie Joe runs away and returns home is her father willing to learn the lessons that the women in his life have been trying to teach him: he diversifies the crops and plows with a team of mules, instead of a tractor: "Maybe the tractor lifted him above the land, / maybe the fields didn't know him anymore. . . . / and why should wheat grow for a stranger?" (226). Billie Joe tells him that he is "like the sod" (205), "steady, silent, and deep. / Holding on to life, with reserves underneath / to sustain him, and me" (202), while she is like the wheat: "I can't grow everywhere, but I can grow here"—especially if she is nurtured by "rain" and "care" and "luck" (205).

Hesse explores the material and discursive relationship between the earth's topsoil and how it is represented as "dust" throughout the narrative. Early in the novel, when dust gets into their food, Billie Joe's father makes jokes attempting to recategorize it as something edible rather than noxious: he calls it "pepper and chocolate" when really "it's nothing but dust" (21). The family frequently ingests it, swallowing dust-covered food and milk turned brown by dust. When one dust storm blows in, Billie Joe senses the storm coming before it arrives; she "heard it / smelled it, / tasted it"; the dust destroys their newly planted crops: "I watched the plants, / surviving after so much drought and so much wind, / I watched them fry," flattened by the dust or blown out of the ground by the wind carrying the dust (31). The dust then "hissed against the windows," and the storm leaves "waves and / waves and / waves of / dust, / rippling across our yard" (33). Another dust storm is "a red dust / like prairie fire, / hot and peppery" (46); later, "brown earth rained down / from sky" (143). During yet another dust storm, the dust "swarmed" (164). Some of the keys on a piano Billie Joe plays are "soured by dust" (49). From inhaling the dust and getting it in his eyes, Billie Joe's father streams "mud" out of his nose and mouth (33). One neighbor is "dazed by dust"; he cannot see, but Billie Joe perceives "our future is drying up / and blowing away with the dust" (39). When Billie Joe hears about a volcano erupting in Hawaii, she compares it to the dust: "sounds a little / like a dust storm" (79). "Dust / piles up like snow / across the prairie"; it rests in "dunes" and "mountains" (102). The dust is represented with many metaphors here: it is food, animal, water, mud, drug, chemical reagent, volcano, snow, sand, mountains; it is a blindingly destructive force.

Billie Joe cannot find peace with herself or heal from her mother's death, however, until she redefines herself in terms of the very dust that has so profoundly changed the course of her life: "And I know that all the time I was trying to get / out of the dust, / the fact is, / what I am, / I am because of the dust" (222). The dust has been external to Billie Joe, and yet she internalizes it when she eats it and breathes it. (Several characters die of dust pneumonia.) The dust is external to her house, but can enter it, burying her piano in dust, during dust storms. The dust is thus both an internal and an external force. When Billie Joe can shift her own self-definition, recognizing that she is both defined by dust and has become a stronger person because of it, she finally achieves a sense of resolution that involves making peace with her father, with herself, and with the vicissitudes the dust brings. Billie Joe initially defines the material—dust—in discursive terms, objectifying it and thinking of it only in terms of her relationship to it as an object. Her initial stance is the stance of a colonizer, imposing discourse on the object with the certainty of a colonizer staking claim to indigenous lands. Eventually, however, the intra-action of the dust as material and the myriad discursive constructions Billie Joe employs to describe it show how the discursive can shape perceptions of the material.

But Billie Joe's embodiment also affects how she understands the dust. She is in the dust, and the dust is in her; she can therefore proclaim, "what I am / I am because of the dust" (222). This *mattering* of dust as object and discourse in a continuous intra-action shifts who Billie Joe believes herself to be. Her *becoming* has been altered by the dust—and she has shifted her father's patriarchal relationship to the land in the process. The novel is one of the earliest ecofeminist children's novels to equate the exploitation of the land with exploitation of women, while it simultaneously interrogates the intra-active relationship of discourse and the material.

A similar equation of the exploitation of females and nature occurs in another novel of historical realism, *The Evolution of Calpurnia Tate*. Calpurnia Tate is the only daughter of a family of white landowners who cultivate cotton in Texas in 1899. Calpurnia wants to dig in the dirt and learn about evolutionary science, but the surrounding cultural environment frequently discourages her. Calpurnia is strong, intelligent, independent—and cursed with six brothers, but emotionally supported by her family's African American cook, Viola, and by her best friend, Lula, who is also coded as a white girl. Most of all, Calpurnia is supported by her curmudgeonly grandfather, a naturalist who takes a shining to Calpurnia when he realizes that she is as interested in learning Darwinian science as he is in teaching it. Calpurnia's ontology and epistemology are linked, especially in the ways that she eventually thinks about how her being is defined both ontologically as female in her world, but also in her wanting to exist epistemologically as a learning-and-knowing scientist. The novel carefully instructs readers that girls can be scientists, too—a rather dated and obvious feminist agenda for a novel published in 2009. Far more interesting, the novel develops an ecofeminist agenda that requires the reader to recognize human activity as a part of nature; that is, in this novel, humans are not separated from nature in a false binary; rather, humans are depicted as one of many species whose agency interacts with the agency of the natural world.

The novel focuses directly on the protagonist's changing ontology as she grows to recognize nature and its agency. Each chapter opens with a quotation from Darwin's *Origin of Species*. Chapter four, for example, has this as its epigraph: "Natural Selection . . . is as immeasurably superior to man's feeble efforts, as the works of Nature are to those of Art" (qtd. 54). This text thus explores how humans and nature interact through natural selection; Calpurnia learns to perceive existence as an ever-mutating series of phenomena in which an organism interacts with, is influenced by, and influences its environment. "Natural selection" serves as the concept through which Calpurnia learns *mattering*. For example, on one early morning ramble with her grandfather, she admires a doe and its fawn. Their beauty makes her speechless, and she wonders how any hunter could possibly want to kill them, but then she observes the fawn shift its identity as it adapts to its environment: "it folded up its front legs, then its hind legs, and sank to the ground where . . . it *disappeared*. The white spots scattered over its brown back mimicked the dappled light so that one second a fawn lay there, and the next second there was nothing but undergrowth" (32, italics and ellipses in the original). The fawn, of course, is still there, but Calpurnia has learned something about the resonances between observer and observed, between an organism and its environment, between her species and nature—and how her species is *part* of nature, not distinct from it.

Calpurnia also learns from Darwin, "As more individuals are produced than can possibly survive, there must in every case be a struggle for existence, either one individual with another of the same species, or with the individuals of distinct species, or with the physical conditions of life" (210). This struggle is both a matter of process and a matter of *becoming*; natural selection is an ongoing process of merging, changing, and adapting. Moreover, the novel clearly connects the idea of natural selection and "struggle for existence" with the injustice and inequities that exist between males and females. For instance, Calpurnia chafes against her mother's strictures about learning traditional feminine home economics: cooking, knitting, embroidery. In this context that emphasizes nature and humanity's relationship to it, Calpurnia thus comes to question what her parents accept as a "natural order" of gender. She begins to understand that this order of things is anything but natural. Her ontological relationship with her world shifts dramatically as she comes to question the social order, even wondering why she herself can't have a wife (223).

Calpurnia, as a budding naturalist, also questions humanity's relationship to nature, asking questions such as one she asks after she reads about kangaroos, "Why don't people have pouches? . . . Answer: [a baby] would never fit under [Mother's] corset" (66). From her grandfather, she learns not only about natural selection, but also about the metric system, the food chain, Newton's law, the rain cycle, the life cycle, and how to use a microscope.

Her cognition, her education, and her changing epistemological awareness are central to the novel's plot. For example, when her dog captures a turtle and she takes the turtle from the dog, she realizes she has interfered with natural selection: perhaps the turtle got caught because it was stupider than the rest of the turtles. She wonders "if I was, in my own small way, promoting the survival of the unfittest" (108). She acknowledges that her dog, as a domesticated animal, fits what Darwin says about domestic animals (in terms that are overtly racialized): "One of the most remarkable features in our domesticated *races* is that we see in them adaptation, not indeed to the animal's or plant's own good, but to man's use or fancy" (259, italics added). Calpurnia is here reflecting on the interactionism of human and nature; in the process, she is implicitly acknowledging the agency of nature. Another of the Darwinian epigraphs reads: "We have seen that man by selection can certainly produce great results, and can adapt organic beings to his own uses" (230). Calpurnia understands well that humans very frequently bend nature to their own will—and not always to positive effect: in one instance, the whiskey her grandfather is trying to distill out of pecans turns out, in his words, to taste like "cat piss" (233).

It's far more important to Calpurnia and her grandfather that they discover a previously uncatalogued plant species of vetch and are thrilled when the Plant Taxonomy Committee of the Smithsonian writes back to verify that it is a new species that will be named in honor of their family, "*Vicia tateii*" (324). She herself decides to become a scientist and finds comfort in the recognition that there are other women scientists who worked in the nineteenth century, such as the chemist Madame Curie and the naturalist Martha Maxwell. Demonstrating both her awareness of her dependence on her cultural environment and its interaction with her natural environment, Calpurnia observes the last firefly of the year: "How sad to be the last of your kind, flashing your signal in the dark, alone, to nothingness. But I was not alone, was I? I had learned that there were others of my kind out there" (258). Seated, as she is, on her family's porch, surrounded by family members, she is at once part of nature and part of human-made culture. The false dichotomy between the two terms seems pronounced in this instance, given that Calpurnia is so invested not only in the natural world, but also in observing it, cataloguing it, and claiming it as part of her culture. Although in this text, natural selection becomes a metaphor for the evolution of strong girls into women who share equal rights and opportunities with men, Calpurnia's ontological awareness expands once she can recognize that human agency is part of the natural world—but that human agency has the potential to be very destructive to the environment, to women of all races, and to men of color.

"An army of colored workers from three counties around" are the exploited laborers who harvest the Tates's cotton (197); their cook, Viola, is a "quadroon" depicted in discourses that complicate the interplay among race, gender, and the environment. Viola is "handsome" and "wiry" and always wears a "clean kerchief" on her hair; Kelly depicts Viola in racialized terms that are usually patronizing. Calpurnia's mother gives Viola "new lengths of cotton in the summer and flannel in the winter, along with her weekly wages. Mother also shared old copies of *Ladies Home Journal*" with Viola—even though she is illiterate (51). Viola lives in the former slave quarters, which were clearly too small for the dozen slaves who were forced to live there: "though it had once housed a dozen or so slaves, it was the perfect size for one person" (50). Calpurnia comments that "Viola's skin was no darker than mine at the end of summer, although she was careful to stay out of the sun," and Calpurnia speculates that because Viola is so light-skinned, she could "pass" in a city like Austin if she wanted, but the risks are too high (50). "An octoroon woman in Bastrop had passed and married a white farmer. Three years later, he discovered her birth certificate in a trunk and pitch-forked her to death. He only served ten months in the county jail" (50). Because of her white privilege, Calpurnia has the luxury of not caring whether her skin tans or not, and she claims that she has "never [seen] any high-handedness" between her mother and Viola (50). Yet Viola is required to care about the color of her skin; Viola cannot read; Viola lives in former slave quarters; and Viola performs hard manual labor so that the white lady for whom she works does not need to. In these passages, the text seems unaware of its own potential to recognize the intersectionality at work in this historical setting.

Another way that Calpurnia defensively implies that Viola is not exploited is to point out that she has help, in the form of the family's Mexican American maid, SanJuanna: "Viola didn't have to do all the heavy cleaning herself—she had SanJuanna for that" (212); if Viola's job is to "cook the mountain of food[,] SanJuanna's was to keep it coming" (237). Calpurnia expresses concern about her family's Mexican American maid, SanJuanna, and her husband, Alberto, who are often left with the "thankless burden of cleaning up" (243). When Calpurnia's grandfather and she hear the news that the Smithsonian has validated their scientific discovery, he insists that both Viola and SanJuanna celebrate by drinking a glass of port with the family, even though Viola demurs: "He ignored her and shoved a glass into her hands and then another into SanJuanna's hands—she looked like she would faint" (325). The novel depicts a hierarchy of intersectionalities in terms of gender, social class, and race: Calpurnia's white father and grandfather have more status than her white mother, but Mrs. Tate has more status than Viola—who, as an octoroon and a cook, has more social status than a Mexican American maid. The chain of exploitation is phenomenal and reflects Darwinian notions of the food-chain about which Calpurnia is learning. But the implied and unquestioned Social Darwinism is more than a little distressing in a novel that is otherwise so careful to trace material feminist concerns about the environment.

Calpurnia's attitudes are very likely a historically accurate reflection of the inherent racism of white people in Texas in 1899. The novel implies that people of color are exploited in this culture but never openly critiques that as a long-term social problem. In a novel that openly objects to the exploitation of women and the environment, it is disappointing that *The Evolution of Calpurnia Tate* cannot also depict the problems with racial exploitation and how it is linked to the exploitation of the environment.

## THE FEMINISM OF ECOGEOGRAPHY AND CONTEMPORARY REALISM

Feminist geography provides another interesting lens through which to investigate realism, particularly contemporary realism (that is, realism set in the era in which it is published). Feminist geographers are linked to ecofeminism in that, rather than focusing on the exploitation of the environment, they investigate how women are exploited through the spaces they occupy. Although geography is delineated and described in discursive terms, place and space are constituted materially, so feminist geography is clearly influenced by ecofeminism and material feminism. Linda McDowell argues that the goal of feminist geography "is to investigate, make visible and challenge the relationships between gender divisions and spatial divisions, to uncover their mutual constitution and problematize their apparent naturalness" (12). Rosi Braidotti believes that understanding the cartographic is imperative to understanding *becoming*: she asserts that understanding the hybridity of human subjectivity requires that we "account for one's locations in terms both of space (geo-political or ecological dimension) and time (historical and geneological [sic] dimension)"; she is therefore interested in "a politically informed map that outlines our own situated perspective" (4). Robyn Longhurst identifies some of the following as practical topics that feminist geographers research: migration and the gendered effects diaspora and postcolonialism have on people and place; work and labor relations as regional and national issues; geographies of women's health and reproduction; and gender as it interacts with such factors as age, race, national identity, and social class to influence how people interact with place (546–49). Longhurst refers to these latter categories as "sociocultural embodied geographies" (544). Relying on the work of feminist geographers such as McDowell, Daphne Spain, and Doreen Massey, Beth Pearce argues that even feminist YA authors, such as Cynthia Voigt, tend to depict young women limited in their options because of the way female characters have historically tended to occupy either domestic spaces or natural spaces in children's and adolescent literature. She argues that, especially among some twentieth-century feminist authors, "female adolescent characters are limited to certain spaces by patriarchal constructions of gendered norms; limiting a character to the natural world is just as damaging as limiting her to the home"—because both options diminish the character's agential options (24).

Female characters in Angela Johnson's contemporary realism *Heaven* demonstrate the changing nature of ecofeminism and feminist geographies in YA literature in that, although the adolescent girl characters have agency at home and in the natural world, they also have agency in liminal spaces that are neither entirely domestic nor natural. *Heaven* is narrated by Marley, who lives in a small town called "Heaven." The geography of the town itself is problematized: Heaven is depicted as both heavenly and not. Marley tells the reader that her family moved to Heaven because her mother saw a postcard of the town and "said she'd been looking for Heaven her whole life" (8). Momma tells her, "Wasn't much to it. Small town, lots of trees and kids running everywhere. There was the cutest little school sitting over by the river. . . . we were in Heaven to stay" (8). But Heaven isn't perfect; it's a "pink flamingo, woolly sheep in the front yard kind of place," not a place for landscaped lawns groomed immaculately (16). Marley's best friend, Shoogy, has repressed enough pain from her family's perfectionism that she cuts herself; one resident's baby has been kidnapped by the family's nanny; and the woman who runs the small grocery store feels great "sorrow" because she is so lonely (76). Marley herself discovers a disconcerting secret that reveals to her that Heaven may be closer to her favorite word, "Hell" (which she shouts on occasion); her parents are not her biological parents (47, 58, 72). Her biological father abandoned her after her biological mother died in a car accident when Marley was an infant. Marley has been raised by her biological father's twin brother and his wife, but they have lied to her and claimed her as their own daughter. The lies they have told her threaten to undercut her confidence in them, in herself, and in everything she believes in: "What if *everything* [they] have been telling me all these years has been one fat lie? I can't trust anything they say now, can I?" (73, italics in the original). The physical environment in which Marley is situated, Heaven, is a major factor in who she believes she is and who she believes she can be.

Margaret Mackey's *One Child Reading: My Auto-Bibliography* provides a possible way to read feminist geography in children's and adolescent literature. Mackey values the importance of situatedness, particularly in literacy acquisition. She argues that where and when a reading occurs affects our memory and understanding of the content of a text. Mackey then borrows from the work of urban geographer Kevin Lynch to analyze literacy in terms of the paths, edges, districts, nodes, and landmarks that shape a reader's world, and she uses her own literacy acquisition in a narrative that demonstrates the situatedness of agency. Mackey defines her reading experiences through the terms that define her path through a city, the boundaries that mark city limits, its sections or neighborhoods, its junctions or intersections, and its landmarks. As a female narrative about the relationship between empowerment and literacy as a form of agency, Mackey's work is effectively—and effective—feminist geography. One can extend her work to argue that because characters are usually depicted in relationship to a physical/material world, the geographic metaphors Mackey employs of paths, edges, districts, nodes, and landmarks can be usefully applied to a reading of gender and geography in children's and adolescent literature. In other words, the paths, edges, districts, nodes, and landmarks with which a character interacts most assuredly affect her embodiment and her interactions with the environment. These principles are true for any novel in which world-creation is well-developed enough, but I find it a particularly useful way to think about contemporary realism, such as *Heaven*.

The opening and final pages of *Heaven* demonstrate Marley negotiating a path through her hometown to the telegraph office. Marley's first words are these: "In Heaven there are 1,637 steps from my house to the Western Union. You have to walk by a playground and four stores—two clothing, one food, and one hardware coffee shop.... Ten steps past the grate is Ma's Superette" (6). The final section concludes: "There are 1,637 steps from my house to the Western Union in Heaven. I've walked by the playground, stores and the coffee shop since I can remember" (135). She has been on a path through Heaven and its environs the entire novel, but this time, she's aware of how the route has changed because she is showing the town to her biological father, Jack, who has finally returned to meet her. The path, she says, "was all old to me until I was suddenly pointing it all out to Jack" (135–36). At the beginning of the novel, she believes, Heaven "was fine for a girl like me" (7); after having followed both the literal and metaphorical path through town, she reinforces this idea, saying: "it's been a fine life, for a girl like me, in Heaven" (138).

The edge of town and its limits also play a factor in helping her understand herself as a member of the community. Although they live "across from the river" (1), she still thinks of herself as someone who was "raised by that river" (138). The river represents an edge, perhaps the boundary that flows between Marley's birth parents and her adoptive parents. She walks by the river as she is reconciling herself to the news her parents have told her about her biological father, Jack. Walking on the river's bank, Marley thinks about Bobby, the man who employs her as his daughter's babysitter. He explains growth to her describing how very young children figure out who their parents by interacting with them and recognizing them over and over: "Then you know who you are. Then you *think* they know who you are" (59, italics in the original). Bobby goes on to explain that children make mistakes, and their parents fix them, but the rupture in the relationship comes when "they get caught doing something stupid" (59). His point is that teenagers, at some point, feel a disconnection from their parents—and that is when they find an edge in their relationship with their parents they may not have known about before. Marley has realized at least some limits in her relationship with her parents, and she is walking on one edge of her town while she reflects on that knowledge.

Mackey also writes about how districts function as both region and in terms of historicity; she defines institutions as a type of district and acknowledges that interacting with these various types of districts "affected my developing powers" (426). Marley has exposure to multiple districts: she ventures into Amish country with Bobby; she also journeys to the beach at Lake Erie, and her family takes a Sunday drive to a different destination every Sunday, so she knows her region of Ohio well. She is also aware of regional differences between Ohio and the South because she is terrified by the terrorist burnings of African American churches that have been occurring in the South.[1] She sees the burnings on the news on television: "I watch another church fall down in flames. Flames that I can feel sitting a thousand miles away. Flames that I will feel long after the TV is turned off. Flames and the looks on the faces of people watching their churches burn down—burning hot into the night, burning dark when the morning comes up" (40). Marley and her brother fear churches in Ohio will be burned, and they donate as much money as they can to the arson relief fund for the African American churches. Her mother tries to analyze "why churches now?" (41), and Marly isn't sure she wants to know the answer, but "I got a feeling I don't have much to say concerning what I learn about the world" (41). Indeed, Marly finds out about her true parentage when the deacon of a church that has burned down in Alabama writes her mother to ask if she can help replace the documents about Marly's biological mother that were destroyed in the fire. Moving north to Heaven has not protected this family from violent acts of racism. As Marly says, early in the book: "the past doesn't always make sense of the present" (26). The history of place influences how people inhabit their geography; in this case, Marly can only learn who she is if she learns her own regional history, including the historical geography of where she was born.

Like many female adolescents in YA novels, Marly inhabits both her home and the natural world; she is at home not only in her bedroom, but also hanging upside down from a tree in her backyard. Nonetheless, she inhabits districts or regions away from the domestic and natural landscapes that also define her and empower her. Perhaps one reason girls are often depicted at home or in a natural setting in adolescent literature involves their lack of employment. They stay home or escape to a green world because these are the only options available to them. In *Heaven*, however, both Marly's and her best friend's mothers have jobs that take them away from the home to help empower their families economically. (Their jobs are never depicted as hardships.) Even more important, Marly has a job babysitting for Bobby's daughter, Feather. Sometimes, Bobby asks Marly to babysit Feather where he is working, which brings her to an alley where he paints. The alley has turned into a sort of city park, so it is part pathway, part district, and part landmark. They are in the alley when Bobby asks Marly to consider forgiving her parents: "Must be hard to hate people you've loved for most of your life" (60). Marly cannot yet forgive them for lying to her, but the experience occurs in a liminal place neither domestic nor natural, and it is a direct result of her employment.

Just as Marly's paying job affects her interaction with the environment, human interaction with geography is also affected by economics. Marly's biological father Jack, for example, has a free-ranging lifestyle, driving all over the country in his pickup with his dog, never settling down, which is possible because he has inherited a large cash settlement from the car company whose defective car killed Marly's biological mother. His ability to live without geographic boundaries is enabled because the settlement leaves him independently wealthy. Marly's ability to interact with Jack comes primarily from the Western Union office and the post office; thus, the intersections that create junctions—or "nodes"—also affect Marly's life in spaces that are more economic than either domestic or natural. The hub of Heaven seems to be the small grocery store, the Superette, where Marley's family wires money to Jack every week. Marly says that she only knows him "through letters and Western Union" (10). He writes her beautiful letters, so that she idealizes him as her uncle, and later, to a lesser degree, as her father. Nevertheless, the Western Union office in the Superette (and the unmentioned post office) are the nodes that prove to be pivotal to her relationship to Jack. Her family would not have settled in Heaven in the first place unless Jack's twin brother, the man who is raising Marly as his daughter, first noticed the Western Union sign in the Superette: "There aren't Western Union offices everywhere, you know" (9). The Superette is an economic node that enables Marly to interact with Jack, regardless of where he is.

Heaven has few landmarks; its most prominent may well be its water tower, where Marly sits with Shoogy, "swinging our legs over the side. Green treetops and electric lines lie under us" (69). They have transcended both "nature" in the form of trees and "culture" in the form of manmade electrical lines. The two girls scream their frustrations about their families, high above a world that can't hear them; Marly's friend smokes and jokes about "keepin' it real" (73). Marly says, "I hate this 'keepin' it real' stuff. What's it all about, anyway? Real *is* what is. If you have to keep something the way it is, then it's not going with the natural flow. That's lying. I mean, if you can't change because you think this is the way it always was and anything else would be phony, that's stupid" (73–74, italics in the original). Marly's ontological explanation of reality invokes both change and the notion of flow—implying time is a river. It is almost as if she has to be sitting in something like a landmark above Heaven, where she can see the edge created by the river, before she can acknowledge that change is a necessary aspect of life and that time is as important to geography as place. In a different scene, she says, "That's the thing about time—it's always long gone. . . . changes can drag you somewhere you didn't want to go" (53). The evocation of time dragging someone somewhere is very situated in a sense of place.

Although *Heaven* can be read in terms of feminist geography, it also validates the concerns of ecofeminism. One group of Amish who live near Heaven has no need for radios to warn them about impending tornadoes: "the Amish trust nature to tell them when a tornado is coming. They trust the air around them and the way their animals behave. They watch the way the leaves blow and how the sky looks and the air feels. They trust nature to tell them what the man on the radio tells us" (49). Because the Amish are not exploiting the land, they don't need a "man" to tell them what nature is doing. Marly respects that and vows to be like them: "I could have that kind of faith—in nature" (49). The implication is that she cannot have that kind of faith in man. Jack also writes to her with ecofeminist advice: "you really can't control nature, Marley. You can reel her in and plow her and even kill a few of her creatures. In the end you can kill everything she offers or you can take what she gives you. It's important to understand the natural world" (83).

Marly clearly agrees that it's important to understand the natural world, although her sense of nature is firmly embedded in Heaven, Ohio. She writes about her hometown in ways that evoke an interest in human interactions with the environment, underscoring ideologies of feminist geography: "People look for what they think they need, I guess. You find what you think you need and what might make you happy in different places with different people and sometimes it's just waiting in a tiny town in Ohio with a cute little schoolhouse by the river" (9). People and place and human desire and happiness are all integral to the ways that Marly describes Heaven. Later, when she finds that her parents have lied to her, she feels displaced: "I didn't have a place anymore. . . . Nothing belonged to me anymore" (52–53). Marly has connected place and time and belonging with her concerns about the historical past, both of her own infancy and of the racist legacy of slavery in the southern United States. She demonstrates how belonging is a form of multi-faceted geography that affects how people interact with their environment and with each other, while she also experiences people concerned about ethical care for the Earth. And although she is empowered in domestic and natural landscapes, she is also empowered in the paths, edges, districts, nodes, and landmarks of her world.

Feminist historical and contemporary realism allows for ecofeminist interpretations that depend heavily on the situatedness of place and how a character interacts with her environment. Like Marley in *Heaven* and Billie Joe in *Out of the Dust*, Calpurnia Tate is influenced by the physical geography of her region and must come to terms with the way she inhabits the space that is afforded to her. The agency of nature also comes into focus in historical novels, perhaps in part because of the ways that natural science and climate science evolved as fields of study during the twentieth century. Both *Out of the Dust* and *The Evolution of Calpurnia Tate* demonstrate that humans can have harmful powers over nature and be subsequently affected by the negative effects of that power. The novels of historical realism, in particular, seem to focus on one specific metaphor—dust, in one case, and natural selection in the other—to emphasize the intra-activity between the material and the discursive as a function of the relationship between the perceiver and the perceived—which reflects advancing ideas about science and scientific observation. The girls in these novels have desires that affect their *becoming*, and those desires interact with the natural world. *Heaven*, on the other hand, directly connects the environment and the cartographic to one girl's *becoming*.

## ECOFEMINISM AND MAGIC REALISM

As with *Heaven* and *The Evolution of Calpurnia Tate*, social justice issues also inform the ecofeminism of *Ninth Ward*, a work of magic realism that examines in mythic terms the life of a mixed-race girl, Lanesha, in the days before, during, and after Hurricane Katrina. Lanesha's mother was seventeen when her daughter was born; she is now dead, and Lanesha can see her mother's ghost still lying despondently on the bed in the home where she lives. Lanesha is cared for by an older woman that she calls "Mama Ya-Ya"; Mama Ya-Ya accepts as a matter of fact that Lanesha sees ghosts, and tells the girl, "Everybody in Louisiana knows there be spirits walking this earth. All kinds of ghosts you can't see, not unless they want you to. But you, child, you see them. You've got the *sight*. It's grace to see both worlds" (2). Indeed, Lanesha's special gift is to see these invisible other-worldly creatures who are, as one of my undergraduates, Lauren Gray, once observed, as invisible in her world as the residents of the Ninth Ward are to the rest of New Orleans and the world. The presence of ghosts in this otherwise realistic novel pushes the boundaries of genre and forces the reader to question the ontological relationship between what is "real" and what isn't. Moreover, intersectionality in this novel foregrounds the multiple oppressions that come from gender, poverty, youth, and ability.[2]

Mama Ya-Ya tells her ward, there are "signs everywhere, Lanesha. Pay attention" (15); "senses tell you everything. See, touch, smell, feel. Trust your senses and you'll never lose your way" (35). Mama Ya-Ya is trying to teach Lanesha about using both her powers of scientific observation and her intuition. In trying to figure out the signs that are the natural world's harbingers of the hurricane, Mama Ya-Ya herself "us[es] her senses: sniffing for sea salt, feeling hot wind, listening for the roar of water" (82). Mama Ya-Ya has visions about the upcoming disaster: "In my dream, Lanesha, storm clouds come; wind comes; rain smacks down; the water clears. Sun comes out. Folks go about their business. Everyone is happy. But then, everything goes black. Like someone pulling a curtain. Or a shroud being pulled over the dead. Or God turning out the lights," but she doesn't have the resources or good health to leave the Ninth Ward (51–52). As the hurricane strikes, Mama Ya-Ya's health deteriorates, and when the floodwaters surge, Lanesha moves the elderly woman to the attic where she dies—but not before she has empowered Lanesha to save herself and a neighbor boy who has found refuge with them. (The boy is often ostracized by his peers because of a physical difference: he has eleven fingers.) After Mama Ya-Ya's death , the two children try to rescue a boat from the floodwaters, but Lanesha ends up underwater in the putrid Mississippi flood waters, trapped by a tree root and unable to swim up for air. Mama Ya-Ya has earlier told Lanesha that her mother's ghost will leave "when she finds her purpose" (54)—which proves to be the case. Her mother's ghost saves her by diving into the water and untangling Lanesha's legs so that she can be reborn to save herself and her friend.

Lanesha's mother and Mama Ya-Ya have decided that Lanesha needs to be "birthed," that is, reborn "like a sweet sixteen [party]. Becoming grown in a new way" because both women want her to be loving and strong—strong enough to meet the tests she still needs to face (157). But when she is underwater, Lanesha sees her mother: "My mother is shining—a bright, radiant light, and I can see. See her long black hair, brown skin, and lips that seem pink with lipstick. But it's her eyes that make all the difference. They aren't dull and blank. They're seeing me" (207). Lanesha's rebirth comes from being submerged in the raging waters of the flooded Ninth Ward: that water is of both natural and man-made origins, and Lanesha emerges from it as a newborn would from a rush of amniotic fluid. Once the two children are safely in the boat, Lanesha sees her mother's and Mama Ya-Ya's ghosts rise, shining above the water. They both tell her that they love her, and Lanesha feels empowered by their love and confidence in her. "Both of my mothers are fading. Then, gone," she thinks; "Yet not. They'll always be together and always be with me" (211).

Throughout the book, Lanesha thinks of herself as being strong in terms of a metaphor that she takes from nature: "Like a butterfly, I am strong" (18). Later, after she and her friend have been towed to safety by Cajuns in a motorboat, she thinks "I feel like I can do anything. Like I'm butterfly strong" (217). Mama Ya-Ya has told her that she is someone who "bridge[s] two worlds" with the "grace to see both worlds" (100, 2). And indeed, Lanesha wants to be an engineer because she is fascinated with building bridges. She and her friend find eventual safety on the Martin Luther King Bridge. Although Mama Ya-Ya's concept of bridging "two worlds" refers to the world of spirits, which is a world she sees as naturally being a part of the world of the living, metaphorically speaking, Lanesha is also bridging the worlds between human culture and the natural world. Hurricane Katrina has been a natural phenomenon, but the flood that devastates her culture has been of man-made origins. Ultimately, Lanesha understands that she is as much a part of the natural world as she is a part of the Ninth Ward and that it is her responsibility to bridge those worlds: she is "born to a new life" and she knows she will "be all right" (217). She is Lanesha, "Interpreter of symbols and signs. Future engineer. Shining love" (217).

*Ninth Ward* has all the elements of twentieth-century feminism: the protagonist is strong, smart, articulate, and cares about the people in her community. What this novel contributes to a discussion about twenty-first century ecofeminism, however, is the novel's awareness of the interrelationships among humans and nature. Nancy Tuana uses Hurricane Katrina as the exemplar at the center of her theorizing about interactionist ontology: "As the phenomenon of Katrina's devastation has taught as all too well, the knowledge that is too often missing and is often desperately needed is at the intersection between things and people, between feats of engineering and social structures, between experiences and bodies" ("Viscous" 189). In *Ninth Ward*, the magic realism allows Rhodes to explore metaphorically the knowledge gaps that Tuana identifies through the mysticism of spirituality. Awareness of the other and of other-worldliness plays a role in empowering Lanesha, particularly in effecting the transformation that makes it possible for her to save herself and her friend; her other-worldliness, in particular, is linked to ecofeminism because it communicates to the reader that everyone exists connected to all living things—as this novel would have it, even to those who have gone before us.

Another work of magic realism that interrogates the gendered relationship of the body to the environment is Margaret Mahy's *Kaitangata Twitch*, which queers embodiment and its relationship to the land. A self-identified "dreamer" named Meredith Skerritt lives with her family overlooking a bay very similar to Governor's Bay, New Zealand, where Mahy lived; in the middle of the bay is an island, Kaitangata, which lies in an evocation of crying, "like a secret, strange tear on the moonlit cheek of the harbour" (22). A greedy real-estate developer, Marriott Carswell, has begun to develop the land around the shore of the bay, and he threatens to build a summer home for himself on Kaitangata.

Kaitangata, however, is evoked in embodied terms. Small earthquakes and land tremors in the area are referred to in a "local joke" as "Kaitangata twitches," which attributes some level of agency to the land (16). Far more ominously, Kaitangata is rumored to have swallowed a young girl fifty years earlier; she was playing on the island during her birthday party and because she claimed the island as her own, "rocks somehow unfolded . . . rose up pointing to the sky like fingers, and then clenched down on her" (166, ellipses in the original). She has never been seen again. Lee Kaa, Meredith's older cousin who more clearly self-identifies as Maori than Meredith does, eventually tells her that this girl's family was also threatening to build real estate on Kaitangata fifty years ago, and so Kaitangata swallowed her to "protect itself" (166).

Kaitangata is more than anthropomorphized in this text; the island is itself definitively established as a living body. The text thus invites readers to contemplate what constitutes a human body: body parts? thinking? sleeping? dreaming? eating? Mahy queers what it means to be a body—how a body is defined and how it is constituted—with extensive descriptions of the island's embodiment. For example, the island whispers to Meredith, "*Need! Feed! Need! Feed!*" (3, italics in the original), and its beaches are named after body parts: "HAND BEACH," "EYE BEACH," "MOUTH BEACH" (150–51). At the "very top" of the island, "grey knuckles of rock broke through the soil and grass. Hundreds of years ago the island had clenched an inner fist and punched up towards the sky" (11). Kaitangata is "watching" Meredith; it has a cliff that "opened a great eye and *looked* at" Meredith (92, 93, italics in the original). The island is "pretty crumbly. It's always falling in on itself—sort of eating itself from inside" (48); it's "as if the island were opening a mouth" during these cave-ins (7).

Indeed, the island is carnivorous. When Meredith bleeds, the island's "bare soil . . . soaked [the drops] up quickly—sucked them up greedily. . . . as if Kaitangata had secretly gasped for breath . . . or for more blood perhaps" (41, ellipses in the original). Meredith's family sings a song about "a cannibal isle" (53); Meredith at one point refuses to go to the island, telling it, "It was *me* you tried to eat last time" (57). Meredith learns that the name Kaitangata comes from the Maori: "*Kai* is the Maori word for food, of course, and *tangata* means people"—or, as Meredith reinterprets the words, "Food-people! People-food!" (101). Flowers bloom as red as human blood on the island:

It suddenly looked as if, there below the fist, crimson were trickling down into a yellow cuff. Kaitangata was bleeding, or perhaps, thought Meredith wildly, the blood that seemed to be trickling from beneath the rocky knuckles was being squeezed from a lost child, secretly crushed for fifty years by the island's clenching fingers. . . . Kaitangata was never as restful as it pretended to be. It was always listening in. (61)

While Kaitangata is not exactly blood-thirsty, it will not allow people to exploit it.

Like Meredith, her cousin Lee Kaa also hears the island's voice speaking to him; his perceptions reinforce the island's embodied, sentient nature for both Meredith and the reader. He tells her to "think of all the things people do to land—clear it, cut it, bruise it, burn it. They smash it around, smooth it down, and all to suit themselves. I reckon that, every now and then, there are a few pieces that want to stay the way they are—maybe get their own back, even. And Kaitangata's one of those pieces. It makes itself powerful by feeding on—well, whatever offers itself" (168). Lee also refuses to label the island "wicked," saying, "Wicked? Good? That's *people*-talk. Kaitangata is something older than people. Beyond them" (168, italics in the original). Significantly, Kaitangata-as-a-body is not gendered, which queers not only the body but also concepts of sex and gender in this book. Kaitangata is neither male nor female; it is neither good nor bad; it simply *is*.

The queering of embodiment evokes predation here, but even predation itself is ungendered. "Everything gets hungry," said Meredith . . . and nothing that gets eaten wants to be eaten" (102). She then runs through a litany of fairy-tales about predatory consumption: "'The Three Billy Goats Gruff,' 'The Three Little Pigs' and 'The Wolf and the Seven Little Kids.' The excitement of nursery tales was all about who managed to eat who. 'Chickens, lambs, fish, none of them want to be eaten'" (102). Marriott Carswell is a predator, but so is Kaitangata. As Mahy explained in a 1987 interview, "many of the first stories we tell to children are still basically concerned with 'who gets to eat who in life.' . . . While we could certainly evolve a totally different literature it wouldn't alter the fact that these predatory relationships do exist in nature" (qtd. in Duder 51). The human body *must* prey on the land, in one way or another, for food—but Kaitangata objects to the concept of ownership, not the concept of supporting life. Ultimately, Mahy's most ecofeminist gesture in this novel may well be the queering of embodiment that emphasizes not reproduction but predation as the most fundamental goal of all human bodies. People prey on the land whether they are cis male, cis female, trans, gender fluid, or questioning, just as all human bodies are vulnerable to infinite forms of predation.

Mahy's character Meredith Skerritt believes herself to be an enchantress who can invoke and summon people, so she calls Marriott Carswell to Kaitangata in an effort to save the island from his predation. She "[feels] the island inside her as well as outside" (155) and is terrified when, in her dream-trance, the island begins to eat Carswell: "Kaitangata embraced him, transforming, as it did so, from pale past child into a dark, muscular lash—a tongue, perhaps—while the great upper lip of the cave protruded above him. ... Kaitangata swallowed him" (159). In this case, the prey eats the predator's body (although Meredith is relieved, upon awakening, to find that the cannibalism is only metaphorical. Carswell disappears because his business has "been swallowed up by someone even bigger than he was" (173); globalized corporations are the greediest fish in this particular food chain.)

The queering of embodiment in this novel also involves the way that Kaitangata has "used the power of [Meredith's] dreams to save itself" (173). Meredith thinks about herself and her cousin Lee Kaa, "*Dreams branch out when you're alone, and dreamers are all islands, really*" (181, italics in the original). The text unfolds in such a way that sometimes the reader is initially unsure what Meredith is dreaming and what is actually happening, but ultimately, her dreams (and the dreams Lee Kaa has had years ago) prove to be as *real* as reality, queering the very concepts of epistemology and ontology. How do we know that dreams are not real? In this novel, reality is so queered that dreams do, indeed, have tangible consequences. Anything seems to be possible epistemologically for a girl like Meredith who listens to her dreams and respects that multiple realties—multiple ways of queering the world—exist. Furthermore, the body—and the mind—are not fixed, stable, concrete entities that can be confined through essentialist terms like "male" or "female." Most important, people must acknowledge their interdependence on the land in order to avoid becoming only predators upon it.

As a genre, ecofeminist magic realism engages readers in ontological speculations that contemporary and historical realism cannot evoke. *Ninth Ward* relies on magic realism to equate the invisibility of the spirit world with the invisible citizens of the Ninth Ward itself; *Kaitangata Twitch* invites readers to queer gendered notions of the land and the relationship of people to predation upon the land. As a genre, magic realism has hybrid possibilities that the demands of verisimilitude don't allow in realism. When deployed in the context of children's and adolescent ecofeminism, magic realism offers stark and powerful social commentary on ecological issues.

## CONCLUSION

Alice Curry identifies the didactic impulse in many post-disaster YA novels that focus on the environment: "Opportunities for narrative didacticism as warning, intimation or moral lesson are overt" (22); the same can be said of ecofeminist YA novels. Nevertheless, *Heaven, Out of the Dust, The Evolution of Calpurnia Tate, Ninth Ward*, and *Kaitangata Twitch* demonstrate the potential that preadolescent and adolescent female protagonists bring to ecofeminism and feminist geography: because these girls are poised in the liminality of adolescence, they understand exploitation and can discern the connections among self and place, self and other, self and nature, the world and other-worldliness, and among cultures, including those that have been othered. The very liminality of female adolescence allows these characters to have changing perceptions of human agency as a potentially destructive facet of nature's agency. Because adolescence is, by its very nature, a time of transition and a time of shifting ontological awareness, it seems only natural that these characters demonstrate an ontology that "takes seriously the agency of the natural" (Haraway, "Otherworldly" 188).

Moreover, these ecofeminist novels value the agency of nature, not only for the way that interacting with it can make people feel they belong (as with Marley in *Heaven*) or stronger (as with Billie Joe in *Out of the Dust* and Lanesha in *Ninth Ward*) or the way that it can teach people (as it does with Calpurnia Tate and the protagonist of *Kaitangata Twitch*), but also for the ways that nature is *not* a human construct to be represented solely through discourse. Billie Joe may play endlessly with language because she is, after all, a piano-player and poet who plays with sound; but far more important, like Lanesha, she recognizes that nature has power greater than that of the humans who have created the environmental catastrophe destroying her world. In *Kaitangata Twitch*, Meredith recognizes the same phenomenon: Kaitangata has far more agency than any human in the novel.

It is this type of agency that allows authors to problematize the troubled duality between materiality and discourse in an ecofeminist YA novel. Initially, Meredith easily recognizes people as predators on the land; only once she interacts with Kaitangata's agency does she recognize the duality of

"Food-people! People-food!" (101). People need food, but they can also serve as food to the land; this is the same type of "ashes to ashes, dust to dust" logic that informs *Out of the Dust*. Farmers have failed to nurture the land, so the land is now becoming the predator of man. The colonizing landholder is being colonized by the land itself in these novels—just as *Ninth Ward* demonstrates the mutually implicating problems that occur because of the interactionisms among nature, humans, and their culture.

Furthermore, like Billie Joe, Lanesha must have an experience of complete silencing—a complete detachment from language—before she can perceive the intra-activity of discourse and materiality. Lanesha is submerged beneath the floodwaters, stripped of her own agency and access to language, just as Billie Joe is silenced by the fire that kills her mother and threatens to destroy her piano-playing hands. While Billie Joe is no longer playing piano, she thinks of the piano as her "silent / mother": "We close our eyes / together / and together find that stillness / like a pond . . . / when the wind is quiet / and the surface glazes / gazing unblinking / at the blue sky" (194). She thinks of the piano as "the / companion / to myself. / The mirror / with my mother's eyes" (194). Silence, nature, music, and culture are entwined in this poem in ways that make it impossible to believe in false dualities between material/discourse or nature/culture.

Thus, in the best of these ecofeminist novels, the protagonists either transcend language and/or employ it to understand their environment. They recognize their embodiment as it is affected by the environment, and they respect the way that nature's agency informs their own existence. In the next chapter, I will analyze a variety of speculative fictions that cross a spectrum of the dystopic and apocalyptic in explorations of embodiment, embodied cognition, biopolitics, sexuality, and neoliberalism; the novels in Chapter 4 are also frequently ecofeminist in the ways that they interrogate both the agency of nature and the intra-activity of discourse and the material *mattering*.

## CHAPTER 4

# SPECULATIVE FICTIONS, EMBODIMENT, AND THE NEOLIBERAL IMPULSE

Most readers of YA literature in the early part of the twenty-first century were aware of the surge of interest in teen dystopian fiction between 2008 and 2012.[1] The subsequent trend included the increased popularity of novels about cyborgs, novels about the supernatural, and novels either apocalyptic or post-apocalyptic.[2] Many of these speculative fictions feature strong and independent-minded girls who save the world from itself, as if the only thing that can possibly reverse the corrupt extremes of the patriarchy is a female. Indeed, Sonja Sawyer Fritz examines how "female protagonists have taken center stage in YA dystopias as girls who resist the forces of their broken and corrupt societies to create their own identities, shape their own destinies, and transform the worlds in which they live"; Fritz refers to these girls as "empowered citizen[s]" and "heroic trailblazer[s]" (17).

Frequently, such novels are categorized as "feminist," simply because they feature a strong female protagonist. Although it is easy to think about speculative YA fiction in feminist terms, in this chapter, I will problematize these novels' depictions of female embodiment in order to interrogate how twenty-first century feminisms sometimes fail in their agendas, particularly within the genre of the YA dystopia. YA dystopias frequently investigate what it means to inhabit a human body; dystopias and other speculative fictions often track how turmoil in the body politic effects subsequent turmoil for the human body itself. My analysis thus relies on material feminism, including ecofeminism, to explore embodiment in literature for the young, and my analysis also examines the nuances of neoliberalism—defined at greater length below—as a concept that complicates twenty-first century feminisms in adolescent literature. In this chapter, I will analyze a range of novels that follow a spectrum from predictable (and not particularly successful) feminism to more innovative forms of feminism. This chapter thus moves from an examination of Suzanne Collins's *The Hunger Games* (2008), to Laini Taylor's *Daughter of Smoke and Bone* (2011), Lissa Price's *Starters* (2012), Adam Rex's *The True Meaning of Smekday* (2007), and Sherri L. Smith's *Orleans* (2013).

## SPECULATIVE FICTION AND EMBODIMENT

Elizabeth Grosz writes about philosophy's long-term failure to grapple with the human body, especially the female body, as a site of knowledge production. She accuses Western philosophy of *somatophobia* and traces this fear of the body as far back as Plato, from whom "matter itself [i]s a denigrated and imperfect version of the Idea. The body is a betrayal of and a prison for the soul, reason, or mind" within Platonic thinking (5). Aristotle gendered the division further by tying that imperfect body to reproduction and specifically pregnancy: "maternity is regarded as a mere housing, receptacle, or nurse of being rather than a coproducer . . . he believed that the mother provided the formless, passive, shapeless matter which, through the father, was given form, shape, and contour, specific features and attributes it otherwise lacked" (Grosz 5). As Grosz notes, Christianity also prepared the way for the Cartesian split by assigning the soul to the mind and sin to the body in a gesture that reified gender binaries, with "Man" serving as the head and "Woman" serving as the body (5–6). Millennia of western thought has thus justified subordinating the female body to notions of putative male rationality. Grosz's call for a feminist rethinking of embodiment insists that the body "must be regarded as a site of social, political, cultural, and geographical inscriptions, production or constitution. The body is not opposed to culture . . . it is itself a cultural, *the* cultural product" (23, italics in the original).

Building on Grosz's work, Susan Bordo questions the poststructural interpretation of the body as an entirely discursive construct. She asks: "If the body is treated as pure text, subversive, destabilizing elements can be emphasized and freedom and self-determination celebrated; but one is left wondering, is there a *body* in this text?" (38, italics in the original). Bordo thus invites us to consider the materiality of the body as a site of knowledge, as an active aspect of agency that is inseparably interconnected with brain functioning, since all brains, after all, are housed in bodies. Yet many of the strong female protagonists of YA dystopias are psychologically at war with their bodies. These protagonists are indeed grateful when their bodies empower them, but they despair or are enraged when their bodies betray them—and even worse, in those moments, they regard their own bodies as objects, not as inextricably one with their minds. As befits the metaphorical nature of speculative fiction, issues surrounding embodiment often serve as metaphorical representations of the embodied issues that girls and young women experience in the twenty-first century.

Furthermore, Alice Curry demonstrates that many dystopias, particularly YA dystopias, offer metaphorical critiques of contemporary disregard for environmentalism, climate change, and the exploitation of resources (23). In other words, ecofeminist dystopias are not predictions about the future; rather, they offer critiques of the contemporary world. Curry notes, "In much young adult fiction, apocalypse as tipping point is shown to result in environmental change, but more radically, perhaps, it is shown to target the very values, relationships and social structures on which human life as we know it is based" (25). For example, I have argued elsewhere that *The Hunger Games* offers a libertarian critique of American teenagers in implying that they rely too heavily on the government and the entertainment industry: in The Hunger Games trilogy, entertainment and government are referred to using a reference to the Roman historian Juvenal's analysis that the Roman Empire became weaker because of citizens' reliance on "bread and circuses"—a line that Collins herself quotes in *Mockingjay* (Trites, "Some Walks" 15–28; Collins, *Mockingjay* 223).

Brian McDonald shows how the dystopic is often ecofeminist because it demonstrates that a downward spiraling of environmental factors "[dominate] every aspect of life" (9). Relying on this idea, Sean P. Connors offers a compelling reading of *The Hunger Games* as an ecofeminist novel that functions in this way. He asserts that Collins "demonstrates how the same oppressive patriarchal conceptual framework that motivates governments and corporations to exploit nature and degrade the environment, both symbols of the feminine, leads them to enact policies that subjugate and exploit disenfranchised groups, including women, minorities, and people in poverty" ("I Try" 138). As Connors argues, the Capitol relies on technology in its role as Colonizer; the Capitol exploits its colonies by forcing people in many of the districts to live in poverty, deprived of the natural resources that have been cultivated in their own district ("I Try" 140–42). To maintain control, the Capitol is willing to dehumanize and sacrifice teenagers, the impoverished, and racially othered peoples; dire poverty occurs in those districts with darker-skinned peoples, such as District 11 and District 12 (Connors, "I Try" 142–43). Connors also traces how patriarchal the culture is; Katniss is notably ruled by men and subject to their gaze ("I Try" 148). The novel positions Katniss as "a metaphor for the damage that patriarchal institutions inflict on young females by inundating them with a steady stream of messages that function to actively limit the subject positions they recognize as available to them" (Connors, "I Try" 139); Collins also "demonstrates how an oppressive conceptual framework that leads governments and corporations to impose themselves on the environment also leads them to enact policies and legisla-tion that actively work to oppress women" (Connors, "I Try" 154). Connors demonstrates elegantly how the dystopic ecofeminist YA novel works: in it, patriarchal forces employ technology and science to exploit women, men of color, the impoverished, the environment—and teenagers.

Curry, moreover, observes that Katniss's embodiment is objectified and regarded as animalistic. Curry demonstrates the novel's "sustained use of animal imagery that represents Katniss as vacillating between the animal and the human" (52), and she observes how the Capitol places Katniss under "erasure" (54). Katniss "link[s] her own plight with that of the animal about to be ingested" when she skewers an apple in a roasted pig's mouth that is about to be served to the judges (53). Curry then argues that Katniss's ani-mal body is subsequently eroticized for the viewing pleasure of the Capitol. *The Hunger Games* thus identifies how "institutional repression of natural embodiment is targeted at the female body and the norms of femininity become a particular locus of control" in ecofeminist novels for the young (47). In an ecofeminist dystopia, readers expect all forms of exploitation, but especially objectifications of female embodiment, to be critiqued. The concerns of ecofeminism thus seem to me to intersect with genre in the ways authors deploy ecofeminism sometimes because of the demands of a genre and sometimes despite it, as I hope to demonstrate in this chapter's discussion of representations of embodiment in speculative fiction.

Collins's *The Hunger Games* participates palpably in the ongoing problem of female protagonists who objectify their own bodies. Katniss is objecti-fied by the Capitol, as a powerless resident of District 12, as a pawn in the Reaping, as a body to be made visually appealing for the Games through the removal of hair and layers of skin, and as a tool objectified by the pan-opticon in the Capitol's Hunger Games.[3] Perhaps then it is no wonder that Katniss would, in turn, objectify her own body. During Katniss's private session with the Gamemakers, she feels "humiliated" initially that she can-not manipulate a new bow and arrow to her liking, but when she gets the rhythm of the new weapon, she is proud of her "excellent shooting" (101). She grows angry, however, because the Gamemakers are feasting on pork and not watching her; they do not see her accomplishments. "Suddenly I am furious, that with my life on the line, they don't even have the decency to pay attention to me. That I'm being upstaged by a pig" (101). Katniss metaphorically draws an analogy between herself and the dead pig while she simultaneously refuses to be thought of as meat.[4] "*Without thinking, I pull an arrow from my quiver and send it straight at the Gamemakers'* table" (102, italics added). Katniss means, of course, that she has completed the action without conscious thought—but the exact wording implies that in this moment of strength, she has relied more on her body than on her brain, as if she has successfully separated her body from her mind and as if anyone can truly fire a weapon "without thinking," without the use of her brain and its cognition. Katniss is exemplifying an impossible mind/body split that demonstrates how Collins participates in ancient dialogues about the female body as being always already only an object.

Later in the arena, when Katniss is chased by fireballs so that she literally does become the Girl on Fire, her recognition of the integration between her body and mind again falters. Her interior monologue demonstrates that she initially perceives her faculties as fully integrated because she "know[s]" that she is "supposed to run" (172); she "know[s]" she should "keep moving" (174). Once she is burned, however, she speaks less about what her mind and body can do together and describes her leg as only a part of her, as one piece of herself: "I roll the leg back and forth on the ground. . . . But then, *without thinking*, I rip away the remaining fabric with my bare hands" (176, italics added). She observes her leg as if it is separate from her selfhood. Notably, when Katniss is in distress, she describes herself as acting "without thinking," discounting her own cognitive abilities.

Katniss again experiences her body as an object when she is stung by tracker jackers. She hallucinates that "ants begin to crawl out of the blisters on my hands and I can't shake them free. They're climbing up my arms, my neck. Someone's screaming, a long high-pitched scream that never breaks for breath. I have a vague idea that it might be me" (194). Tracker jacker venom has been designed "to target the place where fear lives in your brain," so it's not surprising that Katniss hallucinates (195). But the language emphasizes Katniss's sense of being cognitively separated from her own body, especially when she can neither feel herself screaming nor recognize that the screamer's voice is her own. Subsequently, when she loses her hearing after she explodes the land mines at the Tributes' campsite, she again describes her body in objectified terms:

> I find myself pawing at my left ear periodically, trying to clean away whatever deadens its ability to collect sounds. . . . I can't adjust to deafness in the ear. It makes me feel off-balanced and defenseless to my left. Blind even. My head keeps turning to the injured side, as my right ear tries to compensate for the wall of nothingness where yesterday there was a constant flow of information. (228–29)

The way Katniss distinguishes hearing in both ears from hearing in only one is telling: when she is well, her body integrates information without her consciously being aware she is doing so, but when she loses her hearing, she becomes an animal "pawing" at her own ear, or an automaton, repetitively turning her head to one direction in a gesture that implies her brain has no power over her bodily motions. What we know about cognition tells us that it is entirely a function of Katniss's embodied brain that she would instinctively keep turning to listen on the side where she no longer hears. But she reports herself to be powerless over that brain, as if her brain is not part of her body.

Katniss has had her body hair stripped and her skin polished before the Games. The same thing happens again after she and Peeta have been declared victors, but this time, she is both startled her body has been objectified and is nonetheless capable of self-objectification: "I . . . am arrested by the sight of my hands. The skin's perfection, smooth and glowing. Not only are the scars from the arena gone, but those accumulated over years of hunting have vanished without a trace. My forehead feels like satin, and when I try to find the burn on my calf, there's nothing" (351). The Capitol has continuously inscribed itself onto Katniss's skin, before the Games and during the Games when the fire burns her and the tracker jackers sting her. They even have the power of robbing her of her own body's history, erasing scars she held long before she entered the Capitol's arena. Katniss knows the Capitol blames her for being the "instigator," and she uses language self-aware of her own epistemology when she says about the President glaring at her: "That's when I *know* that even though both of us would have eaten the berries, I am to blame for having the *idea*" (364, italics added). Katniss can perceive the Capitol's abuse of power—indeed, she has identified in the first chapter that the Hunger Games are "the Capitol's way of reminding us how totally we are at their mercy. How little chance we would stand of surviving another rebellion" (18). But she cannot perceive what Connors has identified: the gendered nature of the Capitol's abuse of power ("I Try" 138). Throughout the novel, the Capitol inscribes itself on her very skin, but more often than not in these moments, Katniss experiences a body/mind split that reinforces the tendency in our culture to objectify the female body. And Katniss never consciously rebels *per se* against the Capitol as a patriarchy; she rebels against its abuse of power without recognizing how gendered that abuse is.

The novel also demonstrates gender-distinctiveness in its use of what Annette Burfoot refers to as *biopleasure*, which she defines thusly: "Biopleasure speaks to the combined and contradictory nature of biotechnology narratives that simultaneously dehumanizes, demonizes, and eroticizes human beings" (48). The tracker jackers, for example, are genetically mutated animals designed by the Capitol out of their desire to subdue rebel bodies; the desire here emerges from the Capitol's murderous lust for disciplined bodies—even for corpses in the arena of the Hunger Games. Like many dystopias, *Hunger Games* plays with biopleasure in ways both imaginative and terrifying. For example, the "muttations" who kill Cato are horrifying genetic mutations that erase lines between human and animal, especially in the way they bear the eyes of the individual tributes who have died—but their mind/body split is reinforced when we realize how soulless these muttations are.[5] In another example of posthuman biopleasure, the prosthetic leg Peeta eventually receives is a miracle of science and contributes to his ability to continue his role as an object of desire for both the Capitol (who desires to manipulate him) and Katniss (who feels traditional, albeit conflicted, forms of desire for his heteronormative body).[6] It is also significant that Peeta is not left disabled; he must be whole, with what Kristeva might refer to as a "clean and proper" body before Katniss can consummate her relationship with him (Kristeva 78).

If the patriarchal Capitol controls all manipulations of science and technology in the novel, it seems likely that traditional gender distinctions will continue to be reinforced. And Peeta—not Katniss—is the person to insist on, as Susan Hekman would have it, a self-directed sense of self that does not follow a script when he maintains that he wants "to die as myself" (Hekman, "Constructing" 115; Collins 141). When he believes he is dying, he underscores the importance of the discursive in his utterance to Katniss with the words that change everything: "We both know they have to have a victor" (343–44). She takes action only because of his words. Moreover, throughout the first novel in the series, he remains secure in his masculine-but-sensitive identity, unlike Katniss, who must be retrained in femininity for the cameras and yet who must excel as a hunter in the arena. Despite this, Katniss is the object of exchange between men in a traditional love triangle. Of course, since she perceives herself as an object, then it seems inevitable that she would serve as an object of exchange. And indeed, more than one triangle exists in the series: Katniss is an objectified female body triangulated with Peeta and Gale, but she is also triangulated in her relationship that involves Peeta and Haymitch and the fraught relationship between Cinna and President Snow. She cannot even sustain female friendships to offset these homosocial triangles. As Ann M. M. Childs observes, Katniss's relationships with female friends must be sacrificed for her rebellion to be complete, and so Rue must die in *The Hunger Games* and Prim must die in *Mockingjay* (187). And Katniss's reward for all of this rebellion is marriage, two children, and life in a bunkered compound that shelters her from all social interaction. This is hardly a triumph of feminism.[7]

Sara K. Day, Miranda A. Green-Barteet, and Amy L. Montz appreciate the significance of how many YA dystopias like *The Hunger Games* feature strong female protagonists, but they also critique aspects of these novels that are less than feminist. Sara K. Day, for example, examines how sexuality in these novels interpellates young women in terms of whiteness, compulsory heteronormativity, and future motherhood ("Docile" 90), and she argues that many authors of dystopias situate the female teen body in a dystopic future in order to "draw attention to the social mechanisms that not only figure the adolescent woman's desiring body as dangerous but also reinforce to young women that they themselves should fear the disruptive potential of their sexuality" ("Docile" 75). Day concludes: "Thus, the sexist structures that are in place not only in contemporary societies but in the future societies about which dystopian novels speculate may offer young women the possibility of empowerment through sexuality, but the representations that make such promises in fact perpetuate gendered expectations about the adolescent woman's body that continue to render it both docile and dangerous" ("Docile" 91). Day's findings also reinforce Burfoot's work on the heteronormative desires that drive biopleasure.

Similar interrogations of compulsory heteronormativity are elucidated in Childs's examination of how female friendships in YA dystopia are subordinated to heterosexual attractions: "for the male protagonists, saving the day is the ultimate goal, and he is rewarded his love interest for successfully doing so, while the female protagonist saves the day as a part of how she meets her goal of winning her relationship. The female dystopia's protagonist cannot have successful rebellion, deep female friendship, and heterosexual love. . . . One of these three things must fail"—usually the female friendship (199). Thus, both Childs and Day emphasize the YA dystopia's tendency to emphasize heterosexual romance over other considerations. In the process, of course, gender binaries in too many YA speculative fictions are emphasized rather than blurred or queered.

This creates one of the major factors that mitigates against the feminisms that are trying to work in most popular YA speculative fictions. First, too often these female protagonists are objects of male love who are still participating as the object of exchange in the age-old homoerotic love triangle Eve

Kosofsky Sedgwick identified in *Between Men* in 1985. Second, embodiment leads to a fetishizing of the body that works to reinforce gender distinctions, rather than collapsing or even interrogating them in these novels. Finally, some of these young women objectify their own bodies. This is particularly evident in the way that skin is depicted in these novels: it is on the skin that women inscribe their own objectification by means of exfoliation or tattoos or scars. Too often, then, the body thus becomes a politicized object, rather than being regarded as a material reality that interplays through discourse with environmental factors to support and enhance a self-defined identity.

## *DAUGHTER OF SMOKE AND BONE*: CYBORGS AND THE ERASURE OF THE MATERNAL BODY

Day, Green-Barteet, and Montz explain the plethora of female protagonists in recent YA speculative fiction as a function of the way the genre inter-rogates ambiguity and uncertainty. They note that the "emphasis on ado-lescent women reflects an ongoing effort on the part of authors, scholars, parents, and young women themselves to reconsider and redefine adoles-cent womanhood" (5). They highlight the cultural anxieties created by the tension between the emphasis on strength and individuation advanced by the Girl Power movement and the opposing depiction of teen girls' vulner-ability as depicted by *Reviving Ophelia* and similar psychological examina-tions of teen girls. They believe that as a result of these competing forces, "contemporary dystopian literature with adolescent women protagonists places young women in unfamiliar, often liminal spaces—caught between destructive pasts and unclear futures—in order to explore the possibili-ties of resistance and rebellion. . . . [to] participate in the redefinition of adolescent womanhood" (7). Day, *et al.*, highlight how "an increasingly technologically driven and socially complex society" complicates the lim-inality of adolescence even more as young women contend with social media and all of the forces (both positive and negative) that the internet offers (5). Given our culture's dependence on technology, and given the many cultural anxieties that surround advanced technologies, I believe that Day, *et al.*, are right to problematize female rebellion in the YA dystopia as a function of increased cultural attention to the relationship between the body and technology—especially the female body. The same could be said about female rebellion in other types of speculative fiction, such as the apocalyptic and the post-apocalyptic.

Cultural anxieties about the interfaces and interactions among science, technology, human bodies, and language then are distinct factors in driving popular interest in speculative fictions, including the dystopic and the post-apocalyptic. These types of speculative fiction insist on the significance of materiality to daily lives: shattered environments, advanced technologies, sophisticated machines of war, genes as the computer codes of the human body, and bodies that are enhanced by technologies that range from having computerized prosthetic limbs to brain implants, creating multiple scenarios that make it impossible to believe that we are all and only constructed by language—or by bodies alone. In her "Cyborg Manifesto," Donna Haraway employs the cyborg as the metaphor through which she collapses multiple dualities, but especially those of "self/other, mind/body, culture/ nature, male/female, civilized/primitive" ("Cyborg" 189). She writes, "It is not clear what is mind and what body in machines that resolve into coding practices" ("Cyborg" 189) because she recognizes that "communications technologies and biotechnologies are the crucial tools recrafting our bodies" ("Cyborg" 176). Particularly salient to Haraway's logic is the fact that communication and biotechnology (particularly the study of genetics) rely on codes and coding:

> communications sciences and modern biologies are constructed by a common move—*the translation of the world into a problem of coding*, a search for a common language in which all resistance to instrumental control disappears and heterogeneity can be submitted to disassembly, reassembly, investment, and exchange. . . . The world is subdivided by boundaries differentially permeable to information. (Haraway, "Cyborg" 164, italics in the original)

Haraway understands that women throughout the world are victimized by these codings, whether the codes involve language, unspoken social codes, computer codes, or economic codes. "Cyborg politics is the struggle for language and the struggle against perfect communication, against the one code that translates all meaning perfectly, the central dogma of phallogo-centrism" (Haraway, "Cyborg" 188).

Haraway's work on the cyborg has opened up an entire field of interest in the posthuman. Katherine Hayles argues, first, that the posthuman "privileges informational pattern over material instantiation"; second, that posthuman thinking is both implicated in epistemological assumptions about human thought being more important than human embodiment and inherently aware of how people learn to manipulate their own prosthesis (such as eyeglasses) "so that extending or replacing the body with other prostheses becomes a continuation of a process that began before we were born," and finally, that the idea of the posthuman "configures human being so that it can be seamlessly articulated with intelligent machines" (3). Studying YA literature, Victoria Flanagan argues in *Technology and Identity in Young Adult Fiction: The Posthuman Subject* that "posthumanism uses technoscience as the impetus for a radical revaluation of human subjectivity, exploring the many ways in which technological innovations such as virtual reality have changed our understanding of what it means to be human in the modern era" (*Technology* 1). Throughout her work she traces how the originally anti-technological bias of earlier children's literature has become more oriented toward a valuation of technology. Similarly, Fiona McCulloch argues that some adolescent fiction "responds to the posthuman turn by reconfiguring childhood identity beyond the liberal humanist paradigm in ways that interrogate its hegemonic systems" (75). She believes that "at its best, the posthuman turn offers liberty from the shackles of a privileged humanism that casts all others in the role of subhuman; at its worst, it could steer humanity toward a future based upon masculinist power and enterprise" (75). The implications for feminism are clear.

Foucault also provides material feminism with a useful concept when he defines biopolitics as "the attempt, starting from the eighteenth century, to rationalize the problems posed to governmental practice by phenomena characteristic of a set of living beings forming a population: health, hygiene, birthrate, life expectancy, race" (*Birth* 317). Legal codes that regulate food safety, water safety, and female reproduction or laws that require birth or death certificates, mandatory automotive airbags, or warnings on cigarette packages are all examples of the biopolitical. As Burfoot reminds us, "biopleasure" is the extension of biopolitics by which the cyber-body becomes fetishized.

Further building on Haraway's and Foucault's ideas, Burfoot refers to biopleasure as a function of "signification of matter in the context of contemporary technoscientific speculations of bodies as atomized, degendered, and nonhuman" (48). Burfoot explores the ontological status of "human existence" as she interrogates why "matter as a form of biopleasure remains gender-distinct" (48). Biopleasure is a way to "connote a fetishism of the body as components (reproductive cells, uteri, genes, and so on), in which the life-giving qualities of the body are produced in reduced, mechanized, and malleable but mute forms (such as DNA)"; her use of the term "pleasure" in this neologism emphasizes the "sublimated but central role of desire in this production" (29). Like Haraway, she recognizes the commonalities of coding to both genetics and computers.

Laini Taylor's *Daughter of Smoke and Bone* is a speculative fiction in which the technological separation of mind and body is more than a mere metaphor. In this apocalyptic world, after death, souls are captured as "smoke"; they are then resurrected from other people's teeth, the "bone" of the novel's title. Karou is one of these revenants: she has been restored from death back into life by Brimstone, a father-figure who is a chimaera—a type of half-human, half-animal. In the eons-long fight between chimaera and angels-gone-rogue, Brimstone—a resurrectionist—is the chimera who has learned the art of restoring the dead to life by rebuilding their bodies:

> He didn't breathe life back into the torn bodies of the battle-slain; he *made* bodies. This was the magic wrought in the cathedral under the earth. Out of the merest relics—teeth—Brimstone conjured new bodies in which to sleeve the souls of slain warriors. In this way, the chimaera army held up, year after year, against the superior might of the angels. (328, italics in the original)

The biopleasure of having the power to create new bodies for old souls recurs throughout the novel; interestingly, it is initially a male alone who holds that procreative power before he trains his female apprentice. They both report their satisfaction in being able to serve their people as resurrectionists, although the work is wearying, and their desirous warlord borders on lustfulness in his insistence that the resurrectionist work faster to create more bodies for him to use in war. Patriarchal war culture thus drives the need for procreation that, in this case, is divorced from the maternal body.

Much of the plot resides in a love triangle. In her previous life, Karou has been a chimaera named Madrigal (who trained as Brimstone's apprentice). Madrigal has fallen in love with a forbidden lover, the seraph angel Akiva. The resurrected protagonist Karou wears a tattoo that marks the patriarchy's claim on her: she has eyes tattooed on her palms. These eyes signify that she is a revenant, a chimaera resurrected by Brimstone who has a new body into which her former soul has been inserted. Those tattoos of eyes are the greatest weapon she can turn against the angel who pursues her, Akiva, when she does not yet recognize him as her former lover. She thinks of Akiva as someone who has left her "scarred" (194). But Akiva, too, is scarred by the war his father has waged against the chimaeras—because every time an angel kills a chimaera, the angel soldier notches a scar on his or her knuckles. Akiva's hands are blackened with these scars. Unsurprisingly, Akiva is pursuing Karou not to wage war but because he recognizes her as the revenant of the love he lost and has assumed to be dead: Madrigal. Akiva and Madrigal fell in love before she was reborn as Karou, so Madrigal never had tattooed eyes on her palm in that previous life.

The powerful warlord prince of the chimaeras also lusts for Madrigal and, in her first incarnation, has her killed when he realizes she has taken Akiva—instead of him—as her lover. In the subsequent novels, Madrigal (reincarnated as Karou) becomes the object of exchange between these two men who are engaged in battle. They wage war on behalf of their people, but they also wage war on behalf of a claim to a female body—a resurrectionist—that is, one who is capable of giving birth without using her uterus. A different love triangle is invoked by a younger chimaera from her tribe: Kirin, who is also in love with Madrigal/Karou and jealous of Akiva. Karou is as strong, active, intelligent, and self-motivated as Katniss, but she cannot participate in the plot without being at every turn objectified by the male gaze. At least three males gaze upon her with desire: Akiva, Kirin, and their warlord. And in another cliché of adolescent literature, Madrigal is betrayed by a female. Her foster sister, Chiro, is jealous of her—so she betrays Madrigal in an act of stereotypical female vs. female competition—which is why Madrigal dies and must be resurrected as Karou.

Like Katniss, Karou also acts without thinking. At one point when she is startled, "she was *beyond thinking* ... she was all nerve and impulse" (129, italics added); a moment later she throws her ex-boyfriend through a plate-glass window. In her earlier incarnation as Madrigal, when she feels threatened by the leader of the chimaera soldiers, she thinks: "Her heart and body were in revolt.... Her limbs were light, ready to flee. Her heartbeat sped to a fast staccato.... Madrigal recognized the signs in herself, the readying, the outward calm and inner turmoil, the rushing that filled her mind before a charge into battle" (372). Neurological response is here described as physical, as if it were divorced from the brain and from thought; it is her *heart* and *body* that are in revolt—as if they are somehow separate from her brain. Moreover, the first time Madrigal dances with Akiva, she also experiences a "churning of her thoughts, more chaotic than the churning all around her" (353); she is a dancer among other dancers, experiencing herself primarily as a body. And because of Akiva's bodily presence, she claims she cannot think. She cannot perceive her body and brain to be interconnected—but this does not seem surprising, given that in her culture souls can be cultivated from a dead body and reinserted into a new body—as if a body is only a container, nothing more. Indeed, Madrigal thinks of her sister's body as a container: "Chiro's body was a vessel, as Madrigal well knew, having made it herself" (410).

The chimaera themselves are the interesting type of hybrid that evokes Haraway's metaphor of the cyborg. Haraway even notes: "By the late twentieth century, our time, a mythic time, we are all chimeras, theorized and fabricated hybrids of machine and organism; in short, we are cyborgs. The cyborg is our ontology; it gives us our politics" ("Cyborg" 162). Laini Taylor has thus had the opportunity here to create a cyborg-like hybrid and explore its ontology as distinct; she has had the opportunity to dismantle "troubling dualisms" that are "persistent in Western traditions," such as those of "whole/ part," "maker/made" and human/animal (Haraway, "Cyborg" 189). Instead, Karou has been resurrected as completely human. She is a chimaera who is emphatically *not* hybrid, not partially animal, and who therefore does not fit comfortably into the world that is supposed to be her country of origin. She has options the other chimaera don't, such as the ability to move between their world and the world of humans; this ability is an asset that makes her superior to other chimaera. All chimaera share an ontology that is more human than animal; their bestiality is a matter of duality, not a matter of integrated hybridity, because they think as humans, act as humans, and animalistic actions are often described as aberrant. Even more telling is the reason Karou exists in resurrected form. She has been betrayed by her foster sister who was jealous of her for having "high human" form; that is, Madrigal "is of high-human aspect, as was said of races with the head and torso of man or woman. . . . By anyone's measure, she was beautiful" (319). Thus, although Haraway calls for feminists to break down the boundaries between nature and civilization, between animal and human, between whole and part and maker and made, Taylor asserts in a tired and conservative way the superiority of the human form over all other forms of life. The angels, too, of course, are entirely human in their countenance—and they are a race supposedly "superior" to humans.[8]

The chimaera themselves describe how the seraphim regard them: "They needed to believe we were animals, to justify the way they used us" (404); "they told themselves we were dumb beasts, as if that made it all right. They had five thousand beasts in their pits who weren't dumb at all, but they believed their own fiction" (405). In other words, although the chimaera understand that animals have language, the seraphim do not. Nevertheless, it is language on which the chimaera predicate their objections to enslaving animals; they do not object to domination of all matter. Plants, for example, have no language in this world, so no one considers the agency of the botanical in these novels. The linguistic turn is apparent here: discourse is what makes matter worth privileging.

The body as physical matter is also shown to be subordinate to the discursive because resurrections in this world require an offering of physical pain, which Madrigal learns while serving as Brimstone's apprentice: "magic was ugly—a hard bargain with the universe, a calculus of pain" (333); she feels "tremendous satisfaction" when her male mentor approves of her burgeoning ability to create new bodies—which requires her to hurt herself (333). In later novels, Karou pierces her own body with clamps to make the magic of resurrection happen, invoking traditional images of the maternal body both as masochistic and existing solely in the service of others. In this case, the chimaera being resurrected are all warriors (both male and female), so Karou's masochism is serving the patriarchal war machine by providing more bodies to fuel the war. The Madrigal/Karou character is strong, self-reliant, intelligent, and creative. But her potential feminism is undercut by the novel's emphasis on the separation of mind and body, by stereotypical love triangles and female vs. female competition, by the privileging of too many Western dualities, and by repeated images of masochism.

## STARTERS AND NEOLIBERALISM

Compellingly, some authors of YA novels appear to be acknowledging problems with the false binary represented by the mind/body split. For example, Lissa Price's novel Starters is a dystopia that addresses directly the Cartesian split. Price's attempt to critique the notion that mind and body are separate is not always successful, but the novel does problematize the issue far more directly than much recent speculative fiction. The novel is set in a future United States following a pandemic. At the beginning of the pandemic, only enough vaccine has existed for the very young and the elderly to have it—so everyone of any age in between has died. In the culture that is left, "Starters" are the kids and "Enders" are the elderly. Unfortunately, the Enders have grown increasingly jealous of the vitality of the youngsters in their world, so they've developed a technology by which they can temporarily rent a Starter's body and use their own consciousness to control a now youthful body. The Starter remains unconscious during the experience, so the Ender provides the "mind," while the Starter provides the "body," which is then split from the mind. The text positions this practice as ideologically cruel, ensuring that readers understand people are made of both mind and body. But the Enders justify this form of mind-control in economic terms: the deal is a profitable one for the teenager being rented. The protagonist, Callie, is a particularly attractive Starter who learns of an insidious plan by which Enders will permanently take control of bodies of Starters (rather than just renting them for a month or so).

The literary critic Naarah Sawers discusses this type of biotechnology as the "handmaiden of consumer capitalism" (179); she argues that "liberal humanism credits the individual body with dignity and the right to freedom. Embedded in this doctrine is the right not to be used as a 'thing', not to be alienated from the self's body, which would restrict freedom. However, the advent of biotechnologies makes problematic any definitive understanding of the self and subjectivity" (171). She believes that biotechnology in YA novels demonstrates that "agency is crucial to understand how humanity is enacted as performativity in posthuman narratives for children and young adults" (173), as is clearly the case in *Starters*. Biotechnology threatens to rob Callie of her agency. Moreover, the gendering of biopleasure is consistent in this series with the gender dichotomies Burfoot points out at work in texts such as the Matrix and Alien movies: male-dominated technologies are being used to control and circumvent the female body. The man who owns "Prime Destinations"—the body-rental business—is referred to as "the Old Man," signifying his secure position as part of the patriarchy; the other people who play significant roles in the biotechnologies by which the teenaged brains are manipulated are also male. The teenagers who have had computer chips embedded in their heads for rental purposes are nicknamed "Metals"—and at least one type of equality exists here: teenaged boys are as vulnerable to the machinations of the Old Man as teenaged girls. However, everyone is either male or female; no transgendered or agender teenagers appear to problematize the binary or to offer renters the possibility of gender-shifting. Old cis men always rent young cis men; old cis women always rent young cis women. The Enders thus enact numerous binaries, including that of male/female, mind/body, old/young, rich/poor—and the Enders exploit the bodies of adolescents who need the money badly enough they are willing to forsake their own individual identities.

In *A Brief History of Neoliberalism*, David Harvey defines *neoliberalism*, which he believes emerged out of Reagonomics and Margaret Thatcher's economic vision for the UK, as "a theory of political economic practices that proposes that human well-being can best be advanced by liberating individual entrepreneurial freedoms and skills within an institutional framework characterized by strong private property rights, free markets, and free trade" (2). For the purposes of my argument, I want to emphasize Harvey's point that neoliberalism is the doctrine that "individual entrepreneurial freedoms and skills" thrive when they are unfettered by social institutions (2). In other words, neoliberalism purports to empower the individual by freeing every citizen-as-entrepreneur from the shackles of institutionalized regulations. Harvey argues that the *process* of neoliberalism has been a destructive force that dismantled "divisions of labour, social relations, welfare provisions, technological mixes, ways of life and thought, reproductive activities, attachments to the land and habits of the heart" (3). He notes that by the 1990s, many people came to prefer the term "globalization," with its implication that economic growth always benefits everyone (1).[9] Ultimately, neoliberalism privileges the economic power of the individual over the economic power of collective forces, such as governments, in order to position individual entrepreneurship as the economic engine of the world—a process that occurs in *Starters* when older people manipulate younger people into functioning as individual entrepreneurs who sell their bodies.[10] Narratives in every genre of children's and adolescent literature— from the picture book to YA realism—can participate in and/or react to neoliberal trends, but speculative fictions, especially dystopias, seem particularly well-positioned to reimagine (or replicate) the problems inherent in a neoliberal, global economy that fetishizes the body.

Christopher Breu identifies Foucault's concept of biopolitics as a direct product of neoliberalism because of the way people (such as the Starters) have begun to be reconceptualized as tools by which the larger neoliberal economy can expand (15). Biopolitics "present a version of politics in which biological life itself (and its cessation in death) is directly invested and managed by political and economic forms of power" (Breu 14). In addition, according to Breu, in the neoliberal economy, "immaterial production" begins to replace material production as the core of the economy; cities that once depended on "a largely industrial, shipping, and manufacturing base" become "organized around the electronic, service, and financial sectors of the economy" (21, 134). Breu thus extends Foucault's thinking about biopolitics, arguing that Foucault "suggests that a relationship between the biopolitics and neoliberalism can be adduced in relationship to the neoliberal concept of 'human capital' as the means by which human life and biology are regulated under neoliberalism" (15). That is, neoliberalism prioritizes the individual as a cog in the economy such that even the individual's biologically-situated body is regulated through economic forces—a phenomenon that Price demonstrates at work in *Starters*.

The Enders' biopleasure in being able to inhabit young bodies, for instance, is overtly neoliberal. One renter whom Callie meets describes how happy she is to feel young again: "It is flawlessly beautiful, this little body, don't you think?" (66); "It's such fun to be able to wear little things like this again, isn't it? ... Sure beats sitting in a rocking chair, crocheting in front of reruns on a Saturday night" (65). Even though sex is technically prohibited by the renters' contract, desire and the pursuit of embodied pleasures make the renting Enders seem as constantly in need of hedonistic pursuits as the citizens of Panem's Capitol. Enders relish dancing and drinking at clubs with their rented teenaged bodies; they go "joyriding" and refer to it as "real fun" (116, 115); they parasail and bungee-jump, even in violation of their rental contracts. As one Ender tells Callie, presuming that Callie is also a renter, "Well, at least it's not your body" (117). A different Ender warns her to "take it easy your first time out. Nothing too wild. Don't let anything happen to that body, because the fines are simply atrocious" (75). Callie thinks to herself, "She didn't need to tell me to protect this body" (75).

During Callie's first rental, she learns that Helena, the woman who has rented her body, has discovered a means of communicating with her, internally, within Callie's own brain. Callie begins to hear Helena's voice intruding in her own thoughts as a form of direct dialogue: the voice tells her: "*Listen ... important ... Callie ... do not return to ... Prime Destinations*"—the body bank run by the Old Man (72, italics and ellipses in the original). Helena has a friend who is "*a biochip expert. And a surgeon*"; he has been able to redesign the chip in Callie's head (150, italics in the original). Helena underscores the connection between mind and body when she tells Callie (ironically enough, as a disembodied voice emanating from within Callie's own brain) that there were problems with the first redesign of her chip: "*the sporadic blackouts, me getting pushed out of the—your—body, the bouncing back and forth*" (150–51, italics in the original). The fact that Helena herself has to rephrase her words to acknowledge that this is Callie's own body underscores the girl's embodied cognition. Callie understands these words dialogically, using her brain, which is housed in a body that Helena has tried to rent.

The plot is, of course, complicated by a love triangle: although Callie is very fond of a boy named Michael, she falls in love with another one named Blake—a boy she later realizes has been the embodiment of Blake all along, but the brain is not his; it's the brain of the Old Man who runs Prime Destinations. He is inhabiting Blake's mind and manipulating him to blackmail Blake's grandfather—a Senator—into sponsoring legislation that would legalize permanent rentals. Eventually, the Old Man himself inserts himself into Callie's mind, talking to her as Helena has, and asking her questions that make her think about the relationship between her agency and her body: "*I know you better than you know yourself,*" he whispers, inside of her brain (330, italics in the original). He suggests that she has let Helena inhabit her brain longer than was necessary "*so you could live as someone rich, even for a short time*" (330, italics in the original). Callie agrees that is true but rejects his offer of power and of giving her "*a life far more exciting than Helena's*" because she knows that she wants a different life: "Another place, another time. Not with him" (330, italics in the original). Callie can "feel the Old Man's presence lingering in my head. . . . It was the two of us, in a stalemate, in limbo, my own breathing the loudest sound, second only to my heartbeat"—and then she feels him leave her head (331). As the novel ends, however, she hears yet a third voice that makes her question what she knows: "I heard the sound of someone breathing. In my head. My heart quickened. . . . I hadn't heard that voice for a long time. . . . My father? . . . I searched myself. Listened, but heard nothing more" (335). Is Callie still Callie if her brain also contains Helena's thoughts? Or the Old Man's? Or her father's? What constitutes individuality? Independent cognition? A brain that is not shared by others? But aren't we all always defined by our interactions with what is physically external to us? The issues are both ontological and epistemological in nature: how does what we know define our being?

Callie understands that people's brains are inherently embodied, and only from that embodiment can identity be formed and understood. Interestingly, Callie values her own brain; she calls it, "probably my favorite body part. No one ever complained about a fat brain. No one ever accused their brain of being too short or too tall, too wide or two narrow. Or ugly. It either worked or it didn't, and mine worked just fine" (39). When the Old Man tempts her with power, riches, and eternal vitality, she rejects the offer, saying, "I don't want to be anyone else, I just want to be me"—by which she means "me" in both body and mind (330). From watching the Enders justify their unethical behavior in neoliberal terms, she has learned that the Cartesian split between body and mind is a false duality; identity is a matter of embodied cognition and not of mind alone.

The sequel, *Enders*, also emphasizes that we are "more than just our flesh" (94) and that "you can't change who you are" because everyone is constituted by both body and mind (87). This novel also adds direct feminist propaganda about lookism: Callie tells a friend, "Sure, I got a makeover like you did, but it didn't really change me. Someday, we'll both be Enders, and even with green laser surgery, eventually we'll be old and wrinkled. Like everybody. But we'll look a lot better if we're happy inside. If we used our brains and our talents instead of stressing over what someone else defines as 'pretty'" (181). But the sequel includes so many Freudian subplots about teenagers psychically killing their parents that it's not as feminist as *Starters* is. And unfortunately, in both novels, looks *do* matter; people who are better-looking receive more attention and have more neoliberal earning potential than others do. Although *Starters* invites readers to recognize themselves as embodied in ways that many dystopias fail to acknowledge, the novel demonstrates a principle that Stephanie Guerra identifies as a prevalent theme in YA science fiction of "the biotechnical subjection of human matter to market force. Bodies and minds are colonized both as consumers and products, and identities are negotiated in a post-human future where to be 'less than' or 'other than' human is an automatic sentence to product status" (294). She establishes that greed is the neoliberal basis of such novels: "greed alone emerges consistently in these books as the cold, impersonal specter behind corporate evil" (293).

Price's failure to question her neoliberal bias provides a problematic context here: in *Starters*, those Enders who are rich justify their choices as entitlements that they have earned individually; they do not perceive the injustice of the social structures that work to keep the rich rich and the poor poor. And although some Starters are rich because of their grandparents' resources, many Starters are poor—which is what motivates them to become self-selling entrepreneurs in the first place. Benjamin Kunkel demonstrates how many novels that are contemporaneous with *Starters* constitute "a lurid reflection of our distinction between citizens with full legal rights and 'illegal' foreign workers without them [that] hardens into a strict demarcation of castes"; as he puts it, "individuality here means escape from the bad collective (cannibals, the corporate state) but does not entail real *individuation*" (Kunkel, italics in the original). Callie's struggle certainly depicts an underclass of imprisoned workers serving the ruling class—but she also succeeds in defeating these forces because she is the superior individual who can capitalize on her own unique, personal attributes—especially her beauty—to defeat the ruling class when others around her are not as beautiful and therefore not as capable of exploiting their individual assets as she is.

Shauna Pomerantz and Rebecca Raby extend their critique of the influence of neoliberalism on YA literature in a different context: they assess how prominent the figure of the "smart supergirl" (291), which they also refer to as the "post-nerd smart girl" (287), has become in popular culture as a result of neoliberalism. Following Gill and Scharff and Angela McRobbie, they argue:

> Modern-day girlhood is now defined by individualism, consumerism, hypersexuality, and the belief that girls can do, be, and have anything they want without fear of structural inequalities such as sexism racism, or homophobia interfering with their individual efforts to achieve success. As a consequence, such structural inequities have now come to be seen as individual rather than social problems. (288)

In their analysis, characters such as Gabriella Montez from *High School Musical* are supersmart, beautiful, strong girls who succeed within their social context because of their own individual talents—and without ever giving credit to those social structures that have helped make it possible for them to succeed, such as their middle-class status (296–97). They cite Deirdre M. Kelly and Shauna Pomerantz to present an even more damaging effect of neoliberalism: these girls think they are succeeding because of their own individual merits, but they are incapable of critiquing the social structures that oppress them, such as racism in Gabriella Montez's case, and gender in the case of all supersmart nerd girls. Neoliberalist ideologies create "a closed loop that causes female characters to blame individuals rather than implicate broader constructs of power and inequality" (Kelly and Pomerantz xiv; cited in Pomerantz and Raby 301). Thus, Callie can critique the horrible economic rift that the virus has riven between the Enders and the Starters, and she can rebel against the corporate overlord who wishes to exploit this economic situation, but she cannot critique either the sexist structures at work in her situation or solve the overwhelming economic inequities experienced by the underclass of Starters who are not protected by wealthy grandparents.

*Starters* is thus a mixed novel, one that demonstrates well the integration between mind and body but which also privileges the individual's mind/body as an asset positioning some individuals as superior to others. Like Katniss in *The Hunger Games* and Karou in *Daughter of Smoke and Bone*, the protagonist of *Starters* is a superior neoliberal girl—a supersmart girl—who succeeds because of her talents, includeing her intelligent brain, her beautiful body, and a unique array of talents that allow her to triumph when others have no hope of doing so. Although the protagonists in these novels all despair about inequities between various social groups, they prove their neoliberal mettle by being more competitive within the market forces of their economy than any other individual. And as Pomerantz and Raby point out about characters in a different set of texts: while Katniss and Karou and Callie may critique injustices of wealth distribution, their "personal struggles are never connected to sexism, racism, heterosexism" (303). These are all neoliberal individuals charged with saving the world by means of their individual assets; in no case are these characters able to rely consistently on the social structures that support many teenaged readers, such as educational structures; governments that provide infrastructure and regulate food, health, and safety; and economies based on a sound monetary policy. Callie, for example, has access neither to an education system nor to healthcare. The government exists to serve and protect the rich, but not the poor—and yet Callie still manages to pull herself up by her bootstraps. Callie is an entrepreneur, one who can sell her body, and so she uses that talent to overcome her poverty and resist government forces. The biopolitics here are disturbing in that the body is a commodity—and it is often the only commodity that young women in speculative fiction can consistently rely on as entrepreneurs in a free market (neoliberal) economy.

## THE TRUE MEANING OF SMEKDAY AND THE REJECTION OF NEOLIBERALISM

Adam Rex's *The True Meaning of Smekday* is a novel for children in the middle grades that avoids the body/mind split, largely because the protagonist is young enough that neither she nor the people around her have yet begun sexualizing and objectifying her body. The book is narrated by the eleven-year-old protagonist, Gratuity Tucci. The premise of the novel involves her describing her personal reaction to an invasion of Earth by aliens known as the "Boov"; they have renamed Earth "Smekland" and are trying to resettle all citizens of the United States to Arizona so that they can keep the rest of the country for themselves (28). Like many girls in feminist speculative fiction, Gratuity is on a quest to save a family member, in this case, her mother, who has been abducted by the Boov.[11] A rogue Boov who innocently names himself J.Lo helps her redesign her car so that they can fly to Arizona together; with J.Lo and her cat, Gratuity journeys from Pennsylvania to Florida to Arizona, where she rescues her mother *and* the entirety of planet Earth from a second alien invasion by aliens even more vicious than the Boov, the Gorgs.

First, it is significant that Gratuity has no love interest. The romantic subplot the genre seems to require is reserved for her mother, who is pursued and objectified by an adult (human) male—but by the end of the novel, Gratuity's mother has recovered her wits and does not end the novel romantically linked to him. Gratuity's age is perhaps the most important factor in this novel's ability to underplay the romance plot and avoid a love triangle: she is only eleven. In other words, because Gratuity is too young to have a love relationship, she is spared the compulsory heteronormativity of the YA genre. This, then, is something that preteen novels, unlike YA novels, can offer girls: preadolescents can avoid the heteronormative romance plot. Teenagers too often can't.

Second, the man Gratuity's mother is temporarily involved with—who is named Dan Landry—is given credit for saving the planet from two alien races. Gratuity has written her historical account to set the record straight, and she does so with a clear sense of the irony that her accomplishments have been attributed to a white male (who is an adult). She is grateful to have been spared all the media attention Landry has experienced, and she acknowledges that she has "saved the whole human race" when she was eleven. "I could win an Oscar and fix the ozone layer. I could cure all known diseases and I'll *still* feel like my Uncle Roy, who used to be a star quarterback but now just sells hot tubs. I'm going to have to figure out how to live with this, and I sure don't need everyone I meet bringing it up all the time" (423). Unlike an adult male, this preadolescent girl can contemplate living with humility and anonymity. More important, she doesn't position herself as having a unique set of talents that has allowed her to be the savior of the world. Gratuity gives credit to J.Lo and the Native American adult who have both helped her; additionally: "stories poured in from around the world about humans fighting back"—she specifically names as particularly effective defenders of the planet the Chinese and the allied Israelis and Palestinians (421). She knows that the combination of J.Lo's engineering skills and the Gorgs' mysterious allergies to cats have worked more magic in effecting this defeat of the aliens than anything she has done. She thus rejects neoliberal scripts of unique individualism because she prefers to live in the anonymity of a world restored to its previous social order.

Third, nothing is inscribed on Gratuity's skin—although it is interesting that the Boov have implanted a mole-like device on her mother's neck. The Boov control Gratuity's mother through this device. Thus, it is a female old enough to experience a romantic relationship who has the mark of patriarchal control and biopleasure placed on her skin in this novel—not the protagonist. Moreover, although Gratuity's mother is white and her father is black, the text makes little mention of Gratuity's race or her skin. Indeed, the most prominently described skin in the book is the outer shell of the Gorgs' spaceship:

> The big Gorg ball seemed to move on the surface. Its skin seemed to crawl. . . .
> "Yes," said J.Lo. "The shipskin is made of Gorg. Mixed-up Gorg, like from a blender. Is not even that hard—not hard like Boovish metals or plastics—but it heals. They can keep onto [sic] making more and more skin for replacing the old." (198)

In other words, the Gorgs' spaceship is a biological entity—one that is cannibalistically comprised of the very Gorg clones that it carries. The image is meant to be comical; Gratuity compares the way the Gorgs emit "telecloners" from the ship's skin to "popping a zit" (223). Nevertheless, the complexity of the image is intriguing: the shipskin separates the external from the internal, as is the case with human skin, yet it is made out of its own passengers—and it also ejects those passengers intact onto anything it wishes to colonize. The Gorgs' ship contains multitudes, as it were—and the imagery evokes Barad's ideas that I discuss in Chapter 1 about the ways that "primary semantic units are . . . material-discursive practices through which boundaries are constituted" ("Posthumanist" 135). An "ongoing reconfigur[ing] of the world" happens in this "ebb and flow of agency," through which "'things'-in-phenomena" invite us to question both the relationship between the perceiver and the perceived and the instability of concepts like internal and external (Barad, *Meeting* 141; "Posthumanist" 135). Gorgs are in their ship, outside of their ship, and they constitute the very ship itself. J.Lo and Gratuity are able to defeat the Gorg because J.Lo uses the Gorgs' telecloners against the organism's/organisms' skin: "There are ten thousand cloners on the ship. . . . Cloners for to make its skin. I sent a handful of [cat] hair to every one" (418). The Gorg are defeated through their skin by an auto-immune disorder: cat allergies.

Finally, it is worth pointing out that Gratuity, too, does occasionally act "without thinking": she walks with her mother toward the Boov space ship "without thinking" (50), and she ducks once "without thinking" (232). As with Katniss, the words imply that Gratuity is acting by instinct. But more often, Gratuity seems to base her body's actions on cognition: she thinks and acts in a coordinated effort. Furthermore, she is without question the leader of her group of companions, even though she is accompanied by a male Boov. As a species, the Boov complicate gender in ways both poetic and humorous: "The Boov are having *seven* magnificent genders. There is boy, girl, boygirl, boyboy, boyboygirl, and boyboyboyboy" (77, italics in the original). The text thus acknowledges that gender performativity falls along a spectrum, but J.Lo is clearly a male, Gratuity is clearly a female—and in charge. The text also critiques gendered stereotypes, as when one young boy questions Gratuity's knowledge in a way that is meant to be read as obnoxious: "How does some stupid girl know all this?" he asks her, allowing readers to perceive that he is the one in the wrong. In a more comical aside, Gratuity critiques Mark Twain for not being able to "write any decent girl characters" (281), although the novel gives *Adventures of Huckleberry Finn* credit for being an influential antecedent when she decides to protect J.Lo: "I did not think, All right then, I'll go to Hell. . . . I just decided to stick by a friend" (150). Friendship is prioritized over romance in *The True Meaning of Smekday*—although as in most female dystopias, Gratuity does not manage to maintain a friendship with another female. Thus, in terms of interrogating such binaries as internal/external and mind/body, *The True Meaning of Smekday* reflects material feminist concerns about bodies' relationships to the environment, and the novel privileges friendship over romance. Gratuity is concerned about the environmental impact of the Boovs' and the Gorgs' invasions; she is matter-of-fact about race, and she is a leader who emphasizes cooperation over competition. Ultimately, this novel's relationship to material feminism positions it to reject neoliberal narratives of individuals triumphing over the collective because of their unique talents.

## *ORLEANS* AND INTRA-ACTIVITY

Perhaps the most successful feminist speculative YA fiction under discussion in this chapter is Sherri L. Smith's *Orleans*. The premise is post-apocalyptic: New Orleans has been devastated by the six post-Katrina hurricanes that have hit the Gulf Coast by 2019, and a blood-borne virus, Delta Fever, has devastated the entire region. As a biohazard, Delta Fever breaks down false binaries between "nature" and "culture"; the Fever would not exist had manmade conditions not allowed it to spiral out of control as a pathogen. Since no force either natural or manmade can control the disease, in 2025, the United States signs the Declaration of Separation, separating itself from Louisiana, Alabama, Mississippi, Florida, and Texas so that now two countries exist: the Outer States (that continue to function with government infrastructure) and the lawless and ungoverned Delta, in which all institutions and infrastructures are proven to have failed. Fen de la Guerre lives in the region, in the city that used to be New Orleans. Like all people in the Delta, Fen has a tribe. Because her blood type is O positive, she lives with the OP tribe. Delta Fever attacks people differently by blood type, so instead of being segregated by race, people in the Delta have become segregated by blood. People with O blood are less affected by Delta Fever than those with A or B or AB blood, so ruthless blood hunters (complete with blood hounds) try to hunt and capture Os to harvest their blood.[12] The leader of Fen's tribe, Lydia, is attacked during a brutal raid, and she dies in childbirth. She has been Fen's closest friend and mentor, so it becomes Fen's job to rescue the newborn.

When Fen discovers a white scientist, Daniel, who has slipped over the Wall hoping to solve the last missing clue in his efforts to develop a cure for Delta Fever, she realizes that he can take the baby—whom she calls simply "Baby Girl" for most of the novel—back with him over the Wall. Because Daniel tells her that Baby Girl is O positive and has not yet been infected by the Fever, the newborn has a chance of being raised in a world with social institutions that the text openly values—such as schools and churches—instead of growing up off the grid in swamps that are largely devoid of single-family dwellings or electricity and where the only economy is a bartering system.

Protected from Delta Fever by a technically-advanced haz mat suit, Daniel proves to be more inept at dealing with this dystopic world than he has imagined he would be. He is kidnapped by blood hunters; Fen helps him escape. He falls into a sinkhole (where he loses the six vials of still-toxic vaccine he has brought with him) and is attacked by a hideous serpentine reptile of some sort; Fen saves him. He wants only to interact with the professors reputed to be sequestered in the Institute of Post-Separation Studies, believing that they might have the final clue for his vaccine since "the goal of the Institute was to study the closed environment of Orleans—socially and medically," so Fen takes him to the professors (74). Daniel discovers that they are all in self-induced medical comas, and he is horrified when their leader, Dr. Warren, awakes and tells him what Fen already knows: these are not biologists seeking a cure; they are anthropologists who have elected to stay in the Delta to study how a society structured on blood-type rather than race will work:

" . . . They ain't working on a cure here, Daniel. Orleans just a lab to them. We ain't people, we rats."

"If they weren't looking for a cure, what is all this for?"

"Dr. Warren's pet project. . . . He ain't interested in the Fever. He studying tribes."

Daniel frown. "Ending racism," he say. "For the most part, the rules of blood make race irrelevant. Blood types cross all ethnicities."

I nod. "If folks stop hating each other 'cause of skin color, the only difference be blood type."

"A new form of racism," Daniel say. His face go pale. "It's like Tuskegee all over again. They never wanted a cure." (206–7)

Fen knows that the Institute's emphasis on "post-separation" is not a reference to the Delta separating from the Outer States; it is a reference to the separation of the tribes by blood type. She knows this because her parents worked at the Institute as graduate students—and left the Institute with her when she was a young child once they learned how corrupt the Institute's mission was. Within five years of leaving the Institute, Fen's parents have been killed, and she has survived in the swamps first under the corrupt influence of a voodoo priestess who charms children to steal their blood, and later under the wise and benevolent protection of Lydia, the tribal leader to whom Fen has sworn allegiance so strong that she even agrees to protect the dying woman's newborn.

As in most speculative fictions, skin takes on a privileged role of signification. Although blood tribes trump race in this novel, race still exists. Fen refers to one character's "ruddy brown" skin (35) and another's "mahogany face" (249). One woman has skin "too dark for blond hair" (123); one man has "eyes like agate or river rock" and his hair is "in thick, long dreads, all milky brown, like a lion mane" (32). One smuggler is described as "white, whiter than you see in Orleans anymore, with yellow-blond hair stuck to his forehead with sweat" (77–78); moreover, Fen acknowledges that religion in the region has grown as "mixed up as the people" (78). Hers is an acknowledgement of the region's multiplicity. Indeed, one of the only people in the novel described as "pink" (and therefore not someone experiencing multiplicity) is the corrupt priest who tries to use Baby Girl to give himself a blood transfusion (297). Another exception to the creolization of races is Asian-Americans, who are largely immune to Delta Fever and who have developed their own shanty town along the river—although it is a culture among which mixes "Koreans and Japanese, Chinese and Vietnamese and Filipino. But nothing else. Folks in Orleans all be mutts except for the Asians" (144). They have self-segregated by race, which serves as a foil for the society segregated by blood-type and which is also something of a plot device, since this allows there to be a group of people who are "used to trading, so they ain't that territorial" (145). In this regard, the segregated Asian Americans both reinforce Smith's ideological critique of the social construction of race and serve, at the same time, to undermine it.

Throughout the novel, vampire-imagery fuses with evocations of New Orleans's creolized culture: the good guys, including Asians, have developed natural immunities to the disease they carry; the bad guys are corrupted within their very blood to be predators of other people—but race has nothing to do with this predation. Neither does gender: Fen's one-time protector, Mama Gentille, proves to be one of the worst predators in the book. Although Fen is now about sixteen, she has been preyed on in many ways by the environment and by the people in the Delta, but no one is more truly abusive to her than Mama Gentille, who poses as a spiritual healer but who harbors children so that she can sell both their blood and their bodies in prostitution. As a nine-year-old, Fen is raped by a man who has bought her first for her blood and only secondarily for her virginity. When Fen realizes why this man desires her, she wraps her arms around a scalding pot, burning the interiors of her arms so completely that the scarring makes it almost impossible for anyone to draw blood from her arms. Mama Gentille wants nothing more to do with her, since she can no longer be sold, as Fen puts it, "for blood and sex and magic" (115). From that point on, in order for the vampyric predators in the Delta to take her blood, they'd need to take it from her neck and kill her, which most predators are unwilling to do since that would mean that they could only "bleed" her once (17). In this way, Fen has marked herself, using her skin to demarcate her status, as has happened to Karou in *Daughter of Smoke and Bone*. The markings on Karou's skin are about status, but they also indicate which tribe she belongs to. But Fen's marking are not part of her tribal status; her scarring protects her from the corrupt practices that were set into motion by the pre-Separation patriarchy, and this scarring is a way for her to create a status that differentiates her from others in the Delta. It is a way for her to prevent people from—literally—getting under her skin. No one can get a needle to penetrate the thick skin of her scars.

The emphasis on skin in most speculative fiction is a way of distinguishing the human from the environment; in *The Hunger Games*, Katniss's hunting scars have happened away from civilization, while she has been hunting the wild beasts of nature back at home in District 12. They demonstrate her relationship with nature: she is outside of it and dominates it, in a relationship to nature that evokes ecofeminist concerns with humanity's attempts to control and colonize nature (Connors, "I Try" 141–42). Later, Katniss receives a tracker under her skin, injected by the Gamemakers so that they can track her during the Hunger Games, indicating that she is no longer completely in control of her own body. Callie's brain implant and the similar implant Gratuity's mother receives under her skin signify that the character is being manipulated externally in imagery that reifies the false dichotomy of the Cartesian split: the body here *can* operate successfully when it is separated from the mind. Perhaps even more important and more troubling: the hegemonic force that is either a result of the dystopic setting or responsible for it has invaded the individual, rendering her powerless against external manipulation. In these novels, the external dystopia has become internal, which would seem to challenge the false binary of external/internal but which is usually left undeveloped as an idea in the speculative fictions under discussion.

Fen de la Guerre's resistance to her environment in *Orleans*, however, demonstrates how false it is to create a binary between people and nature—or even between people of different races. She knows she is part of nature and that nature is part of her. For example, she resists dystopic predators by a self-sustained manipulation of her own skin. Because she is a carrier of Delta Fever, she knows she has already internalized the dystopic "natural" force that has rendered her culture unstable. As she puts it when she has been steeped in swamp water, "I'm not clean. . . . I'm covered in it. Fever be in the water, the air. In me" (314). Fen perceives the fever to be part of her, as she is part of it; her observation creates the type of intra-activity that involves a changed sense of her own *becoming*. She also recognizes what Nancy Tuana might consider to be Fen's acknowledgment of the "viscous porosity" of her skin; Fen is who she is—as her whole environment is what it is—because of the "rich interactions between beings through which subjects are constituted out of relationality" (Tuana, "Viscous" 188). The dystopic virus is part of Fen, but she is nevertheless capable of learning how to integrate her lived reality with that dystopic presence. Now she must protect herself from a type of ravaging worse than the disease has already caused: the blood-letting of the human predators who would devour her for that which is internal to her skin: her blood. And yet, she is still part of a large community of OP peoples. She relies on the Asian Americans for help, and she knows that she can also get help from the community of Ursuline nuns who succor the sick and dying in Orleans. She is glad to have been part of a tribe, especially one led by a woman, and Fen is devastated when ABs massacre her people, so she is willing to take responsibility for another human life. She knows she is one among many and does not regard herself as somehow "superspecial" and superior to her community. This knowledge is part of what enables her to trust Daniel as the only person who can help get Baby Girl to safety.

Daniel is horrified at the conditions in the Delta. He'd expected few people to be alive, perhaps because the last census has estimated the total population of the area to be eight thousand. He finds the Superdome filled with bones: it has sheltered people through one hurricane; another turns it into a "morgue," and the last hurricane turns it into a "tomb" (107). He then discovers that the Ursuline Sisters have turned it into a "catacomb," an ossuary holding more than a hundred thousand skeletons (112). The building itself demonstrates intra-activity, as its internal contents shift how others perceive it from being a morgue to a tomb to a catacomb. When Daniel arrives in Orleans, his perceptions shift again. He "thought the entire city was a tomb, but Orleans was clearly very much alive" (111); he has found "life of a sort he hadn't expected to find. Thriving life" (146); the "city was alive, and in such variety that it stunned Daniel" (153). Although in the initial hubris of his scientific smugness he has expected to find a "city of the dead" (109), after his encounters with both blood-hunters and the cooperative peoples who barter and run the markets, he learns that it is a "living city of the dead" (163). Sherri Smith is complicating binaries here, demonstrating how interdependent humanity is and how interdependent it is with nature and how perception shifts understanding as the material and discourse interact. Daniel, for example, must wear a haz mat suit to separate himself from the killing forces of this environment, but he is an outsider who must leave. Fen, however, is an insider—she is the human and acculturated embodiment of Delta Fever, which is itself an amalgam of natural and man-made causes.

Even though Fen has learned to survive in the Delta, she critiques the social decay of the region. She is no neoliberal raising herself by dint of her own talents and moral superiority. She knows that everyone "need a tribe," acknowledging the importance of community (260)—but Daniel's comments comparing the Institute of Post-Separation Studies to Tuskegee also critiques racism. Fen is particularly critical of the way that the Delta has been allowed to subsist without infrastructure. Electricity is "rare" in the Delta (23); the only computer that still exists is powered by a foot-pedal sewing-machine (214). She has known about life in the Outer States—the schools, the automobiles, the electricity, the single-family dwellings—because she was once sponsored by a family from the Outer States who sent her clothing and pictures of their home. Daniel tells her about "grocery stores and farms and amusement parks and movies"—but Fen cannot understand why anyone would intentionally want to experience a thrill ride (168). She says, "That be different from Orleans, then, for sure. We got scary, but it ain't no fun" (168).

Fen also knows about the Outer States because of the smugglers she has known: smugglers are a "resource" who can "provide things we ain't got here" (129). One smuggler laments how New Orleans has lost its music, "Jazz and blues, zydeco. The kind of songs that made your heart sing" (17). Fen tells a story, part oral history and part lamentation, that portrays New Orleans in terms of the interactionism of nature and culture: "Once upon a time, there was a magical place called New Orleans. . . . There was magic in the water, magic in the trees, and magic in the people" (42). She tells the story to Lydia to soothe her when the woman is in labor (42); she tells the story again to Lydia's daughter shortly after she renames Baby Girl "Enola"—for the acronym used for East New Orleans, LA (274, 272). Although one scientist Fen knows claims that, with the help of nature, Orleans may be "healing itself" (265), Fen is not content with a world that is dominated by haves and have-nots, as she explains when she tells Daniel that she suspects greed is as rampant over the Wall as it is in the Delta. When Daniel tells her some people in the Outer States don't have enough to eat because not everyone can afford food, Fen thinks, "Every place you go got a price" (143), and she asks Daniel: "Ain't it be like that everywhere? Either you got it or somebody else do" (167). Daniel is forced to acknowledge that she is right in her tacit critique of neoliberalism. Fen also critiques one set of problems with masculinity: "Look like boys be fools on both sides of the Wall. They love the Market and they love looking for trouble. But I got more sense than that" (159).

Fen is bitter because she remembers "when it looked like the Wall weren't gonna be there always, and folks on the other side still cared enough to sponsor kids in Orleans" (24). She knows the Outer States have given up on her infrastructure-less world, and it makes her angry: "Anything be better than this," she tells Daniel (315). When Lydia has lain dying, she tells Fen, "It's too much. Too much to change" (43). By the end of the novel, Fen is thinking similar thoughts: "I be tired of running and hiding, tired of just trying to survive. How can Orleans be a home if it always trying to kill you? How can it be living if you ain't allowed to live? What did Lydia say?

The City takes. Well, I ain't got nothing left to give" (305). This is no perfectionist supersmart girl hero who has triumphed against adversity; this is a young woman worn out by the unjust environment in which she lives, but who nevertheless achieves the most important goal she has set for herself: performing an act of human decency in helping to save Baby Girl's life.

As in *Smekday*, a girl has been the brains behind this operation. Fen values her own thought processes; she is aware of the relationship between her body's actions and her thoughts, and she demonstrates a high degree of analytical thinking in stressful situations. When Fen and Daniel are captured by the blood hunters, she remembers her father's advice: "The first rule of escape: assess your situation"; the second rule is to "identify your assets. Anything that can help you escape," and the third rule is to "assess your weaknesses" (126, 131). When she is ready to give up on Daniel because of his incompetence, she admonishes herself "to think" and calls herself a "fool"—but she recognizes that Daniel is Baby Girl's best chance of survival, so she goes back to help him again (201). After they get separated, however, she turns for help to a priest she has known and trusts. He tells her that Baby Girl is not O positive, as Daniel has said, but that she has type B blood and is infected by the virus. Fen recognizes she cannot raise the child, and the priest agrees to protect the baby. Fen thinks, "I feel like I done used up all I got to give to this life. Maybe this be why we don't grow old in the Delta. There just ain't no point" (303). Fen leaves Baby Girl with Father John and later walks into the cool waters of a swamp, allowing herself to float and be soothed in the gentle waters, "like a baptism"; the water feels warm "like blood" (306). She seems to be giving up: "I lie in the water and let the current carry me away" (306). Fen refers to herself as "an alligator snack" (309); she is "waiting to drown" (310) and wonders why she is not already dead. Her internal dialogue acknowledges that this is "the most peace I ever found in Orleans" (309). In this moment, she is a human fused with and inseparable from nature, and this interactionism shifts her ability to perceive herself in an intra-activity by which she is first a body, then "an alligator snack" and then a potential corpse (309). The epistemology of peace, however, makes it possible for her analytical skills—her powers of deduction—to jump to an intuitive conclusion: the priest has lied to her. Baby Girl is, indeed, O positive, but the priest is infected with the disease and wants to use her blood, just as too many people have tried to use Fen. "You can't trust no one in Orleans. But Daniel ain't from here. I shoulda trusted him" (310). Fen is critiquing her own culture for its non-cooperative, competitive nature, which has implications for the novel's critique of neoliberalism. Only those operating with cooperation and in trusting relationships can achieve their goals in this novel.

This novel's problematization of such Western binaries as internal/external, nature/culture, and individual entrepreneurs vs. collectively-based economies demonstrates the potential of twenty-first century feminisms in helping young readers think differently about cognition, embodiment, and the biopolitical natural and cultural forces that interact to position the subject. Smith even offers an implied interrogation of the heterosexist romance plot that dominates so many YA dystopias. The reader might expect Fen to develop a relationship with Daniel or with a man from another tribe named O-Neg Davis with whom she might well develop a *Romeo and Juliet*-like forbidden love. (Readers deeply immersed in YA dystopian traditions might even expect a love triangle.) Instead, although Fen finds O-Neg Davis attractive in their first one-on-one verbal interaction, she comes to recognize him for the potential predator he is, and she never expresses romantic feelings for Daniel. Neither does he objectify her or attempt to transform her into a romantic partner. She describes herself as skinny, but readers never get a description of her body objectified by his male gaze. Instead, the two join forces to work effectively as a team. They save the baby. Fen shows Daniel how to slip through the Wall that divides the Delta from the Outer States; he can do this because of his haz mat suit. She has him carry the baby through the Wall while she creates a diversion.

Fen is shot during that final scene, when she is wading through the canal by the Wall, holding Daniel's jacket, wadded up over her head as if it were a baby: "A shot rang out. The bundle fell from her hands" (323). The ABs have bought a shipment of guns from the military base, so the neoliberal government seems ready to provide the very guns that will allow the ABs to start the type of genocide Daniel has most feared. He knows that "The United States economy was suffering. If the Delta could be recovered, stripped of Delta Fever and harvested for its natural resources—timber, oil, shipping lands, and more . . . If the military knew about Daniel's virus, they might very well use it. Genocide in the name of money" (47, ellipses in the original). Neoliberalism and its attendant greed are under direct attack here, but it is the government and its military launching this potential genocide in the name of a profit-motive, not the private industry of a free market economy.

Readers are left to decide for themselves whether Fen has died, but she has achieved her highest priority: Baby Girl's life is saved. While a male has helped Fen rescue the baby, he never threatens to take over the plot; he is a partner—even the "junior partner"—who steps out of the way so that Fen can make the sacrifices she needs to make to succeed in her goal. The textual ambiguity of the novel's teleology is one more way that Sherri Smith invites readers to reject binaristic thinking: is Fen alive? Or dead? Or is she already both: a living being carrying death within her blood? Will the culture of Orleans survive, or will it be annihilated by a government with genocidal motives—in which case Fen would die anyway? Is Fen a hero who has saved the members of her new tribe, Daniel and Enola? Or is she another self-sacrificing maternal figure who prioritizes the life of her surrogate child over her own body? The novel offers no clear-cut answers.

## CONCLUSION

At their most feminist, twenty-first century YA speculative fictions with female protagonists reject heteronormative love triangles and destabilize the false dichotomy of the Cartesian split; moreover, they critique neoliberalist ideologies that posit individual agency as a stable and self-defining entity that is by itself capable of improving the world's economy. At their worst, these dystopias objectify the female body so badly that even the female protagonists objectify their own bodies, participating as objects of exchange in male homosocial love triangles—with a general Noah's Ark-ing of the characters, paired off two by two, by novel's end. One standard explanation for the heteronormativity of YA literature involves a combination of readers' expectations of the genre's conventions and the pervasive Romanticism in which many teenagers are still culturally immersed. A more cynical view would acknowledge the neoliberal bias towards heteronormativity. Neoliberal economies depend on expanding economies, and the only way that economies expand is if populations expand. Thus, strong (and fertile) young women *must* find virile men with which to breed in order to feed the machine of the expanding neoliberal market. Were all the strong females to rebelliously refuse to procreate, the market would eventually collapse. Of course, within this cynical model, female embodiment is reduced to a privileging of only one aspect of embodiment: procreation. To my mind, this is very likely why so few neoliberal speculative fictions involve trans women or lesbians as the potential saviors of a corrupted patriarchal world.

I hope I have demonstrated that in these nominally feminist dystopias, the body is privileged over mind because in western thought, females *are* too often defined only as bodies, as Elizabeth Grosz and Susan Bordo have demonstrated; the implication is that somehow females do their best work when they are *not* thinking and/or when their actions lead to heteronormative marriages that imply the continuation of the next generation.

Although the strong and independent protagonists in all of these novels are preferable to the secondary characters dominated by males in twentieth-century YA dystopias, like Orson Scott Card's *Ender's Game* (1985), in which the one female adolescent is overshadowed by her two brothers, or Lois Lowry's *The Giver* (1993), in which the only female adolescent character ends up dead, twenty-first century feminisms are too complex to be reduced to a formula as simple as being feminist because they feature a "strong girl." Physical and mental strength are laudable traits, but material feminism invites us to think about the interrelationships of embodied cognition and the environment in ways that enable us to define agency as something that is—and *should* be—more complex than simply being able to take action or seek heteronormative love.

## CHAPTER 5

# QUEERING ROMANCE, SEXUALITY, GENDER IDENTITY, AND MOTHERHOOD

Sexuality is linked to materiality through the physicality of the human body. How that sexuality is interpreted, represented, performed, and lived involves the discursive—but sexuality itself emerges from physical activities of the human body. This exploration of material feminism would thus not be complete without a chapter that explores the interrelated aspects of sexuality, orientation, and gender identification in YA literature—especially given that these topics have been explored more openly in twenty-first century literature for the young than in books written in the previous century. Literary critics have done a superb job of tracking these trends, so I begin this chapter with a review of the literature and then move into specific sections: first, a section about heteronormative romance and then into sections about novels that queer heteronormativity and gender identification. I conclude with a section on motherhood as a manifestation of sexuality. My premise in this chapter continues the argument that underlies the rest of this volume: gender issues, including those that involve sexuality, are implicated in both the discursive *and* the material. This chapter also serves as a corrective to some of my earlier work, in which I overemphasized sexuality in terms of the discursive at the expense of the material.

## QUEERNESS, SEXUALITY, AND THEORY

There is very little I can offer to a twenty-first century feminist reading of queering and sexuality in YA literature beyond the excellent work already done by Kerry Mallan in *Gender Dilemmas in Children's Fiction* and Lydia Kokkola *Fictions of Adolescent Carnality*. In the latter, Kokkola provides an in-depth examination of sexuality in YA literature. She argues that "the ways in which adolescent sexuality is presented in works intended for young readers reflects changes in the ways society negotiates adolescence, and . . .

the emergence of 'radical' adolescent fiction depicting sexually active adolescents signals an underlying shift in how the social categories of childhood, adolescence, and adulthood are conceived" (9). Kokkola divides her study into chapters that explore sexuality and power, negative consequences of sexuality, queer sexuality, bestiality, and abjection. To date, her study is the most substantive exploration of sexuality in fiction written for teenagers, and her work is informed by her consistent feminism.

Of the five gender dilemmas Kerry Mallan identifies in *Gender Dilemmas in Children's Literature*, three (desire, beauty, and queerness) revolve around issues of sex and sexuality. Specifically, she defines queer theory "as a theory that foregrounds a politics of difference" (125), and she identifies queerness as one of the most important issues in contemporary children's and adolescent fiction. Her goal is "to identify queer moments or spaces in the texts where the *represented content is about resignifying normativity by destablising 'naturalised' identity categories* . . . [in order] to distinguish between those performatives that are subversive of dominant discourse and those that work to consolidate or strengthen them" (*Gender* 128, italics in the original). Like Kokkola's argument about queerness, Mallan argues that "queer sexualities are related to the adult-adolescent binarism" (*Gender* 97); that is:

> Unlike their heterosexual peers, youngsters experiencing same-sex desire are formulated as having undergone some form of transformation even before they act upon their desires. They were presumed to be heterosexual until they "came out" as queer. Their desires immediately plunge them into adulthood, whereas heterosexual desires which are not acted upon do not always signal a transformation into adulthood. (*Gender* 98)

Both Mallan and Kokkola are informed by and acknowledge their intellectual debt to Judith Butler—and both are tracing trajectories between received orthodoxies and those literatures that attempt to subvert and revise binaristic thinking about gender and sexuality.

Following on the work of Judith Butler, Teresa de Lauretis, Eve Kosofsky Sedgwick, and Michael Warner, queer theory invites—even requires—scholars such as Kokkola and Mallan to "queer" the essentialist terms of sex ("male" or "female") and sexuality ("heterosexual" or "homosexual" or "lesbian" or "bisexual"). In 1990, Butler contributed this to then-emerging ideas about queer theory:

> Taken to its logical limit, the sex/gender distinction suggests a radical discontinuity between sexed bodies and culturally constructed genders. Assuming for the moment the stability of binary sex, it does not follow that the construction of "men" will accrue exclusively to the bodies of males or that "women" will interpret only female bodies. Further, even if the sexes appear to be unproblematically binary in their morphology and constitution (which will become a question), there is no reason to assume that genders ought also to remain as two. (*Gender* 10)

In *The Epistemology of the Closet*, Sedgwick also argues:

> many of the major nodes of thought and knowledge in twentieth-century Western culture as a whole are structured—indeed, fractured—by a chronic, now endemic crisis of homo/heterosexual definition, indicatively male, dating from the end of the nineteenth century. . . . an understanding of virtually any aspect of modern Western culture must be, not merely incomplete, but damaged in its central substance to the degree that it does not incorporate a critical analysis of modern homo/heterosexual definition; and it will assume that the appropriate place for that critical analysis to begin is from the relatively decentered perspective of modern gay and antihomophobic theory. (1)

Queer theory is "another discursive horizon, another way of thinking the sexual" (de Lauretis iv); "The preference of 'queer' represents . . . an aggressive impulse of generalization; it rejects a minoritizing logic of toleration or simple political interest-representation in favor of a more thorough resistance to regimes of the normal" (Warner xxvi).

At its core, then, queer theory is concerned with human embodiment and how embodiment is configured. According to David M. Halperin, the lived physical experiences of sexuality and gender are embedded in materiality:

> Queer theory has effectively re-opened the question of the relations between sexuality and gender, both as analytic categories and as lived experiences . . . it has pursued the task (begun long before within the sphere of lesbian/gay studies) of detaching the critique of gender and sexuality from narrowly conceived notions of lesbian and gay identity; it has supported non-normative expressions of gender and sexuality, encouraging both theoretical and political resistance to normalization. (341)

As Sally Miller Gearhart Willits puts it, "Queer theory suggests that every part of our identity is both fluid and mixed, and is thus capable of trans-formation. In other words, it urges us toward the possibility that we are not trapped in those essentialist identities" (xxix–xxx).[1]

Kokkola observes the intellectual conversations between YA critics who are interested in queer theory and those who write about sexuality. She cites, for example, my early work that identifies sexuality in YA literature as a didactic force designed to interpellate the teenager into social conformity (Kokkola 8–9; Trites, *Disturbing* 84–116), but Kokkola also cites Kimberley Reynolds's observation in *Radical Children's Literature* about "sex, sexuality and relationships between the sexes" as "one of the most radically changed areas in contemporary children's literature" (Kokkola 9; Reynolds 114–15). Reynolds rightly acknowledges that in the first decade of the twenty-first century, "the area of greatest change is not about how much sex is taking place but the importance attached to it and the strategies for writing about it" (*Radical* 122).

Kathryn James also builds on work I began in *Disturbing the Universe* to further problematize the relationship between sexuality and death in *Death, Gender, and Sexuality in Contemporary Adolescent Literature*, while Victoria Flanagan queers trans performance in *Into the Closet: Cross-dressing and the Gendered Body in Children's Literature and Film*. Michael Cart and Christine Jenkins's *The Heart Has its Reasons* provides an intricate reading of gay and lesbian YA literature, and the work of Abate and Kidd puts many scholars of queer theory into conversation with each other in *Over the Rainbow: Queer Children's and Young Adult Literature*. Tison Pugh deconstructs the tensions between innocence and heterosexuality in children's literature, arguing that being interpellated into heteronormativity necessarily mitigates against innocence. Claudia Nelson and Michelle H. Martin have explored the nature of sexual pedagogies, especially as a function of empire-building, and in an introduction to the 2012 issue of the *Children's Literature Association Quarterly* that problematizes twenty-first century depictions of childhood sexuality, Lance Weldy and Thomas Crisp address "society's simultaneous preoccupation with and repulsion by the sexualized child" (369). Mary Hilton and Maria Nikolajeva acknowledge the link between politics and sexuality when they argue that: "If political instability in the search for identity can be mapped onto the process of adolescent matura-tion, then sexual awakening and hormonal turmoil is also a marker of the disjunction between child and adolescent" (12). Sara K. Day also exposes the political nature of the sexually exploited female body in dystopian YA novels ("Docile" 75–92). Although sexuality is not the sole defining criterion of YA literature, it does seem to be a topic that has attracted the attention of many feminist and queer scholars of children's and adolescent literature.

## SUBVERTING THE (HETERONORMATIVE) ROMANCE

When I teach any course on children's novels, I invariably end up talking about fairy-tale structures as a way of helping students connect how much fairy tales and folktales still influence children's and adolescent literature; this also teaches students that they can often predict plot outcome based on their knowledge of those structures. For example, stories like "Goldilocks and the Three Bears" and "The Three Little Pigs" have taught them that two characters doing something sets a pattern, while the third breaks it.

Students also easily recognize certain archetypal characters: the prince, the princess, the witch, for example. They can describe the standard characteristics of a witch—but when I ask why the witch is so frequently a female, they often don't have an answer. I then give them a fairly standard viewpoint: princesses are good because they are pure (and virginal and sexually inactive), but witches are evil because they have been sexually active and are therefore corrupt—which sometimes makes some students uncomfortable when they recognize how frequently popular culture promotes stereotypical assumptions about sexuality, especially the notion that female sexuality is a corrupting force.

Interestingly enough, some novels that strive toward feminist goals still find themselves adhering to these same fairy-tale tropes: archetypal princesses who need rescuing by an archetypal prince (who can rescue the girl because he has a mode of transportation that offers them both a form of escape). Deconstructing fairy-tale tropes can thus provide information about how a YA romance is positioning itself vis a vis feminism. Two examples— Fatima Sharafeddine's award-winning Lebanese novel *The Servant* (2013) and Rainbow Rowell's romance *Eleanor & Park* (2013)—both problematize the relationship between the heteronormative romance genre and feminism, but they also rely on heteronormative fairy-tale structures to do so.

Amy Pattee argues in *Reading the Adolescent Romance* that the YA romance novel is an inherently conservative genre, affirming, as it does, heteronormative values (4). She identifies the following characteristics of (heteronormative) YA romances: the novels often occur in domestic and/

or commercial settings, and the heroines "[maintain] that true love—either romantic or familial—[i]s a reward worth work and sacrifice" (4). Both *The Servant* and *Eleanor & Park* follow these patterns, with their domestic settings and hard-working protagonists who are willing to self-sacrifice in the name of love. *The Servant*, for example, is set in the 1980s in Beirut during the fifteen-year Lebanese Civil War of 1975–1990. Faten, a village girl, is sent by her father to work as a servant for a family who lives in an upscale apartment building in the city. All Faten's wages go to her father. Her employer, Mrs. Samira, is demanding and inflexible; she's contrasted to the accommodating employer of Faten's friend Roslyn, who works in another apartment in the same building. Readers can well imagine Mrs. Samira in the role of Cinderella's stepmother, since Faten loves her own mother and misses her deeply. Faten's father shows up monthly to collect her paycheck, and Faten thinks, "Her rights are being stolen. She is being robbed of another month of her life"—so some of her sacrifice is imposed by the patriarchy, rather than being self-imposed (23). Faten only speaks to her mother on the phone occasionally and rarely sees her. Faten's relationship with her father is thus driven by the materiality of economics—and her material living conditions are dependent on his patriarchal decision-making.

Although Mrs. Samira has two daughters of her own, May and Sahar, they only initially fulfill the role of Cinderella's stepsisters. Sahar shares secrets with Faten and laughs with her, helping to cheer Faten at times. The elder daughter, May, questions the ethics of her parents' willingness to sacrifice her own career as an artist so that she can be married in an arranged marriage: May yells at her parents: "For you two my future is only in marriage. Who told you I want to get married? You know very well that I want to get accepted into the institute of modern art, and that I want to paint. I can't imagine studying anything else. . . . I'm not considering marriage at all right now" (36). Not only does May question the ethics of arranged marriage, but she also captures the sadness of Faten's status as an entrapped servant. When May sketches a drawing of Faten, the budding artist depicts the servant's sadness "in Faten's eyes rather than the smile that she glued on her face" (54). Faten cautions May not to throw abandon to the wind and marry the next available suitor, but angry with her parents, May disregards this advice and marries an American medical doctor anyway. A year later, returning home pregnant and lonely but still married, May tells Faten that she should have listened to her servant's good advice: "I regret taking your advice so lightly the day I decided to leave school and get married," May tells Faten, explaining about her husband: "I'm alone during the days and sometimes at night.

He's a doctor and can't manage his time. I miss Lebanon, my family, and my friends all the time" (151–52). May gives Faten two of the pictures she has painted of her former servant, and tells her "do not get married before you get your university degree," a promise to which Faten agrees (153). By the end of the novel, Faten's fate seems more independent and promising than May's.

Throughout the novel, Faten has nurtured two secret dreams: one dream is her ambition to be a nurse; the other is her silent admiration for a young man who lives across the street from the apartment where she works. Faten can only admire the young man from glimpses stolen when he's on the balcony and from hearing him play the piano when the windows are open. Faten is Muslim, and Marwan is Christian, so they appear to be star-crossed lovers.

Faten's friend, Roslyn—the maid downstairs—smuggles a note to Marwan in which Faten asks him to help her with the first of her ambitions. He helps her find information about nursing school admissions and about how to study for the high school diploma on her own, since she does not have the privilege of attending high school. Eventually, Faten and Marwan meet—once over coffee, another time at a wedding. After a friend of Mrs. Samira's catches them on a driving-rendezvous to the seaside, Faten is punished and she does not see Marwan for months. Nonetheless, he has served as her prince because he has a material mode of transportation that makes many things possible: his car makes it possible for them to go on dates, for her to take a solitary (and redemptive) run on the beach, and eventually, for him to drive her to the examinations she must pass before she can pursue her dream to become a nurse. Marwan's car is, literally and metaphorically, her vehicle of escape.

But once Faten learns Marwan is affianced to a girl who shares his economic status and his religion, she ends the relationship. Although she is heartbroken, she decides to continue her plans to study nursing. She passes her diploma exam and finds a job in a hospital as a receptionist. She even decides that she will no longer support her father's unemployment, but will instead give her wages to her mother. She tells a friend, "I have decided not to send money to my father. I'll help Mother with the house expenses and to help with my sister and brothers, but I think it's time for my father to stop sitting in cafés and work more seriously" (140). Her decision to control her income is intertwined with her decision to continue her studies—and just as important.

The final pages of the novel, however, raise again the question of romance. Marwan tells her he has broken off his engagement and is willing to defy his parents in pursuing a relationship with her. Faten's response is ambiguous: she answers in a voice "stronger" than she has used before with him and agrees only to meet him for coffee (157). Readers can decide for themselves whether she is likely to enter into a long-term relationship with a man who has both helped and hurt her—and whether she is sustaining or subverting traditional fairy-tale structures. Either way, she has decided to prioritize her own economic future—in terms both of her education and her income—ahead of romance.

Rainbow Rowell's *Eleanor & Park* follows some of the same patterns. Eleanor and her four siblings live in Omaha in an abusive family situation with a stepfather who is a classic perpetrator and a mother who is a classic victim. The family's status is depicted in clichés of "white trash." All five children share a bedroom in their two-bedroom house; the bathroom has no door; the material conditions in which they live are degrading. Eleanor has no money for new clothes and sometimes goes to school smelling like urine from one of her younger siblings' nighttime bedwetting.

Everyone on the school bus bullies Eleanor, except Park, the son of a white ex-Marine and a Korean mother. By glossing over Park's racial identity to emphasize instead his class status, Rowell implies that social class affects an adolescent's materiality more than either race or gender. Park's parents, for example, serve as the foils to Eleanor's mother and stepfather in that Park's parents are loving, supportive of each other, and share power at different times in the relationship. They've raised the type of son who can't stand to see someone bullied, so Eleanor ends up sitting next to Park on the bus. In the first days of their relationship, they sit in silence. Park soon discovers Eleanor is reading his comic books over his shoulder. The comic book represents materially their exchange of ideas—and eventually their shared emotions, too. After Park sends a comic book home with Eleanor one night, their relationship blossoms. The music they share further blends the material and the discursive: the music is a language to them, but it requires a material object (in this case, a Walkman) and batteries for its discourse to be enacted. The music on the Walkman becomes a form of foreplay between them because they exchange songs to communicate information to each other about their individual personalities. Eventually they kiss and experience sexual intimacy—in the back seat of Park's car (because, of course, Park has his own car). Eleanor thinks: "Nothing was dirty. With Park. Nothing could be shameful. Because Park was the sun, and that was the only way Eleanor could think to explain it" (252).

However, when Eleanor realizes that her abusive stepfather has been writing sexually menacing messages to her on her school books, transcribing the insidiousness of his discursive intent onto a material object, she realizes she has to leave the family situation. She knows she can only save herself, and she relies on the discourse of children's literature to express her self-blame for not being able to save her siblings, thinking that if she "were the hero of some book, like *The Boxcar Children* or [i]f she were Dicey Tillerman, she'd find a way" (294). The ethics of care are also realistic: as young and as resourceless as she is, Eleanor can only care for herself, not for all four of her siblings as well.

Eleanor turns to Park for help, and his parents give her permission to drive her the hundreds of miles to her aunt and uncle's house in Minnesota. Since Park has a car, he can whisk the princess in this story out of harm's way to freedom. But like *The Servant*, the final pages of the story problematize standard fairy-tale tropes. Eleanor indicates to Park that she wants to have sex with him for the first time when they are pulled over to rest during their journey. He tells her they should wait; she insists she does not want to:

> "Eleanor, no we have to stop."
> "No . . ."
> "We can't do this . . ."
> "No. Don't stop, Park."
> "I don't even know how to . . . I don't have anything."
> "It doesn't matter."
> "But I don't want you to get—"
> "I don't care."
> "*I* care, Eleanor—"
> "It's our last chance."
> "No. No, I can't . . . I, *no*, I need to believe that it isn't our last chance . . . Eleanor? Can you hear me? I need you to believe it, too." (302–3, ellipses and italics in the original)

The interstices of the story allow readers to choose whether they believe the two have had intercourse. Significantly, Eleanor doesn't get pregnant or develop a disease. Kokkola writes about the "calamitous consequences of carnality" in YA novels, explaining that "fictional teenagers seem to have a pretty rough time when they lose their virginity. At best, they are

disappointed; at worst, their first sexual experiences are painful and/or associated with violence" (51).

Perhaps the most interesting feminist revision of the fairy-tale structure
here is the control Eleanor has—like the control Faten has—whether to
continue the relationship. In Minnesota, she tells Park the relationship can't
work out, that they need to say good-bye to each other: "That's what people
say—'it's not good-bye'—when they're too afraid to face what they're really
feeling. I'm not going to see you tomorrow, Park—I don't know *when* I'll
see you again. That deserves more than 'it's not good-bye'" (310–11, italics in
the original). He spends months pining for her—until on the final page he
receives a postcard—a material object containing "just three words": presumably the three words she hasn't been able to say throughout the novel,
"I love you" (325).

Before they part, Eleanor thinks about their relationship in terms that
actually deny fairy-tale structures:

> *There's no such thing as handsome princes,* she told herself.
> *There's no such thing as happily ever after.* (310, italics in the original)

Fifteen pages later, their apparent reunion at the novel's ending seems to
contradict that sentiment, although that reunion is enacted into being by a
material object—the postcard—that conveys discursive representationality
of an embodied emotion.

Eleanor's romance, like Faten's, relies on fairy-tale tropes that make the
plots of both novels seem at times predictable. Even in the final pages of
both novels, when the narratives veer from traditional structures and allow the protagonists the power to control their own futures and the power
that comes from ambiguity, each protagonist seems destined for a stable,
heteronormative relationship, albeit with her destiny in her own hands.
Both girls claim material control of their living conditions, wresting power
away from the patriarchal males who have tried to control how they live.
These girls' relationships may not work out, but in each case, the female
protagonist—neither the male teenager nor the father-figure—makes that
decision.

Jackie Horne notes that many YA romances still communicate the ideological clichés she uncovers in Beverly Cleary's *Fifteen* (1956), "messages
that can easily be found in many a romance published for teens and adults
in the years since 1956"; these messages include affirmations about the importance of being self-confident and conforming to social norms while still

somehow maintaining a status as "special": descriptions of competition with other girls for the attention of a boy (who is excused for his behavior based on his masculinity); miscommunication; and enforced heteronormativity as the end-goal of female adolescence (Horne, "Romancing"). *The Servant* and *Eleanor & Park* conform to some of these romance clichés but not all of them; authors like Sharafeddine and Rowell who are recognized as feminist YA authors are clearly trying to change the romance script, even while they are not yet fully successful in doing so.[2] Horne has identified as a corrective to YA romance novels the freedoms that New Adult romance offers: "What is so appealing to readers in the New Adult genre [is] the overwhelming feelings of first, requited lust; the all-consuming focus on a new love; the difficult, often traumatic life circumstances that prevent young love from flourishing; the pleasure-pain of angst when love goes awry" ("Surfacing").[3] While the New Adult novel remains outside the scope of this project, it is worth noting that Horne identifies the following as representative of feminist NA romances: Sarina Bowen's *The Shameless Hour* (2015), Elle Kennedy's *The Score* (2016), Robin York's *Deeper* (2014), and Heidi Cullinan's *Love Lessons* (2014) (Horne, "Slut"; "What"; "Surfacing"; "Paying").

Kimberley Reynolds has observed that "the sexual experiences of young people in a growing number of novels are depicted as pleasurable and consequence-free" (*Radical* 122), although it seems worth noting that much of the sexuality that is graphically depicted in YA literature is heteronormative. Moreover, much of this sexuality involves "first time" sex and a privileging of "penetrative sex," as if all definitions of "virginity" are always culturally stable (Hennessey). Additionally, Claire Hennessey identifies how these novels "[blur] the line between novel and [sex] manual": because they include so much information about sex (and how to have it and how to prevent negative consequences) that some of these books read like "guidebooks." *The Huffington Post* argues that teens are increasingly "turning to literature educate themselves about sex" because "only 22 states require sexual education at all"; that article then lists "books that don't sugarcoat teen sexuality" (Crum). Lists about explicit sexuality can be found on the sites of booksellers (e.g., Fitzpatrick for Barnes and Noble), social cataloging sites (e.g., Goodreads), popular reviewing sites (e.g., Jensen for Book Riot), and traditional reviewing sources (e.g., Wood for YALSA). Yet as Hennessey writes, "what seems to suffer in the more explicit works is story and characterisation: in order to fit in all the necessary clinical information, characters become mouthpieces and textbooks, presenting a world where they cannot be read [like] anything other than role models of some sort" (Hennessey).

Hennessey identifies such novels as Melvin Burgess's *Doing It* (2003), Meg Cabot's *Ready or Not* (2005), Daria Snadowsky's *Anatomy of a Boyfriend* (2007), and William Nicholson's *Rich and Mad* (2010) as books that fall into this category, but these books are hardly pinnacles of feminism. When YA novels focus on training teens about how sex works, attention to the shared empowerment that can come from mutually pleasurable sexuality seems to suffer. Too frequently, male sexuality is still depicted as more urgent and dominating than female sexuality—and when authors conscious of feminism try to correct that pattern, they sometimes end up with novels in which the female completely dominates the male in the sexual experience, as with Lauren Myracle's *Infinite Moment of Us* (2013), in which Wren makes all the decisions regarding the couple's sexual intimacy. Either way, a power imbalance occurs.

When teenaged girls are empowered in their decision-making, their living conditions, and have control of their sexuality, romances seem more feminist than when males control the plot lines. Nevertheless, some YA authors still seem to have a difficult time demonstrating girls sharing power equally with boys, especially when sexuality is involved. Perhaps the pervasiveness of fairy-tale romance tropes still controls the public's imagination about teenagers too much for writers to be truly liberated from the discursive patriarchal power that structures traditional romances.

## QUEERING ORIENTATION AND GENDER IDENTITY

Perhaps the most blatant ways that feminist fictions for the young question traditional Western binaries occurs in those novels that interrogate sexuality, orientation, and gender identity. These books refuse multiple binaries, such as binaries of cis/trans identity or straight/gay identity. At their best, these books show teenagers celebrating their sexuality. As the narrator says in Beth Goobie's *Hello, Groin*: "No matter how much you tell yourself that your body is just a subplot in your life, it isn't. It's the *main* plot"; later, the narrator adds, "we live in our whole body. . . . Our entire body is our mind. . . . We think and feel and hope with our groin, just as much as with our brain and heart" (57, italics added, 252, 256).

Kokkola observes that GLBTQ novels frequently reinforce binaristic thinking about orientation, particularly when they rely on a "butch-femme division" that "reinforces the normative boundaries 'queer' attempts to destroy" (113). Kokkola perceives lesbian novels as themselves having many parallels with adolescent sexuality, particularly in the way that lesbianism and adolescent sexuality are delegitimized by a variety of cultural attitudes (102–3). Relying on the work of Barbara Creed, Kokkola demonstrates that lesbianism and adolescent sexuality fall prey to the following skepticisms: "adolescents like lesbians are questioned as to whether what they do really counts as sex" (102); sexual acts of lesbians and adolescents are "disparaged rather than outlawed" (102); like adolescent sexuality, lesbianism is often portrayed as an immature phase; heteronormativity defines both lesbian and adolescent sexual practices; adolescent and lesbian sexuality are both labeled as "insatiable" (103); and lesbian and adolescent desire are both portrayed as "narcissistic and in need of taming" and in terms of "loneliness" (103). Kokkola firmly establishes that critics of YA literature need to understand these parallels as a way to resist them. Her argument that age-based norms define adolescent sexuality in YA novels will resonate with anyone who recognizes that adult sexual behavior is depicted as stable in adolescent literature, while adolescent sexuality is portrayed as unstable.

Kokkola also traces how lesbian novels must ultimately grapple—as most LGBTQ novels do—with homophobia. Gay sexuality is a "problem" to be solved, and it is invariably "solved" against a homophobic nemesis (98).[4] To Kokkola's outstanding work, I would also like to invite an increased awareness of the material dimensions of lesbianism in at least one novel, Emily M. Danforth's *The Miseducation of Cameron Post* (2012)—a novel in which lesbianism is most assuredly defined against a homophobia that remains regrettably stable, but a novel in which materiality is also clearly linked to *becoming*. For example, Danforth's description of Cameron's first kiss emphasizes the material, the physicality, of the act. She and a friend, both twelve-year-olds, are playing in a barn made excruciatingly hot by a summer heat wave. Cameron does a handstand, which leaves her shirt bunched around her neck, so after she rights herself, her friend asks Cameron to show her the tan line from her swimsuit again. The friend traces the white strip of skin with her finger and says, "It looks like a bra strap" (8). Cameron feels goose-bumps, and they discuss whether they need to wear bras when they start junior high in the fall. Cameron stuffs straw down her friend's shirt—who then finishes drinking her root beer and dares Cameron to kiss her: "There's nothing to know about a kiss like that before you do it. It was all action and reaction, the way her lips were salty and she tasted like root beer. The way I felt sort of dizzy the whole time" (10). The scene emphasizes the heat, the straw, the barn, the root beer, the girls' clothing, and the sensation of their tongues touching each other. The two girls kiss again, making clear that their desire for one another entails more than a mere dare. Later, they discuss whether they would "get in trouble if anyone found out," and they cite how they know the codes of heteronormativity: through television, the movies and "the world. . . . Anything else was something weird" (11). The materiality of their physical expression of desire is defined, shaped, and limited, by the discursive. Cameron's coming-out to herself, her *becoming*, is thus linked to her memories of "the feel of her mouth that day in the hayloft, the taste of her gum and the root beer we'd been drinking. The day she dared me to kiss her. And the very next day my parents' car had veered through the guardrail" (45). Cameron's parents die in the automobile wreck, and she blames herself for their deaths, linking her own sense of sexuality with death in very material ways.[5]

In the first half of the novel, Cameron never quite shakes the sense of shame with which she connects her orientation and her parents' death. Nevertheless, every stage of her coming-out story—that is, every stage of her *becoming* an out lesbian first to herself, then to her friends, and then to a disapproving community—is implicated in the material. When she explores her sexuality with an out lesbian she meets through swim team, she describes:

> our ever-expanding make-out repertoire—hands up each other's shirts while hidden within the blue tunnel slide on the playground next to Malta's pool; Lindsey's tongue in my mouth behind the Snack Shack not five minutes after I won the Scobey meet; . . . pressed together, our swim-suit tops pulled down and the straps dangling from our waists like slack suspenders while we were supposed to be drying off and staying warm in Lindsey's dad's camper during a thunderstorm. (98–99)

Both the materiality of their bodies and the materiality of the locations where they touch each other affects these girls' sense of their shared sexuality.

When Cameron falls in love, it is with Coley, and their sexual expressions of their feelings are also rooted in the material, although Cameron knows she is relying on discourse to describe the experience. She says of their first kiss: "I'm not going to make it out to be something that it wasn't: It was perfect" (182). She then shifts the narration to focus on the material: "Coley's soft lips against the bite of the liquor and sugary Coke still on our tongues. She did more than just not stop me. She kissed me back. She pulled in with her arms, her ankles latching behind my thighs, and we stayed like that until

I could feel my boots sinking so far into the rain-softened clay-thick mud beneath me" (182–83). When they have enough privacy to engage in genital sex, Cameron again focuses on the material: the taste of what they have been drinking, the size and shape of their clothing as they disrobe each other, the contrast of their hot bodies to the cool sheets, the scent of Coley's lotion, the way specific parts of Coley's body feel under Cameron's fingertips and tongue. They acknowledge each other's size and are startled that they both experience each other as "so small" (224). Cameron describes the intimacy of the position they are in when Coley orgasms, acknowledging how "her whole body tensed and her breaths came in ragged jumps and her thighs pressed together against my head. . . . But I didn't know what to do in the aftermath, where to put my body, what to say" (225). Ultimately, Cameron feels awkward and uncertain about both her own materiality and her own discourse—but she has found Coley's *jouissance* pleasurable.

Coley's brother interrupts them before Cameron orgasms, and he forces Coley to admit to their mother what the girls have been doing. Coley relies on discourse to exonerate herself, depicting Cameron in terms of "the pursuer" who has "attempted corruption" of Coley because of Cameron's "sick infatuation" (248). Cameron's aunt decides to send her to a Christian camp dedicated to convincing teenagers that being gay is sinful so they can "break free from the bonds of sexual sin and confusion by welcoming Jesus Christ into their lives" (252). Thus begins Cameron Post's "miseducation." Camp Promise is predicated on the type of religious belief that argues "sin" can be controlled both by cognitive self-discipline and the discourse one uses to think about one's self and that sin. The camp subscribes to the type of "sinful body" argument that Elizabeth Grosz cites as accruing to early Christianity via Plato's thinking, as I have discussed in Chapter 4 (Grosz 5). The camp privileges discourse over embodiment—and Cameron Post directly critiques this type of thinking. At the camp, she makes two friends who smoke marijuana with her and who aren't particularly chatty: "We were good with smoking and not talking. All of us did so much talking at Promise, even those of us who didn't really say anything in all that talking" (310). Talk-therapy constitutes the camp's allegedly therapeutic approach, and Cameron accuses the counselors of making it up as they go, saying "You guys don't even know what you're doing here, do you? You're just like making it up as you go along . . . and you're gonna pretend like you have answers that you don't even have and it's completely fucking fake" (382)—and she rightly labels their methods "pseudoscientific" (421). Using her own words, she labels the counselor's therapy "emotional abuse" (400);

after one boy tries to castrate himself and pours bleach on his wounds to cleanse himself from his allegedly impure gay thoughts, a state investigator comes to interview the residents of the camp. Cameron tells him: "the whole fucking purpose of this place is to make us hate ourselves so that we change. We're supposed to *hate* who we are, despise it" (400, italics in the original). Cameron means that they are supposed to learn the right type of discourse so that they can hate their material bodies and their physical urges.

The text underscores the relationship between Cameron's actions and her emotions in two material ways: through the geography of Montana and through her compulsive decorating of her childhood dollhouse. Throughout the text, she frequently describes Montana's weather—its harsh, dry, landscape-browning summers, its sudden thunderstorms, its vast skies. She claims that Montana has two seasons, "winter and road construction" as a way of showing how a "saying like that encapsulates just how present the natural world is in Montana, and how aware of it you are—the sky, the land, the weather, all of it" (403). Her parents have drowned in Quake Lake, a lake that was created during a massive earthquake when Cameron's mother was twelve; she had been camping in the area flooded by the earthquake the day before. Her best friend's brother has drowned in that deluge, just as Cameron's parents will eventually die in the same body of water when Cameron herself is twelve. Montana's geography is a material presence throughout the novel that is greater than any other force—even the force of young Cameron's sexuality.

Before he died, Cameron's father has built her an elaborate dollhouse. After her parents' deaths, Cameron turns into a scavenger who collects things (and sometimes steals them) to decorate the interior of the dollhouse. Her ill-trained therapist at Camp Promise connects these artifacts to her parents' deaths and tells her that "these material fragments" are "trophies of your sins"; "you collect these items, and then you display them as a way of attempting, I think, to control your guilt and discomfort regarding both these relationships and your behavior" (433). The counselor later admonishes Cameron: "You've so convinced yourself that God was punishing you for your [lesbian] sins . . . that you're blind to any other assessment, and because of that your parents are no longer people to you; they're simply figures that were manipulated by God for his great plan to teach you a lesson. . . . Your parents did not die for your sins. They didn't need to: Jesus already did" (452). With the two close friends she has made at the camp, Cameron then runs away, rejecting her counselor's fundamentalist interpretation of her sexuality and her grief about her parents' death. In a scene perhaps more imbued than it needs to be with symbolic imagery, Cameron swims in Quake Lake, lighting a candle and talking to her parents' spirits and indicating that she thinks they would have liked getting to know her as she is. "Maybe while you were alive I hadn't even *become* me yet. Maybe I still haven't *become* me. I don't know how you tell for sure when you finally have," she tells her parents, immersed in the baptismal lake water, holding a burning candle, looking at the skeletons of trees that grew on the land before the earthquake triggered the mountain to fall and create Quake Lake (468, italics added). The geography and Cameron's materiality have merged, and she has begun to heal—not because she somehow wants to overcome her lesbianism but precisely because her *becoming* entails accepting her orientation.

The novel illustrates aptly what Kokkola demonstrates about the lesbian ghost, a trope of lesbian literature first identified by Terry Castle. "Adolescent desires, especially queer desires, can be rendered invisible—*ghosted*—by a viewpoint that literally cannot see them" (Kokkola 122). As a trope, the ghost problematizes the relationship between the material and the non-material: it is an otherworldly manifestation that presents itself in the physical world but is not exactly material. And ghosts recur frequently in Cameron's meta-phorical language. When twelve-year-old Cameron has a sleepover with the girl who shares her first kiss, they are in bed, and that girl's father knocks on the door; it will be his unpleasant task to drive Cameron back to her grandmother's house to learn that her parents have died. The girls have heard the phone ring late at night; they hear her father approaching the door: "there was empty time between the end of those steps and the heavy rap of his knuckles: ghost time" (24). Their sexuality has been ghosted; it is invisible to the grieving adults around them. After her parents die, while Cameron visits the video store from which she rents as many lesbian-erotic DVDs as she can, she walks "toward the store, hoping my cap would keep me invisible—I felt like a ghost anyway" (34). Cameron enjoys the kitchen of her aunt's church because "I liked being a ghost in this place, unseen" (111). But after Cameron has been outted as a lesbian, it's not so much that she is invisible as that other people try to be invisible around her: her grandmother "ghosted around the house" until Cameron is sent to Camp Promise (261). Her good friend Adam at the camp tells her "I'm the ghost of my former gay self" (310), and the other friend Cameron runs away with, Jane, tells her that the skeletal trees sticking out of Quake Lake look like "the ghosts of trees" (457). Cameron thinks "the wind fluttering" through those trees sounds like "cheesy scary movie ghost whisper that somehow wasn't cheesy at all" (458). Cameron then asks Adam about "that Lakota giant—the one who was supposed to be like visible to man forever ago, but isn't now, and lives on a mountain surrounded by water" (458); Adam teases Cameron, "Why, did you see him?" (459). This is the whole point of the ghost-imagery in *The Miseducation of Cameron Post*: its goal is to make the lesbian visible, no longer a ghost either to herself or to other people.

*The Miseducation of Cameron Post* contains many standard tropes of LGBTQ stories that Kokkola identifies: Cameron's coming-out is the focus of the story; that coming out is predicated against homophobia that is allowed to remain stable and culturally entrenched; Cameron and her most beloved lover create a butch-femme binary; Cameron is warned by an experienced lesbian that her bisexual lover will eventually betray her to embrace heteronormativity, and Cameron's lesbianism is ghosted. Despite relying on these tropes, *The Miseducation of Cameron Post* does not shy away from the materiality of lesbian sexuality, nor does it reduce lesbianism only to discursive terms. Lesbian *becoming*, like lesbian desire, is discursively inflected in this novel but it is also a material phenomenon rooted in the physicality of young women's bodies.

Beth Goobie's *Hello, Groin* (2006) follows many of the same tropes, complete with homophobia left intact, at least one butch-femme binary, and a focus on coming out. *Hello, Groin*, however, problematizes sexuality, wresting it away from the gay/straight binary that troubles many YA coming-out novels. Dylan's love interest is her best-friend Jocelyn, who is dating Dikker—a boy of whom Dylan disapproves perhaps because she is jealous of him and because he makes Jocelyn feel bad about herself. When Dylan suggests they break up, Jocelyn gets angry and says, "For some reason known only to His very divine self, God dumped us *normal* people with a shitload of hormones and you just got a sprinkling, which you take care of with the occasional mastie" (8, italics added). Jocelyn's use of the word "normal" here is very telling: by the end of the novel, she proves to be happily self-actualized and bisexual. It is textually significant that she self-identifies as "normal," even though it takes Dylan a melodramatically long time to accept her own orientation and to recognize what most readers know by the time the two girls kiss: that Jocelyn is bisexual.

Dylan, of course, only has eyes for Jocelyn—and the opening chapter is a poignantly drawn scene that blends fantasy and realism, sleeping and dreaming, the material and the discursive. Dylan is bicycling Jocelyn to school, with Jocelyn clinging tightly to her from behind. The two girls enter a mysterious "white haze that. . . . glowed a brilliant white and was so tall it touched the underside of the bridge and over-rode the nearest bank by at least a hundred feet" (1–2). When Dylan asks Jocelyn what it is, she answers, "the river's dreaming" (1), and the girls walk into the bubbly cloud. "The whole thing was a little like walking through a trance, thinking in soft colors, sweet scents and vague secret murmurings" (3). Jocelyn strips naked, begins to unbutton Dylan's shirt, but instead grabs her by the hand and spins her in circles, "while everything we couldn't seem to say whirled white and sweet around us" (4). The bubbly mist has been caused by a spill upriver from a soap factory, but the girls have experienced a moment of sexual joy enveloped in images of purity. The text is discursively positioning their sexualities as clean, not dirty.

Not everyone in their community agrees, of course. Dylan's work is censored after she constructs a school project of a "girl and a guy" and "the parts of their bodies . . . each have a different book title" (93). The school's administration objects when she places Joyce Carol Oates's *Foxfire* over the girl's groin because Dylan likes the way the book depicts female sexuality:

> Of course it's about sex. . . . Everything we do in life is sex, isn't it? . . . I mean, it all comes from the same place inside you, doesn't it? And that place is either a place of following rules and doing what you're told, or figuring things out for yourself. . . . Because isn't that the way you really learn—about sex, love, justice, reality, anything? I mean, how can you figure out the universal meaning of something if you don't work out the personal meaning for yourself first? (Goobie 60–61)

Dylan's thinking here is fairly binaristic in terms of inside/outside and breaking or following rules, but this is the intellectual starting place from which she begins to honestly interrogate her orientation.

Dylan grows angry as she realizes how much conventional thinking dominates the discourse about teenage sexuality:

> It's like everyone thinks that what goes on between a teenager's legs is dirty. . . . I mean, whether you're having sex with someone or not. That part of your body is automatically indecent *because* you're a teenager. . . . Anyway, why does that part of your body have to be treated like a wild animal that should be caged and controlled? Why can't it be about decency and honor and what's true and good. . . . and wise? (138–39, italics in the original)

When Dylan finally kisses Jocelyn, she asks if they can't spend some time "just *being* like this" before they explore their sexuality further (238, italics in the original). Dylan's ontological request privileges both the material nature of sexual intimacy and the ontological legitimacy of being lesbian.

Dylan does not have the insight to recognize that she is decoupling binaries, but she acknowledges that "we live in our whole body, right? Our whole body is our heart and mind, maybe even our soul. So I think our heart and soul and mind live in our groin, just like anywhere else. And we need to make that part of us be about truth and respect and love, just like our heart" (252). Dylan understands that her *becoming* is integral to her sexuality—a sexuality that her culture may view as queer but that the text itself normalizes, as it also does Jocelyn's bisexuality. *Hello, Groin* celebrates female sexuality across a spectrum of sexualities, while it also depicts strong girls who advocate for themselves and others. Although orientation is only one aspect of identity politics, *Hello, Groin* enacts feminism in depicting female sexuality as a source of empowerment.

Advances in feminism in twenty-first century YA literature owe much to the contributions of gay YA novels to feminist discourse. Indeed, this chapter's reliance on queer theory indicates how many significant contributions gay men have made to destabilizing gender binaries, fighting homophobia, creating a culture of inclusion, and validating the relationship between one's orientation and one's gender identity. For example, Russel, the narrator of *The Geography Club* (2003), is a gay teenager who is afraid to come out in his homophobic high school. He and a group of friends form a gay-lesbian support group that they deceptively call the "Geography Club" to throw off their judgmental peers. Russel's new boyfriend, Kevin, is part of the group, as is his best friend, Min, and her girlfriend, Terese. Russel's narration sometimes reads like the reports of an anthropologist who is observing high school culture in a detached manner, but he also adds notes of critique to his commentary, as when he describes his disgust for how misogynistic the heteronormative athletes are when they talk about girls and sex: "Now that I had some idea what real intimacy was, it just made the guys sound like idiots, and cruel idiots at that" (181). His critique of these boys' behavior establishes the book's feminist ideology. Moreover, the book is as respectful of lesbian sexuality as it is gay sexuality, and the book features several strong female characters, including Min and her partner and a straight girl, Belinda, who joins the Geography Club because her mother's alcoholism has led her to need the emotional support the group offers. These girls are independent, articulate, strong, and decisive—and their characters are well-rounded, unique, and distinct from one another. Indeed, Min proves to be the most ethical and emotionally strong member of the Geography Club because of her insistence that the group has responsibility for the school's social pariah, Brian Bund. The group eventually "comes out" as the Gay-Straight-Bisexual Alliance—but their ability to call themselves what they really are can only happen because of Min's, Russel's and Brian's shared sense of ethics.

Although gender identity and orientation are not the same, the depiction of trans identity in adolescent literature is usually tied to sexuality. Trans characters question not only their gender identity and affiliation, but they must sometimes defend their orientation. In other words, when characters accept the gender they were assigned at birth, whether "Assigned Female at Birth" (AFAB) or "Assigned Male at Birth" (AMAB), they will, during adolescence, likely explore their orientation along the spectrum that includes heterosexuality, bisexuality, pansexuality, and gay or lesbian sexuality. But for trans characters—that is, those who do not experience themselves as the gender they were assigned at birth—issues of sexual orientation become both more complex and more heteronormative.

Don Latham writes about transgender issues in Louise Erdrich's *The Birchbark House* and its sequels. Latham employs the term "gender variant" to describe the two AFAB characters in the series who queer gender norms: Old Tallow and Two Strike ("Manly-Hearted" 131). Old Tallow is an independent and androgynous older woman who loves her dogs more than anyone; she helps Omakayas, the protagonist, and her family. Two Strike is Omakayas's rebellious cousin who ultimately alienates Omakayas by being so competitive—and Two Strike's gender-bending negatively affects her ability to marry. According to Latham, Old Tallow and Two Strike complicate the performance of gender roles in that Old Tallow embraces both the maternal role of nurturing and the patriarchal role of hunter, while Two Strike "represents a rejection of the feminine and an embracing of the masculine" ("Manly-Hearted" 135). For Latham, it is the social roles that these people perform that establish them as gender variants: it is their physical activities, more than discourse, that define these characters as trans characters ("Manly-Hearted" 133). Latham concludes that these novels "explore both limitations of and liberation from narrowly defined gender roles," providing an important contrast to the protagonist's more traditional assumption of feminine roles ("Manly-Hearted" 148–49). Latham's insistence on paying attention to the material (in the form of dress and work) provides a useful way for thinking about gender variation.

Latham's work relies on Butler's theories about performance and on Michelle Abate's work on tomboyism in *Tomboys: A Literary and Cultural History*. Abate, too, invokes Butler, arguing that "the tomboyish character highlights the performative nature of masculinity and femininity" (*Tomboys* 10). Abate's history of the emergence of the tomboy is also sensitive to materiality: Abate tracks how the hoyden figure of the mid-nineteenth century emerged into the tomboy in response to "changes in the nation's social, political and even economic climate"; by the 1920s, for example, "women were voting, engaging in such formerly masculine activities as smoking and drinking, and even asserting their right to participate in the 'male' world of work"—all of which are phenomena linked to materiality (*Tomboys* x).[6] Abate notes, however, that tomboyism was also linked in some eras with "proto-lesbianism," particularly during the Cold War era (*Tomboys* xi, 170). Abate establishes the tomboy as "a powerful concept and a pervasive cultural phenomenon" (*Tomboys* xxiii) that is particularly important for the powerful "gender-bending" that tomboys perform (*Tomboys* xxiv). Finally, it must be noted that Abate directly emphasizes the materiality of the tomboy:

> Tomboyism is also a distinct bodily identity. Together with being linked to corporeal traits like short hair, it is also predicated on such bodily acts as tree-climbing. Contemplating how the body-based realms of gender and race mutually construct and even reinforce each other, my discussion frequently pivots around questions of embodiment and disembodiment. (*Tomboys* xxviii)

Embodied actions and physical activity, as much as discursive phenomena, permit gender-bending to occur.

Mallan observes that stories that queer gender tend to work against a "backdrop of heteronormativity, with the result that the narratives deal with what could be regarded as an uncomfortable subject by providing a liberal account of empowerment and equality, and by emphasizing the difficulties that protagonists from relatively privileged and established social groups endure" (*Gender* 129). She reads Ellen Wittlinger's *Parrotfish* (2007) as a story about a trans male who tries to disrupt gender binaries by finding a "middle" space in between the two genders; Mallan points out that when the protagonist renames himself, he finds a gender-neutral name that

incorporates "gray" as a morpheme: "Grady" (*Gender* 131). Grady problematizes the idea of performing gender when he questions why people have to
"act" like girls or boys and can't just act "like themselves," but Mallan also
notes he cannot escape thinking about identity as a stable construct: "His
suggestion that people should act like themselves has implications for queer
subjectivity as it dismisses gender categories, but at the same time (and
somewhat contradictorily) it insists on a stable subject ('themselves')" (*Gender* 132). Like Latham and Abate, Mallan also observes that gender depends
on discourse, performance, *and* the material: Grady must physically bind his
breasts, and his performance as a male is disrupted when his period starts
unexpectedly at school; he also defines himself in terms of activities that
occur in the material world because he is someone who enjoys "guy stuff":
carpentry and working on cars (Mallan, *Gender* 133). A drag show at school
allows Grady to problematize masculinity and femininity as constructs, but
he falls inadvertently into another gendered binary that Mallan identifies:
gender performance as "inauthentic" or "authentic" (*Gender* 136). Mallan
observes that this binary "reinforces an ontology (as an account of what
gender *is*) that aligns with the dominant discourse of gender binary and
its norms" (*Gender* 136). Even when authors attempt to destabilize gender
binaries by creating trans characters, they sometimes still reinscribe the
performativity and materiality of gender in binaristic terms.

Another novel that reinforces this observation of Mallan's—and her observation that trans characters often reinscribe middle-class values—is the
trans female at the heart of Julie Anne Peters's *Luna* (2004). Luna/Liam lives
in a world with rigid gender binaries: her parents fight about gender roles,
and Luna sometimes hates her sister, Regan, (who narrates the novel) for
identifying with the gender she was assigned at birth. Luna's sister sometimes thinks Luna/Liam experiences a massive Cartesian split: "as if his
body wasn't connected to his brain" (18). Even while trying to problematize
gender binaries, the book reinscribes them, as when Luna's sister thinks of
Luna as "off both [gender] scales" or "between scales"; "he really was off the
scale. Boy by day, girl by night. Except he was a girl all the time, inside. It
was hardwired into his brain, he said, the way intelligence or memory is.
His body didn't reflect his inner image. His body betrayed him" (50–51).
But gender is also performative in this novel: Luna has to "play" to people's
"expectations. Dress the part. Act the role" (51). Luna's *becoming* initially
revolves around material performance—wearing fingernail polish and wigs
and feminine clothes—but when she decides to transition, her *becoming*

involves changes that are permanent, material, and visceral, including having her Adam's apple surgically altered and having sex reassignment surgery. Nevertheless, the novel shares the same reinscription of stable identity that Mallan identifies in *Parrotfish* when Grady asks, "Why couldn't people just be accepted for who they were?" (Wittlinger 51). Kimberley Reynolds acknowledges the "highly unreal dimension to this book" and assesses it as "more about the problems of living a transgender existence than an exegesis of current thinking about gender" (*Radical* 129). Although Reynolds initially argues that the book is "encouraging [readers] to move beyond the binaries of male/female, masculine/feminine into more nuanced ways of understanding sexual difference and orientations" (*Radical* 129), she also perceives that the book ultimately betrays contemporary understandings of gender that are based in queer theory: "it ignores 'the neithers, the boths, the incoherencies' (Rabinowitz 20) that queer theory has worked so hard to bring to our attention" (Reynolds, *Radical* 129–30).

It seems useful then to ask how the book is feminist. In the fact that Luna feels more emotionally and psychologically empowered as a female than a male, the novel demonstrates a young woman identifying what she wants and pursuing the goals, despite the costs.[7] Moreover, the cis female narrator gains respect for her own gender identity as she recognizes that being female is positive and life-affirming. Luna's sister, Regan, also shares an equal relationship with her boyfriend, despite a series of initial miscommunications. Most important, Regan comes to realize that she's wrong to blame her mother for ignoring Luna's transexuality. Once Regan realizes that their mother has known all along that Liam rejected the gender he was assigned at birth, the girl is angry that their mother has not done more to help Luna and guide her father to accept Luna as a daughter. When Regan has this epiphany, she is unsure whether their mother has been secretly supporting Luna or enabling Liam to commit suicide, and she begins to think of her mother as a "monster," but Luna won't allow that (228). "Yes, Mom's always known. She just hasn't known how to cope with it," Luna says, after which Regan can allow herself to question: "Had I jumped to the wrong conclusion about her? I hoped so. God, I hoped so" (241). Although the book is simplistic about everything from social class to gender binaries, at the very least, it demonstrates the complexity of the mother/daughter relationship when that relationship includes a trans daughter.

Mallan and Reynolds both demonstrate that trans novels are not perhaps the best vehicles for advancing queer theory; they are not always the most successful feminist novels, either. Nevertheless, the entire field of adolescent literature has become more sophisticated and inclusive because of the ways that feminism and queer theory have insisted that cultural attention needs to be given to issues of both gender *and* gender identity. Novels about trans teenagers are participating in a complex cultural conversation about the instability of gender, even when the characters themselves appear to accept gender binaries too easily. And while these particular trans novels focus more on gender identity and orientation than they do on sexuality, sexual desire is an inherent part of both plots. Luna, for example, insists that she is not gay, even though she is attracted to cis males: "I'm not gay.... It's not the same. I'm a girl" (94). As Liam, Luna experiences homophobia—his father and a school mate both accuse him of being gay, while Grady in *Parrotfish* first calls himself a "tomboy," then a "lesbian," and is homophobically accused of being a closeted lesbian by his physician because the man can't recognize that Grady is trans (Wittlinger 9, 54). Grady distinguishes gender identity from orientation, and claims that the phase in which s/he "came out" as a lesbian was "just a pit stop on the queer and confused highway" (Wittlinger 18). But Grady is as heterosexual as Luna is, which ultimately reinforces heteronormative sexuality in both novels.

Issues of sexuality seem even more complex for characters who are intersex. Take, for example, I. W. Gregario's *None of the Above*, in which Krissy Latimer, the homecoming queen of her high school, dates a popular and kind-hearted football player. Because they are both athletes, they frequently run together in what becomes a metaphor for how synchronized they are emotionally: "Over hundreds of runs, Sam and I had established a rhythm, a pace that we no longer had to think about, as if we were running to the same internal song" (11). Fully in control of her own sexuality, Krissy decides that they will have sex the night of homecoming; she's had a birth control shot months earlier, and Sam wears a condom, to ensure that she's physically safe. But the experience does not go as she has anticipated. Even though she is sexually excited and trusts Sam, she experiences pain even more unusual than that which usually accompanies the rupturing of a hymen:

> Sam untangled himself to get a condom, and when he turned back the feel of him on top of me was headier than any champagne.
> And then, oh my God. Pain.
> It felt like someone had taken an electric drill to my insides. I gritted my teeth and tried to power past it, but it was too much. Sam shifted, trying to go deeper, and I whimpered. (19)

The young couple decides to wait for another time—and that time is even more painful and leaves Krissy with lacerations that alarm her enough that she makes an appointment to see a gynecologist.

The gynecologist conducts a sonogram and determines that Krissy has no uterus—which explains why she's never gotten her period—and that she actually has two gonads that have never descended, which is why she has no pubic hair (although she does have normal breasts). A urologist confirms the diagnosis: Krissy has androgen insensitivity syndrome (AIS), sometimes also referred to as a "disorder of sex development" (DSD)—a term that the author rejects in the afterword because of the pejorative term "disorder" (332). Krissy is intersex.

It should be noted that the author of *None of the Above* is herself a urologist and that the novel sometimes reads like the type of self-help book that earns "problem novels" a bad name. Gregario provides extensive textual commentary about the nature of AIS, and she critiques the use of the term "hermaphrodite" and all of the many forms of discrimination that intersex people experience. She provides a thorough bibliography, including information about online support groups for people with AIS. She also occasionally pokes fun of conventions in YA publishing: after Sam breaks up with her because he cannot accept that Krissy is intersex, he begins to date "the head of the football boosters club. The only thing that would've been more cliché was if she were a cheerleader" (277). Following another standard trope of YA literature, Krissy's mother is dead (which is part of why she has not heretofore received adequate gynecological care), and the way Sam breaks up with Krissy is also clichéd. He falls into predictably violent homophobia:

> "Get away from me," he said, without even looking up. . . ."I've got nothing to say to you, you homo. . . ." I grabbed at his arm again. . . . He rounded on me. I could feel the muscles in his arm spasm.
> "Sam, please [ . . . ]," I begged. "Let me explain."
> "What the fuck is there to explain? . . . I thought I loved you, you fucking man-whore. And you've been lying to me. I have nothing to say to you. Ever. Again." (114, bracketed ellipses in the original)

More interesting by far than the text's reliance on clichés is the process of *becoming* by which Krissy accepts that she is female because she self-identifies as female. First, she is terrified of the word "hermaphrodite" and grieves that she is "something in between" being "a man or a woman" (54);

she believes that she is "a car that came off the assembly line all messed up. I was a lemon" (58), but her urologist won't let her accept this line of thinking. Krissy asks that doctor, "Am I trans, then? Like a man trapped in a woman's body?" (59), and the doctor answers honestly, "I know it's really confusing, but chromosomal sex, gender identity, and sexual orientation are all separate concepts" (59). The text acknowledges the materiality of hormone-producing sexual organs. Unfortunately, Krissy continues to think of herself as a "freak" for a while (60), even though she can acknowledge: "Nothing about me had changed, either. Yet everything was different" (64). Krissy friends' use of words like "mannish" or "girly" begins to disturb her as she grows to understand how complex gender identity is, and she realizes, "My life had been one big puzzle, except I never knew it" (70)—but she cries with relief when she realizes that because she has no cervix, she will never die of cervical cancer, as her mother has. Fearing a related cancer of the sex organs, however, she elects to have her testicles removed. After the surgery, "I had hoped, expected even, to suddenly feel like I was a girl again. But all I felt like was an empty jar" (147). As long as Krissy still defines gender in black and white terms, her body feels "empty" to her.

By the time Krissy reaches out to talk to her ex-boyfriend again, she has begun to show signs of accepting herself as she is. Sam tells her, "I. Don't. Date. Men.," so Krissy points out that he's seen her naked—so he should know better: "I am *not* a man. . . . You've seen me [ . . . ] *all of me.* How can you not accept that?" (171, bracketed ellipses in the original). Her assertion of her identity matters more to herself than to him. Although he cannot accept her as she is, Krissy is beginning to acknowledge that she is not male. For example, after she picks up a guy in a bar, she worries "*What if he finds out that you're a boy?*" (184, italics in the original), but internally, she shouts back at herself: "*I'm a girl*" (184, italics in the original). She finds out something about the vulnerability of her own femininity when that character tries to molest her: he grows violent and tries to grab beneath her skirt to find her "dick"; she again thinks "*I'm a girl*" (312). She does not experience full catharsis, however, until a childhood friend named Darren rescues her from this violence, like a fairy-tale knight in shining armor, and she realizes she is in love with Darren:

> All the anxiety and guilt and self-loathing that I'd been holding in for weeks came out in the catharsis Dr. LaForte had been hoping for since I started therapy. But it wasn't fear that pushed all my emotions past the tipping point; it was the realization that I was kind of in love

with Darren Kowalski for making me laugh minutes after I'd survived a potential hate crime. I cried like a baby, and as embarrassing as it was to have a meltdown with the object of my affection sitting there patting me awkwardly on the arm to get me to stop, the release was so liberating that I didn't care. (320)

Krissy has accepted herself as a girl, as heterosexual, and as intersex—although it's a bit unfortunate she has to be "saved" by a heteronormative cis male.

In other words, too much of Krissy's story is binaristic. Her self-definition is greatly influenced either by men (such as Sam, Darren, and her father) or by the series of all-female doctors she has (gynecologist, urologist, psychiatrist). On the other hand, the book does acknowledge that gender identity exists on a spectrum, as does orientation. Darren's father is gay, and so Darren sounds wise when he tells her, "If there's one thing I learned from my dad leaving my mom, it's that love isn't a choice. You fall for the person, not their chromosomes" (324). Darren's effort to make loving someone be about personality rather than biology complicates that contentious issue by touching on dualistic thinking about "nature" and "culture." Is a chromosome an indisputable effect of science/nature? This book implies an answer of "no": gender identity is self-defined; it is influenced by multiple factors, including chromosomes, hormones, familial nurturance, self-perception and self-definition during childhood and adolescence, and cultural attitudes. If *None of the Above* falls into too many heteronormative romance conventions, at least Krissy is a strong, loving, and self-defined girl who deserves to be loved by someone equally strong, loving, and self-defined. Moreover, she has moved from thinking about herself as always-already female, to thinking about herself pejoratively as a "hermaphrodite," to thinking about herself as a "man" to accepting herself as intersex in positive terms that allow her to self-define as a girl. The text could not be more clear in its efforts to empower individuals to determine and self-define their own gender identity.

Where YA novels still often fail to be progressive, however, is in their depiction of female masturbation. Katy Stein points out that the inclusion of masturbation as a topic in YA literature is itself a twenty-first century phenomenon, since the depiction of female masturbation in twentieth-century novels was "practically nonexistent" (416); nevertheless, she relies on Foucault's theorizations about sexuality in *History of Sexuality* when she asserts: "Despite the argument that young adult literature is saturated with transgressive content, depictions of female teen masturbation . . . [remain] situated within traditional, adult-centered values intended to continue and ultimately control teenage sexuality" (415); Stein analyzes how various novels that depict female masturbation do so to validate the masculine presence in heterosexuality and to institutionalize anxiety-ridden discourses about female masturbation. Stein identifies a spectrum of textual attitudes towards female masturbation: in Meg Cabot's *Ready or Not* (2005) and Phyllis Reynolds Naylor's *Dangerously Alice* (2006), female masturbation is a "last resort" for sexually frustrated girls (415); in Judy Blume's *Deenie* (1973) and Ibi Kaslik's *Skinny* (2004), masturbation is "deviant" (417); and even transgressive novels like Beth Goobie's *Hello, Groin*, which attempts to normalize masturbation as an individualized issue of teen sexuality, still inadvertently depict masturbation in problematic ways. "In seeking to define, regulate, and normalize sexuality, these institutions thus encourage its overall repression, positioning the teens to seek approval, answers, and forgiveness from the agencies of power for their emerging sexual desires" (Stein 426).

## QUEERING MOTHERHOOD

Since all children are conceived by sexual acts (ideally consensual, but tragically, not always), motherhood is frequently depicted in YA literature as a problematic extension of sexuality. For example, Isabel Quintero's *Gabi: A Girl in Pieces* underscores the feared link between sexuality and motherhood when Gabi, the narrator, explains, "Adults are incredibly naive sometimes" (162). Her mother tells her to keep her eyes "open" and her legs "closed" (7), as if when that mother was young:

> no one had these feelings between their legs that are supposed to be forbidden. Maybe they did just speak to each other from opposite sides of the fence or on a porch under the watch of eagle-eyed chaperones. Fat chance. That sounds like another unlikely adult-constructed scenario. Because if that was the case, there wouldn't be so many young parents or parents who have never been married or divorced or kids in foster care. Young people have always had sex. But no adult will admit it. (162–63)

In this novel, one of Gabi's friends becomes a mother her senior year of high school because, as the text eventually reveals, she has been the victim of rape. Gabi's own mother is again pregnant—and Gabi's father, a meth addict, dies while her mother is still pregnant. A third female, another high school senior, has an abortion, which is described entirely in negative terms: "I know she feels about it. Really bad. But she doesn't have another choice or feels like she doesn't have another choice" (182). All three women regret their sexuality, and all three of their stories serve as cautionary tales about the link between sexuality and motherhood. I thus include motherhood in this chapter on sexuality because YA novels frequently problematize the relationship between sexuality and motherhood in ways that range from the unrealistic to the psychologically damaging.

In *Philosophy and the Maternal Body*, Michelle Boulous Walker argues that most psychological accounts of motherhood have one of two problems: "either they subsume the mother beneath a theoretical concern with the child, or they sustain an oppositional division between mother and child" (159). Within feminist literature for the young, the same dichotomy seems to emerge: mothers are either subsumed by the act of mothering, or they live in conflict with their children, especially if those children are daughters.

For example, Daniel Greenstone reads the *Olivia* books by Ian Falconer as an instantiation of a mother being subsumed by the act of mothering. "If Olivia is cast as a liberated fount of ambition, her mother comes across rather differently," Greenstone argues (28). He demonstrates how Olivia's exhausted mother is at her energetic daughter's beck and call: he calls the picture books "a brilliant, sly, and at times, a winking critique of what might be called the unfulfilled promises of feminism" (27). While Olivia's exhausted mother cooks, cleans, sews, changes diapers, reads to her children, provides them with exposure to the fine arts in the home, and chauffeurs them to endless activities, Olivia stars in the show. Greenstone notes how well Olivia's parents encourage her feminism by exposing her to feminist role models, such as Eleanor Roosevelt. But if Olivia's mother serves as a foil to Olivia, one can only imagine what Olivia herself will be like if she herself becomes a mother. The picture books imply that it's easier to be a six-year-old feminist than it is to be a feminist mother.

Indeed, many of the twenty-first century novels that either indirectly advocate gender equality or directly advocate feminist agendas demonstrate the same basic pattern. Eleanor's mother in *Eleanor & Park* is so enmeshed in her role as wife and mother that she assumes the role of victim rather than disentangle herself from the role(s) that have subsumed her. Deza Malone's mother lives for her family in *The Mighty Miss Malone*, as does Billie Joe's mother before she dies in *Out of the Dust*. The subsumed mother is a stock character, even in books that otherwise display feminist values.[8]

In *Waking Sleeping Beauty*, I referred to mother-daughter relationships in terms of those that are conflict-oriented, which I called "Freudian" (103–6) and those that are supportive, which I called "anti-Freudian" (106–11). Regrettably, in the twenty-first century, it is still easier to find mothers in Freudian conflict with their daughters than those who are supportive of their daughters without being subsumed by the role of motherhood. Walker would identify these Freudian relationships as a sustained "oppositional" divide (159).

For example, Katniss and her mother have a distrustful relationship in *The Hunger Games* (Mitchell 237). Only towards the end of the third novel does Katniss begin to trust her mother, who tends to be subsumed in depression, only to watch her mother "bur[y] her grief in work" after Prim's death (Collins, *Mockingjay* 351).[9] In another example, the mother of twins in Rainbow Rowell's *Fangirl* (2013) is absent from their lives, which is a source of conflict between Cath and her mother. The mother's career is the ostensible culprit in this conflict: the woman has become self-actualized because of her career; her commitment to her own personal needs has created a major conflict with her daughter. The same thing happens in Kate Di Camillo's *Flora & Ulysses* (2013), a novel I will explore at greater length in the next chapter. Flora's mother is a professional writer; the mother and daughter exist in conflict until the moment at which Phyllis is subsumed by the allure of performing motherhood. In Quintero's *Gabi: A Girl in Pieces* the protagonist lives in constant conflict with her mother, not least because her mother believes, "that all of our worth is between our legs. Once a man has access to that, then we are worth nothing, and there is no future for us" (146). Gabi suspects this belief may be why her mother is so incessantly unhappy—but they exist in sharp conflict with one another.

As it happens, yet another type of mother emerges in contemporary YA novels: the sexually active mother who is neither subsumed by motherhood nor oppositionally divided from her child. This is the sexually active mother who views her children narcissistically as a positive extension of herself. Cynthia Kadohata's *Outside Beauty* exemplifies this trend: Helen Kimura has, as the text puts it, "four daughters by four different men" (6). Shelby, the narrator, is the second daughter, who identifies her sisters as "extensions of myself" (6). The girls are also clearly extensions of their mother, who believes beauty is the "most important thing" in the universe (180). This is a woman subsumed not by motherhood but by the Beauty Myth. Helen entices men into relationships so that they can support her financially. Although she has married some of her daughters' fathers, she has not married them all. Her relationships have netted her $150,000 worth of jewelry and gems; when her relationships fall apart, her former lovers are usually more "angry about . . . how much money they had spent" than about losing Helen (10). She has trained her two older daughters, Shelby and Marilyn, to take charge of their younger sisters when they are out in public and their mother gets "distracted . . . by men" (7). All of Helen's maternal energy is focused on ensuring her daughters are beautiful, marriageable, and themselves maternal. Although she does not value their intellects as much as she values their looks, she also does not compete with her daughters. She is proud of how beautiful they are, and because she perceives them as extensions of her own beauty, she is not threatened by them.

Shelby decides to reject her mother's universe, the one in which beauty is the most important value. She tells her mother and her older sister that she herself lives in a "parallel universe where beauty doesn't matter" (190); both Helen and Marilyn deny that such a universe exists (180, 190). Shelby realizes that her love for her sisters and her mother is far more important to her than beauty is, and she also recognizes that her mother—and most of her mother's lovers—are very lonely people. Shelby thinks, "I would never be truly lonely as long as my sisters were okay. . . . If anything happened to any of my sisters, I would be unhappy. You were taking a chance by letting someone make you happy or sad. My mother had never wanted to take that chance, for whatever reason" (265). But although Shelby rejects her mother's values, she does not reject her mother. Shelby still loves and respects her mother, even though she does not want to live the type of hollow and lonely life she can perceive her mother living.

Never once in the novel does Helen Kimura engage in mean-spirited fights with her daughters. They are a team—and Helen has trained them to prefer using the term "we" to the term "I" (17). Their loyalty to their glamorous, sexually active mother and to each other is perhaps the only beautiful aspect of this book that is so focused on beauty. Eventually, after Helen loses some of her beauty in an automobile accident, Shelby later describes her as "still beautiful, just not perfect" (265). Helen may be punished with the fairy-tale justice in losing what she most values about herself; nevertheless, she is still attached to her daughters and embarks on a new sexual conquest at the end of the novel. She remains sexually active—and her daughters know it.

Children's literature critic Dorina K. Lazo Gilmore, writing about picture books, argues that "mothers from ethnic minority backgrounds . . . reject the mainstream 'good mother' model and prove more multidimensional, serving as a different mothering example for the future. These mothers are naturally emotional and resilient, creative, and in touch with their sexual identities" (97). Gilmore bases her argument in the reality that minority mothers must prepare their children for the racism they will experience, so the literary depiction of motherhood in multicultural literature cannot afford the luxury of the "mainstream myth" of the "good mother" (97). Strength, creativity, sexuality are realities for all mothers, but it is possible that novels that depict multiplicity, such as *Outside Beauty* and *Gabi: A Girl in Pieces*, are more honest about all that motherhood entails than those (usually white, usually middle-class) stories that still rely on the image of motherhood as the "angel in the house." Gilmore demonstrates that "the minority mother. . . . is resilient and confident, strong and creative, sexual and smart" in picture books (109). Certainly, Helen in *Outside Beauty* is more resilient than Gabi's mother in *Gabi: A Girl in Pieces*; nevertheless, both mothers are depicted as sexually active caretakers.

Michelle Boulous Walker theorizes that "the mother-daughter bond, with its rich pre-history of tensions, offers an alternative to the one-sided story of patriarchal relations," especially when the mother-daughter relationship allows for "an intense and often harrowing model of continuity in the face of a detached and autonomous self" (162). In *Outside Beauty*, Marilyn offers a "model of continuity" with her mother, and even though Shelby takes her own path, preferring to be a more "detached and autonomous self," Shelby's major sources of conflict in the narrative occur because of her mother's male lovers, not because of fighting with or emotionally separating from her mother or her sisters. While Helen Kimura's relationship with her daughters has its narcissistic elements, Kadohata rejects scripts that involve the mother either becoming subsumed by the child or defined by conflict with the child.

Sexually active and narcissistic mothers, however, can also be toxic, as is the case in Sonya Hartnett's *Butterfly* (2009). The protagonist, Plum Coyle, begins to make friends with the sophisticated young mother who lives next door, Maureen. About to turn fourteen years old, Plum is graceless and unhappy; she secretly steals mementos from her friends to prove to herself that she has power over them. When Maureen takes an interest in Plum, the teenager feels "welcome and pacified" (24). She thinks of her neighbor: "Maureen who understands her, who respects her opinions, never treats her like a baby, doesn't laugh off and forget what Plum says"—as her own family, including her mother, does (148). As it happens, Maureen is having an affair with Plum's beloved older brother, Justin, and she is only using Plum to gain power over him (not unlike the way Plum herself tries to gain power over her friends by collecting things that are precious to them). In Maureen and Plum's final confrontation, Plum thinks that what has connected them has been "mutual loneliness" (220).

After Justin breaks up with her, Maureen sits on the edge of her four-year-old son's bed and thinks, "aloneness presents itself like a rocking raft, something on which she can lie down in the knowledge that he is safe, and she is safe. . . . Maureen often thinks about this raft, which is sometimes a cradle, sometimes a desert, sometimes the moon or the sea, not in order to escape herself, but so she might be escaped from" (228). Throughout the novel, Maureen has draped her motherhood over her arm like a fashionable accessory; she appears to care more about the way her son makes her look than how he actually feels. Indeed, the boy is one way she makes herself sexually attractive to Justin and emotionally available to Plum—and he becomes the victim of her repressed rage (Miller 5). Sitting on her son's bed, this adult woman acknowledges the depths of her passions:

> There is something in Maureen that's too worrying to put into words, something formless like the unseen presence that brushes past in the ocean. Something unsettling, but also pleasant. It is this that's keeping her here in the room, this underlying wrath. It does not want quenching, peace is its enemy. It wants to rake and rake over the hot coals of the day, growing larger and angrier and more unconstrainable. (228)

Maureen cannot contain her passion, neither her sexual energy nor her rage. She thinks about how her love for Justin is so deep that it "*has not the option to die*" (230, italics in the original). Maureen then places her hand "like a white sea-creature across the boy's face," slowly suffocating him, and thinks about how good it would be to start over again with Justin, as if her son had never been born (232). Her delusions are tied to her passion, and thus she becomes the mother-as-narcissistic-murderer. The critic Rose Miller argues convincingly that Maureen is the narcissistic adult Plum could easily become, given the superficiality of the culture in which Plum lives, but it is noteworthy that Plum's mother—albeit an emotionally distant one—never abandons Plum and provides at least a contrast in being a mother who wants to be there for her child (Miller 7).

Brooklynn Lehner problematizes the figure of the murderous "bad mother" as a fetishized result of the social disavowal that surrounds motherhood. She cites at least three institutional structures that make possible the construction of the "bad mother": "the effect of social conditions, the impossibility of motherhood, and the impossibility of class unity" (35). In order to interpret a mother as "bad," we must be able to ignore factors of this sort and insist that, despite how impossible it is under these conditions for anyone to be a good mother, all mothers must nevertheless always be good (Lehner 30–35). Rose Miller brilliantly outlines the social conditions that produce a bad mother like Maureen in *Butterfly*: hers is a story of the suburban gothic, set in the sterility of 1970s Australian conformity in such a way that Maureen herself seems like a Stepford Wife: "Maureen mirrors her house, a smoky image of the ideology of suburbia" (Miller 5). Nevertheless, the horror of Maureen acting as a murderous mother seems to be a direct result of her sexuality—her passion—rather than the repressive conditions in which she lives. Lehner would argue that, as readers, we fixate on a necessary misreading of the mother (as "bad" rather than as subjected to unfair conditions) because it is easier to blame the mother figure for having been too sexual than it is for us to acknowledge the impossible idealisms and pressures heaped on the social construct of motherhood (37).

The relationship between sexuality and motherhood is a vexed one in YA literature. Teenagers who become mothers are pregnant because they have been sexually active—and "bad." Teenagers who get pregnant but have abortions are sexually active, "bad," *and* murderous. Adult mothers who are sexually active are, more often than not, depicted as women who are "bad" because they do not put their children before all other concerns. But mothers who are too sterile or frigid to be sexual (such as Katniss's mother) are also depicted as "bad." Perhaps motherhood is so fraught a construct in children's and YA literature precisely because of the fetishistic logic by which teenagers tend to want to deny knowledge of their own mothers' sexuality. In any event, few feminist YA novels have made a commitment to having strong and sexually active mothers who model sex positivity for their children.

## CONCLUSION

So what does a feminist novel about sexuality, orientation, and/or gender identity look like? Ideally, neither the character's gender identity nor orientation would be an obstacle to the character's happiness; the character would find an equal partner with whom to share sexual intimacy empowering to both characters. This plot, of course, is one that valorizes a specific discourse that lies at the heart of many YA novels: monogamy, which is privileged in

Francesca Lia Block's novels, for example, as both a social construct and a way to minimize the spread of sexually transmitted diseases. But if the goal of a romance is for the character to find committed love, then yes, monogamy will likely continue to be privileged in YA novels.

Ideally, feminist characters can explore and queer their sexualities and identities in supportive environments. Ideally, feminist characters are empowered by their orientation, gender identity, and experiences of sexuality. Ideally, feminist characters enjoy their sexuality but don't treat it as a mechanism for gaining power over others (nor are they punished for their sexuality or orientation or gender identity). But as it happens, children's and adolescent literature depends very heavily on narrative structures that involve conflict and resolution; as Bradford, *et al.*, observe: "adolescent fiction is pivotally preoccupied with the *formation* of subjectivity—that is, the development of notions of selfhood" (12, italics added). A character who is completely in touch with her embodiment, identity, and orientation, who comes from a loving and supportive family, who experiments with and is empowered by sexuality (without becoming diseased, pregnant, or dead), and who can queer how she thinks about herself and others in non-binaristic ways, might not offer the typical YA author enough conflict to sustain a plot. What would need to be resolved? The story might well succeed only as a utopia.

Thus, when I evaluate the relationship between feminism and YA novels, I tend to privilege endings of the books over the beginnings. Have the teen characters, especially the protagonist(s), ultimately been empowered? Have they been supported and accepted? Have they grappled with orientation and gender identity and sexuality in ways that privilege and respect how complex these issues are? Are cis gendered and trans males sensitive, aware, and able to share power in their love relationships, just as the cis and trans females do? Most important, are love and/or sexuality specific sources of empowerment for the characters? As these questions probably indicate, I think preadolescent and adolescent literature has improved on these issues in the twenty-first century but still has a way to go before gender identity, orientation, and sexuality are routinely treated in ways that complicate and debinarize the millennia-old patterns that continually reinterpellate patriarchal relationship structures.

## CHAPTER 6

# CARING, DISABILITY STUDIES, AND NARRATIVE STRUCTURE

In insisting on the intra-activity of the enacted and the represented, Karen Barad advances a philosophy that rejects the linguistic turn and its epistemological emphasis on the primacy of language. Barad's theories, along with the work of such material feminists as Nancy Tuana, Stacy Alaimo, and Susan Hekman, invite us to collapse the Saussurean dichotomy between signifier and signified, which is the very distinction from which much post-structural thinking emerged. Similarly, the concepts of *self* and *other* create another false binary that material feminists, especially ecofeminists, reject because they recognize how interrelated phenomena are. Just as the human subject cannot be defined without the context of the environment, human subjects are not formed solely in opposition to one another in a permanent state of othering. As Barad writes: "Existence is not an individual affair. Individuals do not preexist their interactions; rather, individuals emerge through and as part of their entangled intra-relating" (ix).

Alice Curry demonstrates how ecofeminism and feminist ethics of care are interrelated aspects of material feminism: "Analyses of systemic imbalances of power and privilege at the macrolevel delimit the potential for acknowledgement of gendered power-plays at a smaller scale—within the family, household and the body—and the crucial ways in which such microlevel systems of gender difference impact the formal sphere" (74).[1] Feminist ethics of care acknowledges the importance of multiplicity; feminist ethics of care also recognizes how individuals are shaped by forces that include (and are not limited to) the environment, the material, and interacting with other people. Feminist ethics of care argues, in particular, that identity formation occurs within a matrix of human interactions, including the necessary role of being the "cared-for," as Nel Noddings defines one crucial element in the relationship of care in her book *Caring*; the other crucial element is the "one-caring" (4). She asserts that "human caring and the memory of caring and being cared for . . . form the foundation of ethical response" (1). For Noddings, the word *care* connotes both nurturance and the idea of taking on a burden (9), and all care involves a certain level of what she calls "engrossment" (17). She distinguishes what she refers to as "natural caring," something akin to instinctual care, from "ethical caring," which is the learned art of caring when we don't necessarily want to but know we must: "Ethical caring, the relation in which we do meet the other morally, will be described as arising out of natural caring—that relation in which we respond as one-caring out of love or natural inclination" (4–5). She regards caring as a foundation of human social structures: "Taking *relations* as ontologically basic simply means that we recognize human encounter and affective response as a basic fact of human existence" (Noddings 4, italics in the original).

Both the "one-caring" and the "cared-for" participate in "contribut[ing] to the relation; my caring must be somehow completed in the other if the relation is to be described as caring" (Noddings 4). Although Noddings uses the term "feminine," she makes the point several times that men and women both participate in non-competitive models of caring that she labels as "feminine" (xvi, 2, 8). She also underscores that empathy requires understanding the material condition of the "cared-for": "When my caring is directed to living things, I must consider their natures, ways of life, needs, and desires. And, although I can never accomplish it entirely, I try to apprehend the reality of the other. . . . To be touched, to have aroused in me something that will disturb my own ethical reality, I must see the other's reality as a possibility for my own" (Noddings 14). In other words, empathy is required in an ethics of care, and that empathy is based, in part, on our perception of the cared-for's physical and cognitive world: "Apprehending the other's reality, feeling what he feels as nearly as possible, is the essential part of caring from the view of the one-caring" (Noddings 16).

In *Feminist Morality*, the feminist ethicist Virginia Held also addresses how several aspects of feminist ethics of care are based in the material:

> A feminist view of culture includes, though it may not be limited to, an understanding of the material forms of the production and development of culture, and of the material lives of those who make culture and are shaped by it. A feminist view of culture recognizes the expensiveness of the equipment and the vastness of the economic resources needed to exert influence through the media in contemporary society. It includes recognition of the embodied reality of human life, as women strive to assure the security of our persons and as mothers struggle to earn enough to feed and safeguard the fragile bodies of children. But it includes, as well,

> awareness of the everyday symbolism of such nonhierarchical activities
> as women together doing what needs to be done in caring cooperatively
> for children or publishing a newsletter. And it understands the cultural
> change involved in women and men working together as genuine equals
> in jobs of equal standing—and feeling comfortable doing so. (3)

While Held acknowledges both the importance of men and women working
together and the importance of cooperation (rather than competition), she
also acknowledges the materiality of the adult body, of cultural production,
of media, of security and safety, and of children as embodied beings.

Mary Jeanette Moran demonstrates an ethics of care in which female
characters in children's and YA novels can "unite the personal satisfaction
of intellectual achievement with the communal goal of caring for others,"
while still avoiding "the expectation that they must sacrifice themselves in
the service of their relationships" ("Use" 23). Moran acknowledges, however,
the potential essentialism that an ethics based on caring can hold, writing:

> Although many scholars have found that caring ethics enhance various
> strands of feminist moral thinking and political action, even those who
> embrace this idea tend to recognize the essentializing potential of revalu-
> ing care as an ethical practice—the same potential that inheres in any
> attempt to reclaim a quality that has been associated with an oppressed
> group. . . . To constitute a truly feminist approach to morality, ethics of
> care must consciously deconstruct such essentialist assumptions while
> also challenging the idea that caring acts are less morally and intellectu-
> ally advanced than those based on rationality. ("Use" 23)

Moran observes that those who dismiss ethics of care as sexist are missing
the point ("Mother" 182–87). Feminist ethics recognizes that ethical decisions require both the analytics of "separation" and the emotionality of
"connection": "once we have moved away from a paradigm that values separation above all else, care emerges as a legitimate goal of ethical decisions
in addition to, or perhaps even instead of justice" (Moran, "Mother" 183).

Moran bases her theory in part on Virginia Held's premise that "caring
should not replace thought" (Held 79), insisting that social justice will be
furthered "the more we can conceive of an ethic of care as the product of
choice, the farther we move away from a system that expects women—
and women only—to have the capacity to care for others and to enact that
care no matter what the cost to themselves" (Moran, "Use" 24). Moran then

analyzes the Judy Bolton series to show that non-reciprocal relationships are destructive, that the "one-caring" must also engage in self-care, and that intellectual activity—such as writing, in Judy's case—is the basis of a healthy ethics of care.

In subsequent articles, Moran relies on Madeleine L'Engle's novels to demonstrate how feminist ethics of care can also provide a model for the "relational self" ("Making" 76) and for a rethinking of maternal ethics of care ("Mother" 194–95). Moran refers to ethics of care as a "less oppositional dynamic" than those ethical models that posit the individual as an "independent, autonomous subject" ("Making" 76). She traces how the feminist ethics of care adopts a model by which "the relational self acknowledges its debt to others as well as its responsibility to them—a much less oppositional dynamic" than theories that define the self in opposition to the other ("Making" 76). As an example, Moran shows how Meg Murray and her brothers "defeat evil by recognizing the relational nature of themselves and other people" ("Making" 76); Meg, Charles Wallace, and their twin brothers, Sandy and Dennys, must recognize and accept difference in order to "resist othering those who seem different" and in order to "find ways to connect across that difference" ("Making" 79). Moreover, although Meg's pregnancy in *A Swiftly Tilting Planet* could have proven to be a "restrictive" or inhibiting force, Moran demonstrates that it is actually Charles Wallace "who must relinquish his sense of autonomous self-hood as he inhabits the bodies of people from various time periods," while it is a pregnant Meg who saves him ("Mother" 195). Moran argues that L'Engle depicts characters who "empathize with others . . . to disrupt the antagonistic self-other dynamic" ("Making" 87).[2]

It is the *relationality* of feminist ethics of care that leads me to consider it as a form of material feminism because relationships require a physical component—an element of human interaction that Noddings's emphasis on the physical aspects of caring as a primary parent-child relationship makes clear. Thus, analyzing the rhetoric of connectedness (as opposed to the rhetoric of competition and/or separation) and the rhetoric of caring can help us understand more about feminist agendas in twenty-first century preadolescent and adolescent literature. As Moran writes, "the development of care ethics constitutes feminist philosophy's most distinctive and significant contribution to the field" ("Mother" 182).

In this chapter, I will thus rely on Moran's theories about ethics of care in children's and adolescent literature to analyze rhetorics of caring and cooperation as they occur both in feminist intersections with Disability Studies and in feminist intersections with narrative theory and reader response theory. As enacted in the twenty-first century study of children's and adolescent literature, Disability Studies, feminist narrative theory, and feminist reader response theory all tend to emphasize material aspects of caring, relationality, and cooperation. To demonstrate how interactions between feminist ethics of care and Disability Studies work, I will analyze *Cinder* (2012), a novel by Marissa Meyer that problematizes disability in feminist terms. Narrative layering also helps authors interrogate levels of care, so the remaining novels I have selected for analysis in this chapter include embedded narratives—stories within the story—that help the protagonist grow in her ethics of care. Thus, to explore how feminist narrative theories of children's and adolescent literature are imbued with ethics of care, I will provide readings of Jennifer Donnelly's *Revolution* (2010) and Kate DiCamillo's *Flora & Ulysses* (2013). And in the final section, to interrogate feminist reader response theory in the YA novel as a function of ethics of care, I will investigate Linda Sue Park's *Project Mulberry* (2005). What all of the theorists and all of the novels I have included in this chapter share is a valuation of caring and relationality.

## DISABILITY STUDIES AND THE ETHICS OF CARING

Disability theorist Rosemarie Garland-Thompson asserts that one defining principle of feminist disability studies "is to augment the terms and confront the limits of how we understand human diversity, the materiality of the body, multiculturalism, and the social formations that interpret bodily differences," and she rightly insists that "integrating disability as a category of analysis and a system of representation deepens, expands, and challenges feminist theory" (15). Central to her argument is the implication that discrimination against the disabled requires that certain rhetorical structures remain in place. Garland-Thompson effectively establishes the connection between feminist ethics of care and feminist disability studies: both involve a belief system that privileges understanding, acceptance, and valuing other people. She also specifically cites feminist disability analysis as a type of material feminism in the way it can "illuminate . . . the investigation of the body: its materiality, its politics, its lived experiences, and its relation to subjectivity and identity" (22).

One theorist of English Education, Patricia A. Dunn, also makes clear the connection between Disability Studies and ethics of caring as a form of material feminism in *Disabling Characters: Representations of Disability in Young Adult Literature* when she writes: "Many barriers contributing to disability are material or attitudinal; either way, they are built. They are constructed. And whatever is constructed can be named, mitigated or removed" (1). Dunn's concern here is with both rhetorical and physical structures. With this succinct analysis, Dunn demonstrates the intersection of the linguistic turn and the material turn: as she notes, "barriers" are constructs that come in two forms: the "attitudinal" and the "material." Dunn argues in favor of a consciousness that recognizes the power of both the discursive and the material as constructs with which people with disabilities engage. She argues that "one of the main features of a disability rights perspective is that it turns the spotlight of critique on society" (19). Dunn's work thus invites us to critique rhetorics that stigmatize disability in YA literature.

Dunn analyzes Harriet McBryde Johnson's *Accidents of Nature* (2006), which focuses on Jean, a protagonist who has cerebral palsy, and on the caustic friend she meets at a summer camp, Sara, whose primary form of mobility comes from maneuvering a wheelchair. At first, Jean is uncertain how to respond to Sara's anger and cutting wit, but she begins to understand that at the heart of Sara's rebelliousness is an anger that "norms," as Sara calls them, perceive themselves as better than the campers (whom Sara defiantly refers to as "crips"). As Dunn sees it, the novel critiques ableist attitudes, including the following: "that 'just trying harder' will 'fix' anything, that people with disabilities are sexless beings, and that walking is the ultimate goal" (Dunn 20). Jean begins to question independence as a value, recognizing instead that being in a wheelchair may be the most efficient mode for her own mobility. Dunn believes that Jean has learned to value "interdependence" more than independence—and that is why I believe that the heart of Dunn's argument resides in an ethics of care, an ethics that insists that both the temporarily able-bodied (as Dunn refers to herself) and people with disabilities work together "to imagine—and help build—a different world view"—one that is more inclusive, accommodating, and ethical (Dunn 12).

Garland-Thompson argues that the "ability/disability system" has four facets: "first, it is a system for interpreting and disciplining bodily variations; second, it is a relationship between bodies and their environments; third, it is a set of practices that produce both the able-bodied and the disabled; fourth, it is a way of describing the inherent instability of the embodied self" (17)—and she cites Haraway, among others, to note that "current feminist work theorizes figures of hybridity and excess such as monsters, grotesques, and cyborgs to suggest their transgressive potential for a feminist politics" (Garland-Thompson 21).

Marissa Meyer's *Cinder* is a cyborg novel that interrogates disability in almost exactly these four terms.[3] Cinder lives in New Beijing, a city in a dystopic future, where "humans" are a distinct class with higher social status than hybrid-human "cyborgs," who, in turn, have higher status than completely mechanized androids. The "ability/disability" system set in place in this novel allows the human residents of New Beijing to "interpret" themselves against cyborgs—and when necessary—to discipline them. The system helps all three types of sentient beings establish themselves within an environment; humans and cyborgs and androids know who they are by defining themselves in opposition to others. Most important, Meyer uses the unstable body of the cyborg Cinder to demonstrate Garland-Thompson's concept of the "inherent instability of the embodied self" and to critique the social practice of defining ability in opposition to disability.

Cinder's multiplicity as a cyborg first became necessary because she was disfigured and partially dismembered in a horrific fire when she was a very young child. Although Gooderham argues that fantasy is a "metaphorical mode" by which we can explore complex social issues via fantastic worlds (173), Cinder is no metaphor for a teenager with a disability. She is a human being who has been physically disabled by this fire: she has a robotic hand and an artificial leg to replace those she lost in the fire; the foot on that leg does not always function properly. Cinder later discovers that her brain has been rewired, and she has four metal ribs and metal vertebrae. Medically, she is "36.28 not human" (82). All of her cyborg parts were designed to replace body parts lost in the fire—although the text makes clear that her reproductive organs are intact and fully functioning (116). (In other words, she is a disabled teenager who will be able to be both sexually active and to procreate.) Meyer here is connecting disability and ability; Cinder's cyborg abilities, including the wiring in her brain, are part of what give her almost super-human powers as a mechanic and as a technician: "Most of her customers couldn't fathom how a teenage girl could be the best mechanic in the city, and she never broadcast the reason for her talent. The fewer people who knew she was cyborg, the better" (10). Cinder hides her cyborg status because she regards it as a stigmatizing disability. When she looks in a mirror, she thinks, about herself: "Her mechanical parts were the only disturbing thing in Cinder's reflection" (190). Readers are meant to empathize with Cinder, and they quickly understand the book's message: that any society that would discriminate against cyborgs is in the wrong. Meyer uses the trope of the cyborg to communicate about the wrongness of discriminating against difference and/or disability. As Flanagan observes, although Cinder is "disabled," the novel is "indicative of the posthuman body's propensity for renewal and rejuvenation" (*Technology* 64).

Cinder's multiplicity becomes even more complicated when she learns that she actually belongs to another human race that has populated the moon for centuries: the Lunars. The news astounds her, and she uses technological rhetorics—especially rhetorics involving mechanics, mathematics, and discourse itself—to explain how her brain processes this information. For example, when the doctor tells her she is Lunar, "the word washed over Cinder as if he were speaking a different *language*. The *machine* in her brain kept ticking, ticking, like it was working through an impossible *equation*" (175, italics added). Lunars have special abilities that allow them to manipulate other people's "bioelectricity"; that is, Lunars have the ability to brainwash and manipulate people through mind control. The Lunars view as inferior any Lunar who is born cognitively incapable of submitting to bioelectricity; they call such Lunars "shells"—and shells are either killed at birth or segregated from others, isolated in orphanages where they serve as fodder for the government's biopolitical experimentations. In other words, shells are the Lunar equivalent of cyborgs: they are the disabled bodies against which "normal" people define themselves. When Cinder first learns she is a Lunar, she believes that she is a shell, but it turns out that her bioelectrical powers were disabled by the doctors who performed the surgeries that transformed her into a cyborg because they wanted her to live on Earth undetected as a Lunar. Cinder is thus not only a cyborg and a Lunar, but she is also an illegal alien—one with a great potential for mind control. She is horrified by the knowledge of how multiply-othered she is: "To be cyborg *and* Lunar? One was enough to make her a mutant, an outcast, but to be *both*? She shuddered" (178, italics in the original). Her self-perception shifts radically as she realizes that "everything she knew about herself, her childhood, her parents, was wrong. A made-up history. A made-up girl" (179). Cinder's body is, indeed, a hybrid "made-up" of both human tissue and technology.[4]

Cinder and her adopted family fear a Lunar plague that has begun to infect the Earth. Although she is actually a foster child in this family, the relationships are clearly those inspired by Cinderella motifs of stepmother and stepdaughter. The plague Cinder and her foster family face evokes all the dystopic fears common to an ecofeminist novel: this plague has the potential to annihilate much of the world's population, and it is being used as a biopolitical weapon by the Lunars against the Earthens. Cinder was adopted at the age of eleven by a man who died soon after from this plague, and early in the novel, one of her two foster sisters, Peony, dies of it, too. One of Meyer's most significant rewritings of the Cinderella tale-type is to depict Cinder in a loving and caring relationship with this sister, Peony. In her anger at Peony's death, Cinder's foster mother sells her cyborg foster daughter to the government for plague research—and the researchers discover that Cinder is immune to the plague. The chief researcher, Dr. Erland, immediately begins to suspect that she is immune not only because she is Lunar, but also because she might also be the moon's lost Princess Selene, who is believed to have been burned to death years earlier by her evil aunt, who now rules the moon as Queen Levana.

Cinder's relationship with Levana and with her foster mother provide the clichéd woman vs. woman competition of the ancient Cinderella tale. Meyer, however, focuses more on the ethics of care in this novel than she does on female competition. She depicts female vs. female competition as problematic. Cinder, for example, cares deeply for her stepsister Peony and tries to bring her a cure for the plague. When Peony dies in her arms, Cinder gives the antidote to a young boy she knows, caring for him despite the way his mother has discriminated against Cinder for being a cyborg. Cinder also serves as the "one-caring" for her feminized android, Iko, after the wicked stepmother dismantles her. Cinder finds a way to salvage the computer chip on which Iko's personality is stored and eventually restores her to life, albeit in an altered embodiment. Most of all, Cinder takes on the role of one-caring for the emperor's son, Prince Kai, on whom she has a crush, just like most of the girls (and Iko!) in New Beijing—and also because this is, after all, a dystopic YA novel, apparently it *must* include a heteronormative love story. Kai brings his personal android, Nainsi, to Cinder; Cinder is able to both repair the feminized android and make sure Kai knows that Queen Levana will kill him if he carries through on the marriage Levana has proposed with Kai as a diplomatic alliance. Cinder is one-caring for many.

Kai only considers accepting Levana's marriage proposal because of his emerging sense as the newly-crowned emperor: he must be the one-caring for the entire population of his empire. His father has only recently died of the plague, and Kai will do anything that it takes to rescue his people, including marrying Levana so that she will give him the Lunar antidote to this biopolitical crisis. Cinder tells Kai that she perceives him as a caring leader: "You're going to be one of those emperors that everyone loves and admires. . . . I mean it. Look how much you *care*, how hard you're trying," and she points out to him the relationality of his role: "It's not like you're alone. You have advisors and province reps and secretaries and treasurers"

(228, italics added). Kai reciprocates Cinder's feelings, and it is very clear that he wishes to build a relationship with her. He asks her to the festival ball several times and tells her he does not want to marry Levana because he "might have actual feelings for someone"—Cinder herself (295). He gifts her with a pair of elegant gloves, in case she chooses to join him at the ball, despite her rejections of his many offers to join him there.

Cinder's ability to perceive herself as one-caring for Kai is wrapped up in both issues of intra-activity and her perception of herself as racialized as a Lunar and disabled as a cyborg. At times she perceives her cyborg body parts as loathsome, but at others, she can recognize that their meaning has shifted for her because they have empowered her so greatly. Cinder's *becoming* shifts throughout the novel through the process of her own identity leading her to desire to merge with a new identity. For example, Cinder has first learned she is "36.28% cyborg" when she sees a holograph of her own body; her observation of that image shifts her perception of herself, demonstrating that the intra-action of matter and meaning are processual, ongoing, and affect agency. She thinks to herself, ". . . her chest. Her heart. Her brain. Her nervous system. What *hadn't* been tampered with?" (117). She thinks these thoughts only moments before Prince Kai sees the same holographic image—and then Cinder thinks about what she believes he is perceiving as he "recoil[s] from the image" (126). He is seeing "a girl. A machine. A freak" (126). Her sense of who she is shifts even more greatly when she realizes that she is Lunar, knowledge that she also believes she must protect Kai from. "He thought she was a mere mechanic, and he was, perhaps, willing to cross *that* social divide. But to be both cyborg and Lunar? To be hated and despised by every culture in the galaxy? He would understand in a moment why he needed to forget her" (292). Cinder believes that she must protect Kai from the knowledge that she is multiply-othered, thinking at one point, for example, "She hadn't considered that being noticed by the queen could put Kai in jeopardy too" (223).

After Cinder learns Levana will kill Prince Kai once they have married, Cinder delivers that news to Kai during the ball at great personal risk to herself. As Cinder reclaims her bioelectric powers of mind control at the ball, she thinks of it as her "awakening gift" (354) and is grateful that she can neither blush nor cry, so she thinks her "hateful cyborg body was good for one thing," at least, when she confronts Queen Levana (355). Cinder tells Levana she is not a shell, and against all odds, Cinder is able to overpower Queen Levana's highly potent bioelectricity. "Fire exploded in her spine, racing along her nerves and wires, slithering down the metal braces in her limbs. . . . It felt as if her body were trying to dispel all her cyborg parts—explosions and sparks and smoke tearing at her flesh" (363). But instead of expelling her mechanical enhancements, her body grows so overheated that she melts the gloves Kai has given her to wear to the ball. "She felt different. Strong. Powerful. On fire" (364). Her desire to defeat Levana has shifted her *becoming*. Moreover, she is defined in this moment of *becoming* by her embodiment—including her embodied cognition.

When Cinder then flees from Queen Levana's mind control and runs down the steps of the palace, her entire cyber-foot (rather than just her slipper) falls off. She is revealed to the prince for what she is: a Lunar, a cyborg, a human hybrid, and she stands in the mud on only one foot, disabled. She assumes he can never love her now that he knows these things about her, and she believes it would be even worse for him if he knew she were both "cyborg and Lunar" (292). Because of his own limitations, Kai cannot yet accept all of Cinder's differences. Valuing his role as one-caring for a nation more than his role of one-caring for *her*, Kai allows Queen Levana to capture Cinder and keep her as a prisoner. As Flanagan observes, this narrative "rewrite[s] the humanist [ending] of its [pretext]" in that the novel closes "with a form of narrative closure that defies the liberal humanist traditions" that demand stories about young women end in heteronormative marriage (*Technology* 65). The sequels, however, reveal that Kai is able to overcome his prejudices and become one-caring to both Cinder and his nation, just as Cinder will continue as one-caring for him and become one-caring for her nation: the moon. She never does stop caring for Kai, however, despite how her shifting perceptions of her body's *mattering* affect her *becoming* throughout the series. Ultimately, Cinder's life is changed by the intra-activity of matter and meaning, especially in the ways that she comes to value being a cyborg and Lunar, but despite all of the changes she undergoes, she never abandons her feminist ethics of care. By the end of the series, Cinder forsakes competitive models of female vs. female competition and advocates a cooperative ethics of care, based in relationality and respect for difference. Her perspective is the ethical stance that advocates for disability rights, especially given that by the end of the series she has helped those who stand in for the disabled in this novel—the cyborgs and the mutants—to gain equal rights on both Earth and Luna. Androids are, unfortunately exempted from this attention to equal rights, presumably because they are entirely mechanized.

## ETHICS OF CARING AND NARRATIVE STRUCTURE

Any number of feminist theorists in children's and adolescent literature have engaged with feminist issues of narrative structure. Not least among them are Lissa Paul in "Enigma Variations"; Holly Blackford in *The Myth of Persephone in Girls' Fantasy Literature*; Kerry Mallan in *Secrets, Lies, and Children's Fiction*; and Sara K. Day in *Reading Like a Girl*, all of whose theoretical models intersect in some way with the ethics of care. What unites the work of these critics with Mary Moran's and Patricia Dunn's work on adolescent literature then is these narrative theorists' underlying use of the rhetoric of care; that is, these feminists who explore children's and adolescent literature all make arguments that in some way foreground caring and relationality.

For example, as early as 1987, with her essay "Enigma Variations: What Feminist Theory Knows about Children's Literature," Lissa Paul published an influential essay about caring and the interrelationships between feminism and children's literature. In that essay, Paul explores three specific forms of entrapment children, especially girls, experience: physical, linguistic, and economic entrapment. She then writes about the literary strategies by which child characters (especially girls) escape entrapment: through a combination of deceit and trickeries and through imaginative energies that help them envision a way to transcend their situation. Significantly, Paul praises Margaret Mahy's *The Changeover* (1984) for the way the novel enacts a specifically feminist quest: the novel is about one girl's effort to rescue a family member from entrapment. Relying on Annis Pratt and archetypal theory, Paul identifies an important narrative pattern in children's literature. She says of the protagonist of *The Changeover*, her "quest is personal and domestic, she fights for someone she loves. She uses the tricksterish tactics of the weak and powerless. . . . The values in Mahy's book are connected with individual humanity rather than public glory" (198). Although Paul does not connect her own work to feminist ethics of care, the link is clearly there in Paul's privileging the importance of personal interrelationships and cooperative models of sharing power. Thus, as early as 1987, Paul began encouraging the entire field of children's and adolescent literature to value as feminist those fictions that demonstrate relational selves interconnecting in the roles of one-caring and cared-for.

Holly Blackford's *The Myth of Persephone in Girls' Fantasy Literature* also traces a significant narrative structure that has played a pivotal role in fantasy novels with female protagonists since at least the Victorian age.

Blackford observes that many Victorians were influenced by the myth of Persephone and Demeter; these Victorians shifted traditional attention from the role of the grieving mother to the role of the daughter separating from her mother (1). Although the ethics of care are not the specific object of Blackford's concern, the myth is nevertheless imbued with issues about the dynamics between Demeter, as the one-caring, and Persephone as the cared-for. Persephone's separation from her mother allows her to individuate and to become in turn the one-caring for Hades during the seasons of the year she spends in the Underworld. The myth, moreover, illustrates the distinction Noddings makes between "natural care"—or care that comes from the primacy of the parent-child relationship—and "ethical care," the care we learn to give others outside of that relationship—and sometimes, even when we do not necessarily wish to be the one-caring. Noddings identifies Demeter as the prototypical "one-caring" who demonstrates what natural caring is (40–41), while Persephone demonstrates the cared-for becoming the one-caring as an act of ethical caring in the way she takes care of Hades six months of a year, despite having been kidnapped and not originally wishing to be married to him.

In Blackford's analysis of the narrative structures influenced by this mythology, the pattern is a "perpetuation of a very old fertility ritual. Girls go to the underworlds so they can partially return and fuel the perpetuation of more Demeters" (4). The girl is initially tempted by some sort of toy—in Persephone's case, a narcissus—and in children's literature, the variants often include a "pair of Hades figures, one a mysterious adult and one a brooding though irresistible boy" (5). Blackford cites Barrie's *Peter Pan* (1911), Burnett's *Secret Garden* (1911), and Rowling's *Harry Potter and the Chamber of Secrets* (1998) as fantasy stories that follow this pattern. Sometimes, the girl must also face a "Black Demeter": a mother figure who is infuriated by her daughter's absence, as Mrs. Darling and Mrs. Weasley are (4). "These texts dwell on the psychological conditions of Persephone figures who invariably reach for 'the lovely toy' or narcissus because they are developmentally ready to do so, unfortunately without the slightest understanding of consequences. Chasms open to reveal dark lords who threaten to subsume the girls: the ancient paradox of Persephone's plight" (4). It should be noted that it is only through a compromise by which Persephone can balance her duties as one-caring and one cared-for that order and balance are restored to the seasons.

Lissa Paul praises the protagonist of *The Changeover* for becoming, in effect, both the one-caring to her little brother and Demeter to that boy's Persephone. Her little brother has been abducted by a Hades-like incubus who is sucking his soul; the protagonist must save her brother from this underworld. The narrative crisis in Jennifer Donnelly's intricately-plotted *Revolution* is also triggered by a little brother: Andi is consumed with grief because her younger brother, Truman, died when a crazed man grabbed him on the streets of New York and stepped in front of a speeding delivery van; Truman and the man are both killed. Two years later, Andi is slipping deeper and deeper into a grief-induced depression, and so is her mother. Both of them are mentally ill, and neither one is fully capable of filling the role of one-caring for the other, although Andi does manage to keep her mother fed. (This novel lends itself easily to a story about disability rights for those with mental illness. Andi and her mother are making their world work, despite their differences from societal norms.)

The novel unfolds on three different levels. The first level of narration is set in modern-day New York. Andi's memories of Truman make him the brooding boy who sets Andi on her quest to regain faith in the meaning of life; Andi's father is the Byronic dark figure who whisks her to another world where she does not want to be when he insists that his daughter will accompany him to Paris during Christmas break because he does not like how poorly she is doing in school He simultaneously has Andi's mother committed to a psychiatric hospital during their absence, so Andi is relieved of her duties as one-caring, albeit against her will (and her mother's). Hades has thus stolen Persephone and banished Demeter from his world.

Andi wears around her neck a small key that her brother gave their father long ago. Andi's father is a geneticist who told his family when the children were younger that he was looking for "the key to the universe. To life" (28). While he is still quite young, Truman finds an ornate and elegant antique key to give his father, earnestly believing that since his father now has the key, their father will spend more time with them and less time at the lab. After Andi's father wins the Nobel Prize and is even more absent from home, Truman steals the key back from him—and so after his death, Andi wears it on a ribbon around her neck as a way of remembering her sweet brother.

During the Christmas break two years after Truman's death, Andi is resentful about being dragged to Paris to work on her senior project. The project involves her studying a specific chord progression created by an eighteenth-century French musician, Malherbeau, whom Andi believes has influenced contemporary musicians from Leonard Bernstein to John Lee Hooker and from Miles Davis to Radiohead. Andi and her father are staying at the home of a historian who has summoned her father to Paris to examine the genetics of a heart believed to be that of the late Dauphin, who would have grown to become Louis XVII had he survived the French Revolution. Among the historian's collection of French Revolutionary artifacts is an elegant antique guitar, which Andi—a disciplined and trained guitarist—plays beautifully. But her brother's key serves as the "toy" that helps her open the story into the second plot level—one which also involves the dynamics of ethical caring.

Truman's key helps Andi open a false bottom in the antique guitar case, where she finds the diary of Alexandrine (or Alexe), a teenaged performer who eventually serves as a paid companion to the Dauphin, Louis-Charles. Andi reads Alexe's diary and learns that this girl, too, has great love for what becomes a little-brother figure to her, the young Dauphin. He is the brooding boy who draws Alexe into the role of Persephone in a secretive underworld of caring for the young prince once his parents are imprisoned. His uncle, the Duc d'Orléans, serves as the Byronic hero who pulls Alexe deeper into the conspiracy: he pays Alexe to be a spy because he wishes himself to become king. Orléans's heart is black, just like his eyes, which are compared to "midnight" multiple times (175, 180, 218, 317, 343). He beats Alexe almost senseless at one point for not following his orders, but she nevertheless continues to care for Louis-Charles as best she can. The mother for whom Alexe grieves, however, is not her own mother, but Marie-Antoinette, who plays the role of Demeter in this second level of the narrative. After Louis-Charles has been separated from his mother and imprisoned, Alexe tries to say good-bye to the queen: "But she did not hear me. She heard only him, her child, crying for days on end from his new room, on the floor beneath hers. She would not speak. She would not eat. She would only stare at the wall and rock" (327). Marie-Antoinette gives Alexe one of the King's ornate guitars—the same one Andi eventually plays—and begs Alexe to play for her son: "Play for him. Keep his poor heart merry. Then she sank to the floor, wrapped her arms around her knees, and keened" (327). Marie-Antoinette's ethics of care define who she is within this novel: her self-care suffers because she cannot serve as one-caring for her son, Louis-Charles.

Alexe knows that Louis-Charles loves not only music, but he also loves fireworks. She conspires to buy fireworks that will go off outside of his window in the fortress where he is held so that he will know someone loves him and is thinking of him. She is aware that her activities are illegal. The final entry in her journal describes how a guard has attacked her, fatally wounding her. Alexe runs down to the catacombs, where she writes her last journal entry and hides the diary in the guitar case's secret panel. The historian who is friends with Andi's father had bought the guitar years earlier, amazed that the guitar and its case had been preserved so well in a chamber of the catacombs that had been sealed by "layers of bones" (67). Because this twenty-first century historian knows how depressed Andi is, he is delighted that the guitar inspires her to play her music. But the eighteenth-century diary Andi finds inside the secret base of the guitar proves to be even more important to her healing because of the story she learns about another teenager who has cared for someone who is like a brother to her.

The novel moves into its third and most intricate narrative level in ways that are also motivated by issues of caring. Andi has made friends with a group of musicians, including one named Virgil, on whom she has a crush. He leads her into the catacombs where he wants her to play with his band—which includes a friend named Charon, so the intertextual references to Dante's *Divine Comedy* are clear. (The book is also divided into three parts: Hell, Purgatorio, and Paradise, with everything prior to Andi's time travel corresponding to Hell; her time travel to eighteenth-century France signifying Purgatory, and her return back home being Paradise.) At the catacombs party where Andi descends into the underworld of eighteenth-century Paris, she tells readers that she has taken way too many of her antidepressants, and so she should not have drunk the wine she drinks at the party—which proves to be not unlike ingesting forbidden pomegranate seeds. She knows that her antidepressants do not mix well with alcohol, and the combination leads her to be so befuddled that she concusses herself while running away from a police raid.

Andi returns to consciousness in Paris in 1795. The brooding and Byronic musician Malherbeau himself serves as the person who saves her. After several days in which Andi can't decide if she's having bad dreams or a "vision quest" or is in a coma, Andi comes to believe that she really is in eighteenth-century Paris and that it is Alexe's spirit who has drawn her back into the past so that Andi can finish the work that Alexe has left undone with her death. Andi takes over the role of one-caring for Louis-Charles: she plays guitar under his window and sets off fireworks to cheer him. Andi knows that he will die in six days, so she realizes that Alexe is asking her to be the one-caring for the Dauphin only temporarily. Nonetheless, Andi has herself entered another dark underworld. In the catacombs, she sees and smells stacks of headless, rotting corpses. She is attacked by lewd revelers when she plays her guitar to make money for herself and Malherbeau to eat. And she witnesses first-hand the brutality and corruption of the guillotine and Robespierre's era of the Revolution. The imagery surrounding Andi's sojourn to the past depicts Paris as dark, dank, rank, and sinister.

The Duc d'Orléans has told Alexe, "The world goes on, as stupid and brutal tomorrow as it was today" (344), but inspired by Alexe's guidance, Andi realizes that, although the world may go on being stupid and brutal, she does not need to be stupid and brutal herself.

> It goes on, this world, stupid and brutal.
> But I do not.
> *I* do not. (471, italics in the original)

Andi has despaired, and she has grieved—as Alexe has—that the Dauphin—a boy as young as Truman—"lies dying. Alone. In the dark. Insane. In pain. Afraid" (446). Andi wants "to scream. To howl. . . . to wake up the priest in the rectory. The people in their houses. The whole street. The city. I want to tell them about Louis-Charles and Truman. I want to tell them about the Revolution" (447). And then she utters the statement that is the core of this novel's ethics of care: "I want to make them see that nothing is worth the life of a child" (447). Andi has come to value her own life and is no longer suicidal, but she can also perceive that children are the group most vulnerable to the tumult that revolutions create. Malherbeau has told her that "the orphanages of Paris are full now. . . . [The orphans'] parents were guillotined, perhaps, or their fathers killed in the wars. Danton and Desmoulins, fathers both, tried to stop the worst of Robespierre's excesses. . . . But Robespierre, Saint-Just, Couthon—none of them had children, only ideas, and there is little mercy in ideas" (385). Malherbeau creates a false equivalence in equating ethics only with parenthood; people without children can be ethical (just as people with children are not always ethical). Donnelly's concern, however, seems to be more with child safety than with parenting, especially in her insistence that children are even more vulnerable to the ravages of war and corruption than adults.

Similarly, the crazed man Max who has pulled Truman to his death under a twenty-first century delivery truck in Brooklyn has done so in the name of "the Revolution"; Max, who suffers from schizophrenia, wants "to kill the rich and give the city back to the people" (368). But in Paris, Virgil teaches Andi that, although "life's all about the revolution," the real revolution is "the one inside" (471). Andi learns from many people in her descent into the underworld: Alexe and Malherbeau are particularly instrumental in teaching her how to be emotionally generous again. But her greatest source of comfort comes from Virgil, who himself is willing to serve as one-caring for Andi.

Not insignificantly, by the end of the novel, Andi is reunited with her mother, who checks herself out of the psychiatric ward and begins to heal emotionally from her "collapse" (370). Andi's worry for a long time has been that her mother's heart is not holding together. She reminds her father of Truman's favorite fairy-tale, "The Frog Prince," in which the prince is turned into a frog, and so his beloved servant's heart breaks and can only be held together by "three iron bands" (91). Andi's father bluntly tells Andi that it is not the daughter's place to try to heal her mother: "You think you can fix it. Fix her" (91), but Andi makes it clear that she wishes she "could make it heal" (157). And, indeed, Andi has written a song for her mother called "Iron Band":

> If I had coal and fire
> And metal fine and true
> I'd make an iron band
> An iron band for you
> I'd pick up all the pieces
> From where they fell that day
> Fit them back together
> And take the pain away (157)

At the end of the novel, Andi is still estranged from her Byronic father, but she is reunited with her grieving mother, who tells her daughter that "I was her iron band all along, didn't I know that?" (467). Demeter and Persephone are reunited, and in their reunion, they can serve as one-caring for each other and finally begin to heal from the grief of Truman's death: "Truman is part of the picture now, not the whole picture anymore. There's room for other things in my mother's life again. There's room for me. Which is nice. Because I need her now. I'm really busy" (467). Thus, on three narrative levels, *Revolution* demonstrates how Blackford's theory about the Demeter-Persephone cycle is still at work in twenty-first century feminist fantasy YA novels—and how intertwined that cycle is with feminist ethics of care.

Kerry Mallan demonstrates another strand of the relationship between caring and narrative structure in her book *Secrets, Lies and Children's Fiction*. Mallan identifies as the "key concepts" in her work "secrets, lies and deception" and she notes that these concepts are "linked by a notion of survival" (*Secrets* 11). In other words, like Lissa Paul, Mallan observes the fundamental relationship between deceit and survival; like Paul, Mallan also writes about interrelationships—because lies and secrets are fundamentally communal activities that involve how people interact with others in ways that are both self-protective and protective of others. Mallan identifies as a central metaphor in her work the veil as a "material object as well as a trope that evokes multiple interpretations. It hides a mystery and signifies a host of oppositional binaries: difference or recognition, exotic or traditional, freedom or oppression . . . the veil, as both a noun and a verb, can reveal or conceal truth" (*Secrets* 15–16). Mallan notes how diverse the purposes are of the veil for "striptease performers, dancers of the seven veils, *femme fatales*, nuns, Muslim women and girls"—and of course, the veil here is entirely gendered as a feminine material object (*Secrets* 15).

In a related essay, Mallan expressly links survival to gender issues, explaining that she is "interested in how literature for young people depicts survival as a complex activity that negotiates silence, subjugation and subjectivity"; she is also "interested in how secrets and femininity are theoretically linked with truth and concealment"; as she adds, she is seeking to identify the connections among "truth, femininity, fiction, and concealment" ("On Secrets" 36, 38). She argues that "texts that thematize secrecy work to withhold and disclose their secrets as part of the process of narrating and sequencing" ("On Secrets" 38). She perceives secrets as "fall[ing] between truth and lies, copying a kind of limbo"; in this economy, secrets do not serve as the active agents that lies are (*Secrets* 213). Marjane Satrapi's *Persepolis* memoirs serve as two of her most vivid examples: in order to survive, the narrator must learn how to lie effectively to other Muslims, to her parents, and even at times to herself. Her family keeps secrets from the neighbors; she keeps secrets from her family; and the government keeps secrets from its citizens. The literary goal of depicting all of this lying and all of these secrets, ironically enough, is to move the reader towards a greater understanding of truth and what it means to Marjane to survive and be true to herself.

Mallan observes that "truth is often regarded as something that can be discovered, revealed or hidden. This suggestion implies that truth has a tangible quality, a core essence, which is both problematic and impossible . . . truth is not monolithic, and . . . the connection between unveiling and the truth is a tenuous one" (*Secrets* 41). Mallan's project thus intersects with material feminism in at least two ways: in her observation that too often truth is falsely depicted in children's literature as having a "tangible quality" and also in her observation that the metaphors that surround truth-telling and deceit, such as veiling or cloaking, are indeed very material. Mallan's narrative theory invites us to "complicate" what she reveals to be the "simplistic idea of concealment as deception, and unveiling as truth, by taking into account how subjects transform themselves in their quest to find the truth" (*Secrets* 16).

The ethics of care is also at work here because deceiving and self-deceiving characters are relational beings whose deceptions involve interacting with others, often in relationships of care, and because self-knowledge (as opposed to self-deception) is linked to Noddings's principle that ethical caring requires the one-caring to also be self-caring. "Self-deception has the potential to destroy the ethical ideal. The one-caring, then, must look clearly and receptively on what is there-in-herself. This does not mean that she must spend a great deal of time self-indulgently 'getting to know' herself before reaching out to others. Rather, she reflects on what is inside as she relates to others" (Noddings 108). Few scholars of children's literature would portray any young person's efforts to know themselves as "self-indulgent," but when connected with Mallan's work on self-deception, this principle from feminist ethics of care has validity for children's literature. Mallan identifies a "paradox of self-deception" that occurs when we lie to ourselves because "the lies we tell ourselves may bring short-term feelings of psychological well-being, and enable us to adapt to a situation, but do not change anything in the long run" (*Secrets* 159).

Mallan also notes that survival often includes the liar protecting someone else, especially when the one-caring must lie to ensure the survival of the cared-for: "In these instances, the truth could harm; it could be dangerous or lethal to speak. In circumstances of oppression, unspeakable trauma or a dying loved one, truth is swept under the cover of deception" (*Secrets* 213). I thus combine the idea of the relational self as the one-caring with Mallan's narratological inquiry into secrets, lies, and truth to examine the way that they function as narrative structures. Kate DiCamillo's *Flora & Ulysses* provides a clear example of a girl protagonist who lies but who also finds strength in allowing herself to be both the one-caring and the cared-for—and to become in her process of growing more relational.

In *Flora & Ulysses*, Flora's next-door neighbor, Mrs. Tickham, accidently vacuums a squirrel up with her new "Ulysses" brand vacuum-cleaner; the traumatic brain injury the squirrel experiences gives him the powers of a super-hero, including super-strength, being able to fly, and being able to type poetry. Flora names him Ulysses, after the source of his super-powers, and decides to keep him. (The book is a playful parody of comic books; therefore, many of its conceits involve super-hero tropes, including the trope of a super-hero having a secret identity.) Flora lies to her mother about Ulysses, just as she lies to her mother about not reading comic books.

Flora also requires Mrs. Tickham to lie to Flora's mother about the squirrel's super-powers. Flora's mother is a novelist who does not think a squirrel has a place in their home, a situation that necessitates the narrative element of lying: Ulysses's only real chance at survival requires Flora to lie because otherwise, her mother will have Ulysses killed. Flora justifies herself by thinking about "doing impossible things, *surviving* when the odds were against her and her squirrel" (84, italics added). Flora's mother eventually forces Ulysses to type a lie to Flora, and Ulysses thinks, "It was as if typing the lies, the wrong words, had depleted him of all ability to act" (183). When Flora reads the lie that Ulysses has "chosen" to run away, she thinks, "it was the biggest lie that Flora had ever read in her life" (186). In this moment, she knows that her mother is attempting to kill Ulysses—and, of course, Flora's mother has lied to her daughter about not having murderous motives. When she confronts her mother about this lie, Flora says, "It's the truth" (149). Her mother does not disagree.

Another important form of deception in this novel, however, is self-deception. Flora deceives herself into believing that she is a cynic. Flora loves to read comic books and frequently thinks about the lessons she learns from them about controlling the "criminal element" because these stories reinforce her sense of herself as cynical (53). These stories also teach her that "the human heart is a deep, dark river with hidden currents" (91). Nevertheless, she is deceiving herself because it's clear that she *wants* super-heroes to exist: "Not that Flora really believed in superheroes. But still" (9). Flora's reasons for feeling cynical emerge from her relationship with her mother. Because Flora's mother is self-absorbed and seems to perform the role of mother in a perfunctory way that emerges more from a sense of obligation and more as a misguided perception of ethical-caring than natural-caring, Flora convinces herself that she, Flora, is a cynic who expects little from the universe and nothing from her mother. "Flora's mother had often accused Flora of being a 'natural-born cynic.' Flora suspected that this was true.... *Yep*, thought Flora, *that's me.*" (6, italics in the original); "'Do not hope; instead, observe' were words that Flora, as a cynic, had found useful in the extreme" (33). Flora does not allow herself to hope, to believe, or to have faith in much of anything because she is not able to participate as the object of her mother's caring, as the cared-for in their relationship. And Flora deceives herself into believing she is not affected by her mother's apathy.

Flora's cynicism and lack of faith in her mother is reinforced by a material object—an ugly shepherdess lamp that her mother has named "Mary Ann" (80). Flora is convinced that Mary Ann is the daughter her mother has always wanted. The lamp has been ordered from a store in London, and when it arrives, Flora's mother says, "Oh, she's so beautiful. Isn't she beautiful? I love her with all my heart" (30). Flora thinks to herself, "Flora's mother never called Flora beautiful. She never said that she loved *her* with all her heart. Luckily, Flora was a cynic and didn't care whether her mother loved her or not" (30, italics in the original). Flora, of course, is lying to herself. "Sometimes she felt as if Mary Ann knew something that she didn't know, that the little shepherdess was keeping some dark and terrible secret" (30); Mary Ann has "a look on her face that said, *I know something you don't know*" (141, italics in the original). Flora hates Mary Ann for having the kind of secret that Mallan argues is implicated in the relationship between gender and survival. Mary Ann—a lamp—is thus the material object onto which Flora can project her anger, her sense of injustice, and her own dishonesty.

Two secrets emerge, however, that affect Flora's relationality and allow her to begin to have faith and hope again. First, she learns that her father—who is divorced from her mother—misses Flora terribly and grieves that he no longer lives with his daughter. His neighbor, Dr. Meescham, delivers this news to Flora, telling her that her father is "capacious of heart" (129). Hearing these words brings Flora almost to tears, but she stops herself from crying by remembering "I'm a cynic!" Dr. Meescham tells the girl, "Bah. . . . Cynics are people who are afraid to believe" (129). Flora, however, believes her mother has been harboring another secret when she hears her mother say that it would make "my life much easier" if Flora would just move in with her father (150). Only once her mother truly despairs that Flora has run away does the woman reach out for her daughter, calling her "my baby," demonstrating the type of love that seems to feel to Flora like natural-caring (225). Flora cries tears of joy, and it is clear that the girl has learned to have faith in her mother and hope for herself again. She is now completely willing to believe in "the possibility of impossible things" (171).

If lies, self-deception, and secrets shape the narrative form of this novel, the search for truth resides in the novel's ethical core. For example, when Ulysses is confronted with his first word-processor, he knows he can type, but he does not know what to write. He thinks to himself:

> What could he do? . . .
> There was nothing he could do except to be himself, to try to make the letters on the keyboard speak the *truth* of his heart, to work to make them reveal the essence of the squirrel he was.
> But what was the *truth*? (62, italics added)

Flora has also learned from her comic books that people can learn truths from listening. She has read in a comic book, "All words at all times, true or false, whispered or shouted, are clues to the working of the human heart" (72). Additionally, Dr. Meescham talks about truth, telling Flora that in the village of her youth, "the words on the sign were often not the truth. And I ask you: What good does it do you to read the words of a lie?" (117). When Flora wants a typewriter so that Ulysses can tell them what Flora's mother has done, she says, "We need a typewriter so that we can get to the truth," but her friend, William Spiver, tells her, "The truth . . . is a slippery thing. I doubt that you will ever get to *The* Truth. You may get to a version of the truth. But *The* Truth? I doubt it very seriously" (221, italics in the original). One conceit driven by the novel's embedded narrative level—a pastiche of comic-books—is the false binary that implies all criminals are dishonest and non-criminals are honest. Flora must learn exactly what William Spiver asks her to recognize: that truth is complex—and it may even include the fact that dishonesty is sometimes the best strategy for survival in certain situations.

Symbolically, as the novel ends, Flora finds herself "wedged" so that she no longer slides off Dr. Meescham's horsehair sofa; she is wedged between her mother and Mrs. Tickham's great-nephew, William Spiver, who has become a good friend (226). William Spiver is another self-deceiving character; he believes he is blind, even though he is not. He insists that he is telling the truth: "I am telling the truth, my truth. I cannot see" (205). When Flora asks him to take his dark glasses off, he maintains that they've been glued to his head: Flora responds: "You lie," and he admits: "Yes. No. I don't. I do. I'm engaging in hyperbole" (81). His blindness is a metaphor for another type of cloaking or veiling; he cannot allow himself to see the truth that he is the person who has damaged his own relationship with his mother (by pushing his stepfather's truck into a pond). William Spiver is highly articulate and occasionally annoying; nevertheless, Flora grows to care about his opinion and to trust him. At one point, she is surprised to learn that she misses him (174) and even more surprised to realize that she trusts him (187). By the end of the novel, she is holding his hand, telling him not to "squeeze" her hand so tightly, but still herself holding on tightly to him (230).

William Spiver and Flora have a reciprocal relationship in that they take turns being the one-caring and the one cared-for. The same is true of Flora in her relationship with Ulysses. Initially, Flora is the one-caring for Ulysses as she nurses him back to health, but she thinks in relational terms:

"Together, she and Ulysses could change the world. Or something" (39). By the end of the novel, Ulysses is caring for her and loving her beyond measure.

Metaphors about relationality and the human heart occur when Flora takes time to place her hand on her father's chest so she can feel his capacious heart and when she and William Spiver later fall down together and she feels his beating heart. The fall breaks his glasses, so they no longer cloak him in the darkness that allows him to convince himself he is blind, so he, too, is freed from self-deception and now more free to love. Readers also learn that Flora's mother has been motivated to protect Flora from the "strangeness" of Ulysses because she does not want her daughter to "end up unloved and all alone in the world," as she fears herself to be (196). In the novel's most poignant image, Dr. Meescham explains that her late husband painted a giant squid devouring a lone boat on the ocean to symbolize the loneliness of the human heart: "The giant squid is the loneliest of all God's creatures. He can sometimes go for the whole of his life without seeing another of his kind," Dr. Meescham tells Flora—who proclaims the squid a "villain" (124). And Dr. Meescham answers her: "Yes, well, loneliness makes us do terrible things" (124)—such as perhaps valuing a lamp more than one's daughter or saying hurtful words to her or trying to kill her dearest friend, just because he's a squirrel. The wise woman Dr. Meescham articulates many of the novel's themes about love and relationality, including one about the reason to open a door hopefully: "Always . . . you opened the door because you could not stop hoping that on the other side of it would be the face of someone you loved" (219–20). In this novel, no relationship is perfect, especially not the fraught mother-daughter relationship, but relationality, nonetheless, is valued as the highest ethic. Paradoxically enough, as Mallan's work demonstrates happens often in children's literature, secrets and lies help lead the way to that truth. The metaphors about relationality in *Flora & Ulysses*, in particular, demonstrate how saturated children's and adolescent literature can be, as Mary Jeanette Moran has established, with the rhetoric of feminist caring.

## NARRATIVE INTIMACY AND ETHICS OF CARE

Sara K. Day defines "narrative intimacy" as a textual construct by which "many contemporary American novels for and about adolescent women actively encourage . . . blurring of boundaries" between reader and narrator "by constructing narrator-reader relationships that reflect, model, and reimagine intimate interpersonal relationships through the disclosure of information and the experience of the story as a space that the narrator invites the reader to share" (*Reading* 3). Day's work involves both narrative theory and reader-response theory. She is especially interested in the relationality between narrator and reader.

Day observes that the core element of narrative intimacy is "the creation of an emotional bond based on trust and disclosure" (*Reading* 4). When a text relies on narrative intimacy, the narrator generally expresses a desire to share intimate details with the reader, and that narrator generally is reluctant to share those feelings with characters in the book, which creates a narrative bond between narrator and reader based on trust, knowledge, vulnerability, and power (Day, *Reading* 4–6). Relying on the work of psychologists Carin Rubenstein and Philip Shaver, Day demonstrates how gendered American concepts of intimacy are because young women "have historically been raised to nurture and care"; female adolescence has historically been a time in which young women were indoctrinated to prepare for adult roles as wives and mothers (Day, *Reading* 9). Narrators and readers, of course, can never really "know" one another, so Day focuses on Seymour Chatman's distinction between the narrator and the real reader and the "logical gap" that Peter Lamarque perceives separating them (Day, *Reading* 18; Lamarque 114–15). Without directly saying so, Day implies that an interest in ethics is at the heart of her argument because in the relationship of narrative intimacy, "the reader may experience intimacy without risk, just as the narrator seeks to do"—which creates a paradox in suggesting "that the only 'safe' space within which to fully explore the possibilities of intimacy is the impossible narrator-reader relationship" (*Reading* 28).

Day analyzes a variety of novels, such as Sarah Dessen's *Keeping the Moon* (1999), Natasha Friend's *Perfect* (2004), and Lizabeth Zindel's *The Secret Rites of Social Butterflies* (2008), to demonstrate how narrators create intimacy; she concludes that these books reflect a *Zeitgeist* that intense adolescent friendships prepare teenaged girls for intimate adult relationships—but that they do so depicting friendship as a "double-edged sword" that can both empower and disempower a female (*Reading* 30). "The implicit relationships between narrator and reader in these novels . . . [model] a sort of 'ideal' interpersonal relationship—the narrator may reveal anything and everything to the reader without fear of being betrayed or facing unexpected consequences. The very boundary between fictional narrator and real reader . . . actively reinforces contradictory messages about intimacy" (*Reading* 63). At the core of Day's argument is an ethics that questions any relationship that *cannot* be reciprocal, given that the real reader cannot meaningfully affect a narrator. As Noddings argues, "Each of us is dependent upon the other in caring and moral relationships"; even when relationships are asymmetrical, ethical care includes at least some measure of mutuality and reciprocity (48). Since the narrator cultivating intimacy cannot engage in mutuality, Day is implying that such novels do not and cannot engage in a feminist ethics of care.

Linda Sue Park's *Project Mulberry* attempts to grapple with the ethics of narrative intimacy, albeit not altogether successfully. The narrator, Julia Song, directly addresses the reader to establish their relationship, saying things like, "I always want to thread a needle on my first try—it's a thing with me" (8–9) and telling the reader that, after a kid on the playground in elementary school yelled "Chinka-chinka-Chinamen" at her, "it made me feel really bad inside—so bad that I hated thinking about it" (29). Julia and her best friend, a white boy named Patrick, want to work together on a project for a club much like 4-H. Patrick thinks they should work on silkworms, but Julia doesn't know how to tell him that would be "too *Korean*"; she wants "a nice, normal, All-American, red-white-and-blue kind of project" (29, 30, italics in the original). As she tries to find ways to throw up obstacles for embarking on this project, she begins to think of herself as a "secret agent working undercover—thinking one thing while acting and saying the opposite" (53). Rather than confiding her doubts in Patrick, she confides in the reader, establishing what Day would identify as narrative intimacy—and as Mallan might note, Julia establishes that intimacy through secrecy and deceit. Eventually, however, Julia works through her doubts, and the friends do work on a silkworm project. Some level of reciprocity occurs between Patrick and Julia when she discovers late in the novel that he has also been keeping a secret from her: he has a "worm phobia" (157). Patrick, however, confides this to Julia, not directly to the reader.

Park complicates the issues of Julia and reciprocity with a series of interstitial dialogues between herself-as-the-author and Julia-as-a-character. The dialogues are written in the form of a play script, with Julia still narrating in the first person, underscoring the artifice at work here: Park may be the author, but readers are interacting with her as a character in her own novel. Moreover, Park is depicting the author and the character as having a reciprocal relationship. Julia frames the first section, telling readers, "I've got another story to tell you, and I'm going to do it here, between the chapters. Every story has another story inside, but you don't usually get to read the inside one. . . . if you're interested in learning how this book was written . . . you've come to the right place. . . . It's mostly conversations between me and the author, Ms. Park. We had a lot of discussions while she was writing" (12). The conceit is that Julia is both a muse to Ms. Park and has, as a character, taken on her own life.

> **Me:** Do you want my opinion? I am not happy with the way things are going here. I hate the project idea. . . .
>
> **Ms. Park:** Actually, no—I don't want your opinion. In fact, I have to admit, this is weird for me. I've written other books, and only *once* has a character ever talked to me. You talk to me *all the time*, and I'm finding that hard to get used to. . . .
>
> **Me:** Well, I don't care whether you want my opinion or not—you're getting it. *That was a terrible chapter.*
>
> **Ms. Park:** Would it help if I said I'm sorry you're having such a hard time. . . .
>
> **Me:** But it's *my* story. I should have a vote. (34–35, italics in the original)

In a nod towards Julia's ontological status, when Julia tells Ms. Park that she wants "plenty of time in the story to practice my embroidery," Ms. Park answers Julia as if she were a real child: "It's your responsibility. You have to organize your schedule, get your homework and your chores done, and not dilly-dally around. You should have plenty of time to do embroidery if you plan your time efficiently" (44). Park seems to be shifting Julia's ontological status precisely to demonstrate that their interactions have reciprocity, even though they don't.

Julia, however, purportedly believes Ms. Park has too much agency because she accuses her of being bossy, and Ms. Park explains, perhaps coyly, "Neither of us is the boss. The story is the boss. . . . It's kind of hard to explain. Sometimes the story takes over, and I end up writing things I didn't expect" (45). Park is playing into Romantic constructions of creativity with her insistence that the story "tells itself." Julia asks the fictionalized author, "even though I'm part of your imagination, I'm my own person, too?"—to which Ms. Park responds, "You think I'd deliberately invent a character who was as much trouble as you are?" (97). Park will grant herself the agency of making revisions—"I *like* finding my mistakes and trying to make the story better—changing little things here and there, taking some words out, choosing others" (127), but she maintains the fiction (one that could perhaps be considered deceitful) that Julia is somehow *real* throughout their dialogues.

Only through this false attempt to establish ontological reality can Park demonstrate any sense of reciprocity in their relationship. Ms. Park, too, has a secret, which Julia ostensibly discovers: like Patrick, the author also has a phobia of worms that she has kept hidden from Julia (and the reader).

When Julia doesn't like the way the story is going, she gives Ms. Park the silent treatment for a month. After Julia begins to talk again, she pleads with Ms. Park to end the story right there with an inderminant ending. Ms. Park then shifts the ontological source of reciprocity, telling Julia: "You have to care about the readers. Because without them, you won't exist. . . . You exist while the story is being written . . . but pretty soon the story will get made into a book. And after that, it's the readers who will bring you to life" (191). While it's true that readers "bring Julia to life" when they read, the relationship is still unidirectional. The author can change who Julia is and what she does, but readers cannot. This is what Day refers to as the "impossible narrator-reader relationship" (*Reading* 28).

Day's concept of narrative intimacy can be tied in this novel to a certain type of knowledge. Park asserts that readers who can deal with the complexity of how a book is written, especially one with multiple narrative levels, will have a cognitive advantage over readers who take everything in a book at face value:

> **Ms. Park:** I think it's good for people to know that there *is* an inside story, and to decide for themselves when it's important to know.
> **Me:** Isn't it always important?
> **Ms. Park:** That's a tough one. I think . . . in life, yes. The more you know about things, the more you can appreciate them. (219)

Through the dialogues between Julia and Ms. Park, Linda Sue Park—the (real) author—intensifies levels of narrative intimacy. Julia has confided in the reader, and Ms. Park confides in Julia, reinforcing what Day says about the interrelated nature of disclosure, vulnerability, trust, and intimacy (Day, *Reading* 62–63). Moreover, Park emphasizes the mutuality of the creative process: books require readers to complete the meaning. Nevertheless, despite Park's attempts to protest otherwise, the ethics of reciprocity can never be complete because no reader can make herself vulnerable to Julia by trusting her with the intimate details of the reader's own confidences. The relationality of a novel is a one-way street.

Day argues convincingly that "the complicated and often contradictory messages about intimacy that are propagated by contemporary culture shape representations and experiences of interpersonal relationships across genres, as well as across age, gender, race, and class" (*Reading* 202). Drawing from fiction, fanfiction, film, and self-help books, Day shows how teenaged girls "have become one of the groups most immediately influenced by the understanding that intimacy simultaneously depends upon disclosure and represents a threat *because of* disclosure" (*Reading* 202, italics in the original). When she talks about "disclosure," Day is referring to how girls make themselves vulnerable with their honesty. Day concludes:

> Ultimately, because the content of these novels so frequently presents warnings about disclosure within interpersonal relationships even as they construct narrator-reader relationships based upon the assumption that the narrator can confide all of her thoughts, feelings, and experiences to the reader, *narrative intimacy particularly acts as an embodiment of contradictory expectations regarding disclosure and discretion in young women's relationships.* (*Reading* 203, italics added)

Day's work is particularly useful in helping us examine one specific way that the ethics of feminist care can never be enacted successfully as a narrative device: the creation of narrative intimacy is always already a non-reciprocal relationship, even when the text creates the illusion of what Day might refer to as "trust" through disclosure.


## CONCLUSION

When I realized that many of the feminists I most respect are writing about preadolescent and adolescent literature in terms that evoke the ethics of care, I was at first surprised. While it seems logical to me that disabilities rights advocates would focus on care, it seemed more unusual to me that narrative theorists would. In retrospect, I should not have been surprised. Blackford, Mallan, and Day all focus demonstrably on narrative structures that involve relationality. The net effect surfaces the inherent feminist ethics of care at work among those adolescent literary theorists interested in rhetorics of disability, narrative structures, and reader response theory.

After conducting this study, I have become convinced that material feminism and ethics of care are mutually implicated in shaping twenty-first century children's and adolescent literature as both a genre and as a field of study. Moreover, the relationship between material feminism and ethics of care is reflected in Nel Nodding's belief that "it is the recognition of and longing for relatedness that form the foundation of our ethic" (6). Material feminists also insist on the primacy of relationality. For example, in Chapter 1, I wrote about how Barad's theories of intra-activity depend on the ongoing relational processes by which meaning is defined. In Chapter 2, I demonstrated that Critical Race Theorists acknowledge how forms of oppression are multiplied by the relationality between people, especially as they are classified into groups in terms of social identities. Chapter 3 shows how ecofeminists' insistence on the interactionisms among people, living beings, and the environment involve fundamentally ethical acts. I personally find speculative fictions that emphasize individuality over the relationality of the collective to be unethical, as I observe in my critique of neoliberal interpretations of embodiment in Chapter 4. Chapter 5 examines sexuality, orientation, and gender identity as a function of embodiment and human relationships. And this chapter has openly linked relationality to narrative constructions that include novels implicated in Disability Studies and the work of various narrative theorists in children's literature.

My own inquiry into material feminism began with a study of how cognitive theory can better help us understand children's literature, but I soon realized cognition is an embodied activity, which lead me to learn more about materiality. Cognition, embodiment, the environment, and the meaning-systems by which we interact with each other and our world are interdependent, processual, and cannot be understood in terms of discourse alone. In *Flora & Ulysses,* William Spiver makes an observation that evokes the most basic principles of material feminism when he says, "My mother says that . . . I live in my head as opposed to living in the world. But I ask you: Don't we all live in our heads? Where else could we possibly exist? Our brains *are* the universe" (191, italics in the original). Without our embodied cognition and without perception, we would have no relationship to the universe. The squirrel Ulysses underscores the necessary connection between relationality and the universe in the final poem of the novel. Ulysses has learned from William Spiver that the universe is always expanding, so he writes his love to Flora with the words: "You are the ever-expanding universe to me" (233). The universe in this novel is defined in terms of relationality and care.

The legacy of various feminisms in twenty-first century preadolescent and adolescent literature includes the emphasis on relationality, especially those that resonate among embodiment, the environment, technology, and discourse. Novels that acknowledge intra-activity, interrelationships, and the importance of social support systems may well empower cis and trans girls far better than the twentieth-century feminist model that emphasized discourse as the primary form of empowerment. Discourse is, indeed, an imperative element of empowerment, but it is not the only factor involved in creating feminist literature for the young. Novelists and critics alike in the twenty-first century have become increasingly aware of our relationship to what DiCamillo calls the "ever-expanding universe" (*Flora & Ulysses* 233). The result is a lens through which we can view the many ways empowerment enacts itself in relational interactions with other people, with the environment, with technology, with our own embodiment and embodied cognition, and with our social identities. All of these concepts promise to complicate and expand how gender issues manifest themselves in children's and adolescent literature for many years to come.

# NOTES

## INTRODUCTION

1. According to Foucault, if language is "the concrete link between representation and reflection," then discourse is the "sequence of verbal signs," the movement between linguistic signs, that makes meaning possible (*Order* 83).

2. Johnson avoids the use of capital letters throughout her text. I have taken the liberty of capitalizing characters' proper names; all other quotations reflect Johnson's stylistic usage.

## CHAPTER 1

1. For more on the destabilization of gender binaries in *The Hunger Games*, see Meghann Meeusen's "Hungering for the Middle Ground" (45–61).

2. The following definitions inform my work: *female YA novels* are those that are written for and marketed to adolescent girls; *adolescent literature* is the broader category of novels that appeal to adolescents (Trites, *Disturbing* 7). *Children's literature* is an umbrella term that can encompass all texts that children and adolescents experience. *Adolescence* is the discursive description of those biophysical changes that occur during the "second decade of life" (Lerner and Steinberg x). *Material feminism* is "about the materiality of the body as itself an active, sometimes recalcitrant force. Women *have* bodies. . . . We need a way to talk about these bodies and the materiality they inhabit" (Alaimo and Hekman 4, italics in the original).

3. See, for example, Derrida (49) or Foucault, *History of Sexuality* (17–36).

4. Scholars such as Caroline New dispute Butler's self-assessment, however, arguing that, although Butler "admits the materiality of the body" in *Bodies That Matter*, her sense of the materiality of the body "remains formless, its only causal powers emanating from its discursive construction" (67).

5. Historically, philosophers have complicated how perception works when they question whether it 1) occurs through a process of "sense datum" in which material objects trigger cognitive processes or 2) whether qualia—"qualities of experience" within the brain itself—trigger perception or 3) whether perception is "a form of intentionality or mental representation," that is, a mental state of "aboutness": "An intentional mental state is normally understood . . . as one which is about, or represents, something in the world" (Crane). In this latter definition of perception, perception itself *is* the process of representation (Crane). Laurence BonJour categorizes the first of these theories of perception in terms of *indirect realism*, as the belief that external objects trigger cognitive knowledge of experience; the second as *phenomenalism*, in which experience itself defines the external object, and the third as *direct realism*, "the view that physical objects are after all themselves directly or immediately perceived in a way that allegedly avoids the need for any sort of justificatory inference from sensory experience to

physical reality" (BonJour). Readers of this volume do not need to determine for themselves which of these views of perception is the correct one; rather, readers need to understand that all definitions of perception acknowledge it as a cognitive activity. As Barad would have it, the knower interacts with the known to produce knowledge (Barad, *Meeting* 46–47).

6. Barad further defines *mattering*: "The world is an ongoing open process of mattering through which 'mattering' itself acquires meaning and form in the realization of different agential possibilities. Temporality and spatiality emerge in this processual historicity. Relations of exteriority, connectivity, and exclusion are reconfigured. The changing topologies of the world entail an ongoing reworking of the very nature of dynamics. In summary, the universe is agential intra-activity in its becoming" ("Posthuman" 135).

7. See, for example, Coats and Trites (148–53).

8. Michael Hames-García defines identities as "emerg[ing] from, on the one hand, the mutual constitution of various social group memberships and, on the other hand, the mutual constitution of individuals and their environment, including social structures" (5). According to Braidotti, "The definition of a person's identity takes place in between nature-technology, male-female, black-white, in the spaces that flow and connect in between. We live in permanent processes of transition, hybridization and nomadization" (*Metamorphoses* 2).

9. Further explanations about feminist epistemology include the following: "Feminist epistemologists, in holding gender as a central analytic category, investigate the influence of conceptions and norms of gender and gender-specific interests and experiences on accepted accounts of knowing and on the actual production of knowledge" (Tuana, "Introduction" 2); "a feminist epistemological project involves finding resistant logics, engaging to transform them to liberatory ends, and in particular resisting the logic/language-games of hegemonic medical, legal, and scientific models" (Crary 134).

10. "Power produces knowledge (and not simply by encouraging it because it serves power or by applying it because it is useful); . . . power and knowledge directly imply one another; . . . there is no power relation without the correlative constitution of a field of knowledge, nor any knowledge that does not presuppose and constitute at the same time power relations" (*Discipline* 27).

11. Barclay writes, "To Braidotti, identities are always in process and 'becoming is a question of undoing the structures of domination by careful, patient revisitations, re-adjustments, micro-changes' [*Metamorphoses* 116]" (147). It is my hope herein to complicate Barclay's convincing but nascent use of material feminism in the interpretation of *Beauty Queens*.

12. For more on hailing, see Althusser (116–18).

13. Bray is playing the same sly game that Mark Twain plays in his "Notice" to readers about ignoring "motive" and "moral" in *Adventures of Huckleberry Finn* (5).

14. In Barclay's reading, the most important form of indeterminacy the text raises is gender indeterminacy (144–45); *Beauty Queens*, however, also interrogates the indeterminacy of being itself.

15. Influenced by Elizabeth Grosz's reading of Darwin, Barclay argues: "This understanding of transforming, evolving, mutating identities and futures renders a transforming Petra powerful" (146); moreover, "Petra also seems to give 'permission' to the other girls to cross boundaries" (147).

## CHAPTER 3

1. One hundred forty-five African-American churches were burned between 1995 and 1996; the vast majority of these were located in southern states (Lavelle).

2. I am grateful to Michelle H. Martin for pointing out that Lanesha has been born in a caul—a traditional symbol thought to prevent sailors from drowning. Lanesha's caul functions both as symbolic foreshadowing and as an element of the novel's magic realism. She is special—and can see ghosts—in part because she was born with a caul and in part because she is mixed-race and thus automatically inhabits two social spheres (Martin, 9 June 2015).

## CHAPTER 4

1. Joseph W. Campbell argues that the central concern of dystopia is its insistence that readers "look critically at the power structures that envelop and seek to construct them" (2); Jack Zipes notes that dystopia "often includes a critique of 'postmodern,' advanced technological society gone awry" ("Foreword" xi). Hintz and Ostry assert that dystopia depicts cultures "in which the ideals for improvement have gone tragically amok" (3), and they note that dystopia can be a "powerful metaphor for adolescence," since the genre depicts growing pains, rebellion against authority, and the thirst for increased "power and control" (9). Kay Sambell distinguishes differences between dystopias written for adults and adolescents: "Whereas the 'adult' dystopia's didactic impact relies on the absolute, unswerving nature of its dire warning, the expression of moral meaning in the children's dystopia is often characterized by degrees of hesitation, oscillation, and ambiguity" (164). Clare Bradford and her colleagues describe dystopias as "stories that contrast the failure of the main character with the unstoppable advance of society towards totalitarianism," and they note how in adolescent literature, "a dystopian world literature must strive for a form of subjective agency" (Bradford, *et al.*, 28, 29). These critics thus acknowledge, in one way or another, the ideological function of dystopian literature, especially when its intended audience is children or adolescents.

2. *The Hunger Games* hit the *New York Times* Best Sellers List on 28 September 2008, exactly one week after the financial events that triggered the Great Recession ("Bestseller"); *Publisher's Weekly* identified a "shift in attention" away from dystopias toward the paranormal and thrillers in March, 2012 (Sellers and Roback).

3. For a Foucauldian reading of the panopticon and its work in The Hunger Games trilogy, see Wezner (148–57); for an intricate complication of Foucault that relies on de Certeau to problematize strategies by which citizens of Panem resist the panopticon, see Connors, "I Was" (85–102).

4. See also Curry (53–54).

5. The muttations' mind/body split and their soullessness was first suggested to me by Sean P. Connors (email 26 September 2015).

6. For a reading that applies Elizabeth Grosz's theories to *The Hunger Games* in order to demonstrate how this series "explores social anxiety about breaking down binaries between [the] constructed and embodied self by melding the cognitive with culturally constructed forces," see Meghann Meeusen's "Hungering for Middle Ground" (45).

7. Veronica Roth's *Divergent* is a derivative dystopia that my feminist teenaged daughter refers to as "Hogwarts meets *The Hunger Games*." It is worth no more than a footnote here for me to point out that the novel also includes a love triangle, the inscription of identity in the form of tattoos on the skin, a neoliberal female hero pulling herself up by her own bootstraps so she can save a failed society made corrupt by the patriarchy—and who describes her own mind/body split when she acts as if she's capable of acting without thinking (58, 306, 459). The novel even includes an extreme case of a mind/body split when the intellectual Erudite rely on biopleasure to transform the Dauntless into unthinking bodies who fight for the Erudite. Indeed, the whole premise of the bioengineered society is based on the concept of biopleasure and neoliberal economic desire.

8. First suggested to me by Sean P. Connors (email 26 September 2015).

9. Or, as Benjamin Kunkel puts it, "You called this tendency globalization if you liked it, neoliberalism if you didn't." Bradford, *et al.*, define globalization in this way: "Global capitalism has engendered world-wide divisions of labour along with a reduced and politically weakened workforce, a growing number of people in need of social services, and an information-based system that relies on systems of control, surveillance, and exploitation" (36); they also observe that "one of the problems associated with the widespread use of the term 'globalisation' ... as an all-encompassing signifier [includes that the term] evades charges of ethno-euro-anglocentrism" (41).

10. Moreover, as Alice Curry notes, neoliberalism situates care and caring, such as the care of a parent for a child, as "a privatised activity," which negatively affects perceptions about the role of social responsibility in children's care-taking (94).

11. For more on the female adolescent's quest to save loved ones, see Lissa Paul, "Enigma Variations" (198).

12. Stephanie Guerra interrogates "biotechnical methods" for demonstrating oppression and exploitation in YA novels, noting that "if the method of oppression is familiar, it is because biotechnology has allowed the creation and identification of a new minority group; if the victims are familiar, they are being oppressed through new biotechnical methods or denial of access to necessary biotechnology" (290). *Orleans* falls into the former of these two categories in that the biotechnology behind Delta Fever and blood hunting creates two new minority groups: both the ABs, who are the blood type most prone to the fever and thus the most blood-thirsty for constant transfusions, and the people they hunt, the O positives and O negatives, who thus become a different type of exploited and oppressed group distinct from the ABs.

## CHAPTER 5

1. For more on queer theory in children's and adolescent literature, see Coats (*Looking Glasses* 110); Latham ("Melinda's" 371–73); Abate and Kidd (1–11).

2. *The Servant* was named a 2014 Amelia Bloomer novel for its feminist content by the ALA (Nataraj). Rowell self-identifies as a feminist; as she Tweeted on 12 November 2014: "You're sick of 'feminism'? Well, I'm sick of making less money, feeling like my body is community property, and feeling shamed & harassed" (Rowell, "Tweet Message").

3. According to Horne, "most definitions of the emerging category 'New Adult' focus on the age of a book's characters"—approximately 18–25 years-old ("New Adult").

4. See also Thomas Crisp (333–48) and Corrine M. Wickens (148–64).

5. For more on the relationship between sexuality and death, see Trites (*Disturbing* 122–23) and Kathryn James' excellent *Death, Gender, and Sexuality*.

6. Crucial to Abate's work is her important observation about how racialized the tomboy character was: the tomboy's first manifestation was invested in racial purity: "From their inception, tomboys demonstrated how unruly female behavior that was formerly seen as socially 'bad' could be racially good" (xii). Abate finds it paradoxical that "this code of conduct that was intended to strengthen white women, and by extension, the white race was consistently yoked with various forms of nonwhiteness" (xii). She observes that "both syllables of the term 'tomboy' evoke common racial pejoratives" (xii).

7. Luna's tripping off to an apparently happy ending, made easy by the availability of money and one supportive trans sponsor evokes Michelle Abate's comments about Carlton Mellick's reappropriation of such terms as "fag" and "faggiest." Abate writes: "While these lines may be meant to encourage and even empower, they ring hollow. Contrary to Mellick's remarks, combating heterosexism, ending homophobia, and allowing non-gender normative individuals to gain acceptance requires a great deal more than merely thinking 'really happy thoughts'" ("Faggiest" 410). Luna, too, seems to be thinking "really happy thoughts," which I'm sure every reader of this book wishes were enough to make life end happily ever after for all trans teenagers.

8. As Fraustino and Coats observe, "the figure of the mother carries an enormous amount of freight across the emotional and intellectual life of a child. In her materiality as well as in the child's imaginary landscape, she plays many roles and bears many burdens" (3).

9. See also Alice Curry for a description of Katniss's shifting perception of her mother's emotions (74–75).

## CHAPTER 6

1. Curry further connects ecofeminism to caring in the following passage: "If a feminist ethic is to re-envisage environmental thinking—most ecofeminists argue—it must do so by establishing conceptual frameworks that are non-oppressive and nonsubordinating and effectively freed from oppositional thinking. Such an ethical re-visioning must confront the cultural normativity of a masculinised public sphere and a feminised private sphere, and interrogate the political context and conditions of knowledge production" (74). Curry also critiques "the tendency in justice ethics towards the abstract and universal" (76).

2. According to Moran, "Maternal care ethics has enormous potential to help us rethink cultural attitudes toward mothers and to reshape relationships and institutions according to a model of care" ("Mother" 195).

3. Victoria Flanagan asserts that "one of the most notable achievements of *Cinder*" involves "the way in which [its] consideration of the 'othered' posthuman body advocates a variety of ethical social transformations" (*Technology* 60).

4. Flanagan links Cinder's cyborg foot to the ancient Chinese practice of manipulating the structure of the human body through foot-binding (*Technology* 62–63).

# WORKS CITED

## PRIMARY SOURCES

Alcott, Louisa May. *Little Men*. Boston: Roberts, 1871.

Anderson, M. T. *Feed*. New York: Candlewick, 2002.

Barrie, J. M. *Peter Pan*. 1911. New York: Puffin, 1986.

Blume, Judy. *Deenie*. 1973. New York: Delacorte, 2003.

Bowen, Sarina. *The Shameless Hour*. Rennie Road, 2015.

Bray, Libba. *Beauty Queens*. New York: Scholastic, 2011.

Burgess, Melvin. *Doing It*. London: Anderson, 2003.

Burnett, Frances Hodgson. *The Secret Garden*. New York: Stokes, 1911.

Cabot, Meg. *Ready or Not: An All-American Girl Novel*. New York: HarperTeen, 2005.

Card, Orson Scott. *Ender's Game*. New York: Tor, 1985.

Cleary, Beverly. *Fifteen*. New York: Morrow, 1956.

Collins, Suzanne. *Catching Fire*. New York: Scholastic, 2009.

———. *Hunger Games*. New York: Scholastic, 2008.

———. *Mockingjay*. New York: Scholastic, 2010.

Cullinan, Heidi. *Love Lessons*. Samhain, 2014.

Curtis, Christopher Paul. *The Mighty Miss Malone*. New York: Random, 2012.

Danforth, Emily M. *The Miseducation of Cameron Post*. New York: HarperCollins, 2012.

Dessen, Sarah. *Keeping the Moon*. New York: Speak, 1999.

DiCamillo, Kate. *Flora & Ulysses*. Illus. K. G. Campbell. Berryville, VA: Candlewick, 2013.

Donnelly, Jennifer. *Revolution*. 2010. New York: Ember, 2011.

Erdrich, Louise. *The Birchbark House*. New York: Hyperion, 1999.

Friend, Natasha. *Perfect*. Minneapolis: Milkweed, 2004.

Goobie, Beth. *Hello, Groin*. Victoria, BC: Orca, 2006.

Gregorio, I. W. *None of the Above*. New York: HarperCollins, 2015.

Hartinger, Brent. *Geography Club*. New York: HarperCollins, 2003.

Hartnett, Sonya. *Butterfly*. Berryville, VA: Candlewick, 2009.

Hesse, Karen. *Out of the Dust*. New York: Scholastic, 1997.

*High School Musical*. Dir. Kenny Ortega. First Street Pictures, 2006.

Hoose, Phillip. *Claudette Colvin: Twice Toward Justice*. 2009. New York: Square Fish, 2011.

Johnson, Angela. *a cool moonlight*. New York: Dial, 2003.

———. *Heaven*. New York: Simon & Schuster, 1998.

Johnson, Harriet McBryde. *Accidents of Nature*. New York: Holt, 2006.

Kadohata, Cynthia. *Outside Beauty*. New York: Atheneum, 2008.

Kaslik, Ibi. *Skinny*. New York: Walker, 2004.

Kelly, Jacqueline. *The Evolution of Calpurnia Tate*. 2009. New York: Holt, 2011.

Kennedy, Elle. *The Score*. CreateSpace, 2016.

L'Engle, Madeleine. *A Swiftly Tilting Planet*. New York: Farrar, 1978.

Lowry, Lois. *The Giver*. New York: Houghton, 1993.

Mahy, Margaret. *The Changeover*. New York: Scholastic, 1984.

———. *Kaitangata Twitch*. Crows Nest, NSW: Allen, 2005.

McCormick, Patricia. *Cut*. New York: Scholastic, 2000.

Mellick, Carlton. *The Faggiest Vampire*. Portland, OR: Spunk Goblin Press, 2009.

Meyer, Marissa. *Cinder*. New York: Square Fish, 2012.

———. *Cress*. New York: Macmillan, 2014.

———. *Scarlet*. New York: Macmillan, 2013.

———. *Winter*. New York: Macmillan, 2015.

Myracle, Lauren. *Infinite Moment of Us*. New York: Abrams, 2013.

Naylor, Phyllis Reynolds. *Dangerously Alice*. New York: Simon Pulse, 2006.

Nicholson, William. *Rich and Mad*. London: Egmont, 2010.

Oates, Joyce Carol. *Foxfire*. New York: Dutton, 1993.

Park, Linda Sue. *Project Mulberry*. New York: Random, 2005.

Peters, Julie Anne. *Luna: A Novel*. New York: Little, 2004.

Price, Lissa. *Enders*. New York: Random, 2014.

———. *Starters*. New York: Random, 2012.

Quintero, Isabel. *Gabi: A Girl in Pieces*. El Paso: Cinco Puntos, 2014.

Rex, Adam. *The True Meaning of Smekday*. New York: Hyperion, 2007.

Rhodes, Jewell Parker. *Ninth Ward*. New York: Little, 2010.

Roth, Veronica. *Divergent*. New York: Katherine Tegen Books, 2011.

Rowell, Rainbow. *Eleanor & Park*. New York: St. Martin's, 2013.

———. *Fangirl*. New York: St. Martin's 2013.

Rowling, J. K. *Harry Potter and the Chamber of Secrets*. 1998. New York: Scholastic, 1999.

Ryan, Pam Muñoz. *Becoming Naomi León*. 2004. New York: Scholastic, 2007.

Satrapi, Marjane. *The Complete Persepolis*. 2000, 2003. New York: Pantheon. 2007.

Sharafeddine, Fatima. *The Servant*. 2010. Toronto: Anansi, 2013.

Smith, Sherri L. *Flygirl*. 2008. New York: Penguin, 2010.

———. *Orleans*. New York: Penguin, 2013.

Snadowsky, Daria. *Anatomy of a Boyfriend*. New York: Delacorte, 2007.

Steptoe, John L. *Stevie*. New York: Scholastic, 1970.

Taylor, Laini. *Daughter of Smoke and Bone*. New York: Little, 2011.

———. *Days of Blood and Starlight*. New York: Little, 2012.

———. *Dreams of Gods and Monsters*. New York: Little, 2014.

Travers, P. L. *Mary Poppins*. New York: Harcourt, 1934.

Twain, Mark. *Adventures of Huckleberry Finn*. 1885. Berkeley: University of California Press, 2003.

Westerfeld, Scott. *Uglies*. New York: Simon & Schuster, 2005.

Wittlinger, Ellen. *Parrotfish*. New York: Simon & Schuster, 2007.

Woodson, Jacqueline. *Brown Girl Dreaming.* New York: Penguin, 2014.

York, Robin. *Deeper.* New York: Bantam, 2014.

Zindel, Lizabeth. *The Secret Rites of Social Butterflies.* New York: Viking, 2008.

## SECONDARY SOURCES

Abate, Michelle Ann. "'A Grand Amount of Fagginess': *The Faggiest Vampire*, Bizarro Fiction for Children, and the Dehomosexualization of LGBTQ Terminology." *Children's Literature Association Quarterly* 37.4 (2012): 400–414.

———. *Tomboys: A Literary and Cultural History.* Philadelphia: Temple University Press, 2008.

Abate, Michelle Ann, and Kenneth Kidd, eds. *Over the Rainbow: Queer Children's and Young Adult Literature.* Ann Arbor: University of Michigan Press, 2011.

Alaimo, Stacy, and Susan Hekman, eds. "Introduction: Emerging Models of Materiality in Feminist Theory." *Material Feminisms.* Bloomington: Indiana University Press, 2008. 1–19.

Alcoff, Linda. "Cultural Feminism Versus Post-Structuralism: The Identity Crisis in Feminist Theory." *Signs* 13.3 (1988): 405–36.

Althusser, Louis. *Lenin and Philosophy and Other Essays.* Trans. Ben Brewster. New York: Monthly Review Press, 2001.

Altmann, Anna E. "Welding Brass Tits on the Armor: An Examination of the Quest Metaphor in Robin McKinley's *The Hero and the Crown*." *Children's Literature in Education* 23.3 (1992): 143–56.

Anderson, Elizabeth. "Feminist Epistemology: An Interpretation and a Defense." *Feminist Theory: A Philosophical Anthology.* Eds. Ann E. Cudd and Robin O. Andreason. Oxford: Basil Blackwell, 2005. 188–209.

Asch, Adrienne. "Critical Race Theory, Feminism, and Disability: Reflections on Social Justice and Personal Identity." *Ohio State Law Journal* 62.1 (2001): 1–17. moritzlaw.osu.edu/students/groups/oslj/files/2012/03/62.1.asch_.pdf. Accessed 26 September 2016.

Attebery, Brian. *Decoding Gender in Science Fiction.* New York: Routledge, 2002.

Barad, Karen. "Getting Real: Technoscientific Practices and the Materialization of Reality." *Differences: A Journal of Feminist Cultural Studies* 10.2 (1998): 87–128.

———. *Meeting the Universe Halfway.* Durham, NC: Duke University Press, 2007.

———. "Posthumanist Performativity: Toward an Understanding of How Matter Comes to Matter." *Material Feminisms.* Eds. Stacy Alaimo and Susan Hekman. Bloomington: Indiana University Press, 2008. 120–54.

Barclay, Bridgitte. "'Perpetually Waving to an Unseen Crowd': Satire and Process in *Beauty Queens.*" *Female Rebellion in Young Adult Dystopian Fiction.* Eds. Sara K. Day, Miranda A. Green-Barteet, and Amy L. Montz. Burlington, VT: Ashgate, 2014. 141–53.

Basu, Balaka, Katherine R. Broad, and Carrie Hintz. *Contemporary Dystopian Fiction for Young Adults.* New York: Routledge, 2013.

Beauvoir, Simone de. *The Second Sex.* 1949. Trans. Constance Borde and Sheila Malovany-Chevallier. New York: Vintage, 2011.

Belsey, Catherine. "Constructing the Subject: Deconstructing the Text." *Feminist Criticism and Social Change.* Eds. Judith Newton and Deborah Rosenfelt. London: Methuen, 1985. 45–64.

"Best Sellers List: Children's Books." *New York Times*, 28 September 2008. nytimes
.com/2008/09/28/books/bestseller/bestchildren.html. Accessed 8 July 2015.

Beyoncé. Video Music Awards, 25 August 2014. vimeo.com/127017886. Accessed 26 September 2016.

Bishop, Rudine Sims. *Free Within Ourselves: The Development of African American Children's Literature*. Westport, CT: Greenwood, 2007.

Blackford, Holly. *The Myth of Persephone in Girls' Fantasy Literature*. New York: Routledge, 2012.

BonJour, Laurence. "Epistemological Problems of Perception." *Stanford Encyclopedia of Philosophy*, 2007. plato.stanford.edu/entries/perception-episprob/. Accessed 4 November 2015.

Bordo, Susan. *Unbearable Weight: Feminism, Western Culture, and the Body*. Berkeley: University of California Press, 1993.

Bottigheimer, Ruth. *Grimms' Bad Girls and Bold Boys: The Moral and Social Vision of the Tales*. New Haven: Yale University Press, 1987.

Bradford, Clare, Kerry Mallan, John Stephens, and Robyn McCallum. *New World Orders in Contemporary Children's Literature: Utopian Transformations*. New York: Palgrave, 2008.

Braidotti, Rosi. *Metamorphoses: Towards a Materialist Theory of Becoming*. Malden, MA: Polity, 2002.

Breu, Christopher. *Insistence of the Material: Literature in the Age of Biopolitics*. Minneapolis: University of Minnesota Press, 2014.

Burfoot, Annette. "Human Remains: Identity Politics in the Face of Biotechnology." *Cultural Critique* 53 (2003): 47–71.

Butler, Judith. *Bodies That Matter: On the Discursive Limits of "Sex."* New York: Routledge, 1993.

———. *Gender Trouble: Feminism and the Subversion of Identity*. 1990. New York: Routledge, 2007.

Cadden, Mike. *Ursula K. Le Guin Beyond Genre: Fiction for Children and Adults*. New York: Routledge, 2005.

Cadogan, Mary, and Patricia Craig. *You're a Brick, Angela! A New Look at Girls' Fiction from 1839–1975*. London: Gollancz, 1976.

Campbell, Joseph W. The Order and the Other: Power and Subjectivity in Young Adult Literature. Dissertation, Illinois State University, 2010.

Cart, Michael, and Christine A. Jenkins. *The Heart Has Its Reasons: Young Adult Literature with Gay/Lesbian/Queer Content, 1969–2004*. Lanham, MD: Scarecrow, 2006.

Castle, Terry. *The Apparitional Lesbian: Female Homosexuality and Modern Culture*. New York: Columbia University Press, 1993.

Chatman, Seymour. *Story and Discourse: Narrative Structure in Fiction and Film*. Ithaca: Cornell University Press, 1978.

Childs, Ann M. M. "The Incompatibility of Female Friendships and Rebellion." *Female Rebellions in Young Adult Dystopian Fiction*. Eds. Sara K. Day, Miranda G. Green-Barteet, and Amy L. Montz. Burlington, VT: Ashgate, 2014. 187–201.

Christian, Barbara. *Black Women Novelists: The Development of a Tradition, 1892–1976*. Westport, CT: Greenwood, 1980.

Clark, Beverly Lyon. "Domesticating the School Story, Regendering a Genre: Alcott's *Little Men.*" *New Literary History* 26.2 (1995): 323–42.

———. *Regendering the School Story: Sassy Sissies and Tattling Tomboys*. New York: Routledge, 1996.

Clark, Beverly Lyon, and Margaret Higonnet. *Girls, Boys, Books, Toys: Gender in Children's Literature and Culture*. Baltimore: Johns Hopkins University Press, 1999.

Coats, Karen. "Identity." *Keywords for Children's Literature*. Eds. Philip Nel and Lissa Paul. New York: New York University Press, 2011. 109–12.

———. "Keepin' It Plural: Children's Study in the Academy." *Children's Literature Association Quarterly* 26.3 (2001): 140–50.

———. *Looking Glasses and Neverlands: Lacan, Desire, and Subjectivity in Children's Literature*. Iowa City: University of Iowa Press, 2004.

Coats, Karen, and Roberta Seelinger Trites. "Where Culture Meets Biology." *Canadian Children's Literature* 32.1 (2006): 148–53.

Collins, Patricia Hill. *Black Feminist Thought: Knowledge, Consciousness, and the Politics of Empowerment*, 2nd ed. New York: Routledge: 2000.

Connors, Sean P. Email to the author. 26 September 2015.

———. "'I Try to Remember Who I Am and Who I Am Not': The Subjugation of Nature and Women in *The Hunger Games.*" *The Politics of Panem*. Ed. Sean P. Connors. Amsterdam: Sense, 2014. 137–56.

———. "'I Was Watching You, Mockingjay': Surveillance, Tactics, and the Limits of Panopticism." *The Politics of Panem*. Ed. Sean P. Connors. Amsterdam: Sense, 2014. 85–102.

Connors, Sean P., ed. *The Politics of Panem: Challenging Genres*. Amsterdam, Sense, 2014.

Crane, Tim. "The Problem of Perception." *Stanford Encyclopedia of Philosophy*, 2011. plato.stanford.edu/entries/perception-problem/#2.1. Accessed 4 November 2015.

Crary, Alice. "What Do Feminists Want in an Epistemology?" *Feminist Interpretations of Ludwig Wittgenstein*. Eds. Naomi Scheman and Peg O'Connor. University Park: Pennsylvania State University Press, 2002. 97–118.

Creed, Barbara. "Lesbian Bodies: Tribades, Tomboys, and Tarts." *Sexy Bodies: The Strange Carnalities of Feminism*. Eds. Elizabeth Grosz and Elspeth Probyn. London: Routledge, 1995. 86–103.

Crenshaw, Kimberlé Williams. "Demarginalizing the Intersection of Race and Sex: A Black Feminist Critique of Antidiscrimination Doctrine, Feminist Theory, and Antiracist Politics." *University of Chicago Legal Forum* 140 (1989): 139–67.

Crisp, Thomas. "From Romance to Magical Realism: Limits and Possibilities in Gay Adolescent Fiction." *Children's Literature in Education* 40.4 (2009): 333–48.

Crum, Maddie. "Eight Books That Don't Sugarcoat Teen Sexuality." *The Huffington Post*, 6 November 2015. huffingtonpost.com/entry/teen-sexuality-in-books_us_563a7321e4b0411d306f6cd5. Accessed 16 February 2016.

Curry, Alice. *Environmental Crisis in Young Adult Fiction: A Poetics of Earth*. New York: Palgrave, 2013.

Daly, Mary. *Gyn/Ecology: The Metaethics of Radical Feminism*. 1978. Boston: Beacon, 1990.

Day, Sara K. "Docile Bodies, Dangerous Bodies: Sexual Awakening and Social Resistance in Young Adult Dystopian Novels." *Female Rebellions in Young Adult Dystopian Fiction*.

Eds. Sara K. Day, Miranda G. Green-Barteet, and Amy L. Montz. Burlington, VT: Ashgate, 2014. 75–92.

———. *Reading Like a Girl: Narrative Intimacy in Contemporary American Young Adult
Literature.* Jackson: University Press of Mississippi, 2013.

Day, Sara K., Miranda G. Green-Barteet, and Amy L. Montz, eds. *Female Rebellions in Young
Adult Dystopian Fiction.* Burlington, VT: Ashgate, 2014.

De Lauretis, Teresa. "Queer Theory: Lesbian and Gay Sexualities." *Differences: A Journal of
Feminist Cultural Studies* 3.2 (1991): iii–xviii.

Deleuze, Gilles. *Essays Critical and Clinical.* "Literature and Life." 1993. Trans. Daniel W.
Smith and Michael Greco. New York: Verso, 1998. 1–6.

Derrida, Jacques. *Spurs.* Trans. Barbara Harlow. 1978. Chicago: University of Chicago Press,
1979.

Diamond, Irene, and Gloria Feman Orenstein, eds. *Reweaving the World: The Emergence of
Ecofeminism.* San Francisco: Sierra Club, 1990.

Duder, Tessa. *Margaret Mahy: A Writer's Life.* Auckland, NZ: HarperCollins, 2005.

Dunn, George A., and Nicolas Michaud, eds. *The Hunger Games and Philosophy: A Critique
of Pure Treason.* Hoboken, NJ: Wiley, 2012.

Dunn, Patricia A. *Disabling Characters: Representations of Disability in Young Adult Literature.* New York: Lang, 2015.

Faludi, Susan. *Backlash: The Undeclared War against American Women.* 1991. New York:
Random, 2006.

Fitzpatrick, Shaun Byron. "Thirteen Banned YA Novels We Love." *B&N Reads,* 23 September
2014. barnesandnoble.com/blog/13-banned-ya-novels-we-love/. Accessed 17 February
2016.

Flanagan, Victoria. *Into the Closet: Cross-Dressing and the Gendered Body in Children's
Literature and Film.* New York: Routledge, 2008.

———. *Technology and Identity in Young Adult Fiction: The Posthuman Subject.* New York:
Palgrave, 2014.

Foster, Shirley, and Judy Simons. *What Katy Read: Feminist Re-Readings of "Classic" Stories
for Girls, 1850–1920.* New York: Palgrave, 1995.

Foucault, Michel. *The Birth of Biopolitics.* Ed. Michel Senellart. Trans. Graham Burchell.
2004. New York: Palgrave, 2008.

———. *Discipline and Punish: The Birth of the Prison,* 2nd ed. 1975. Trans. Alan Sheridan.
New York: Vintage, 1995.

———. *History of Sexuality, Volume 1: An Introduction.* 1976. Trans. Robert Hurley. New York:
Vintage, 1990.

———. *The Order of Things: An Archaeology of the Human Sciences.* 1966. New York: Random House, 1970.

Fraustino, Lisa Rowe, and Karen Coats, eds. Introduction. *Mothers in Children's and Young
Adult Literature: From the Eighteenth Century to Postfeminism.* Jackson: University Press
of Mississippi, 2016. 3–24.

Fritz, Sonya Sawyer. "Girl Power and Girl Activism in the Fiction of Suzanne Collins, Scott
Westerfeld, and Moira Young." *Female Rebellion in Young Adult Dystopian Fiction.* Eds.

Sara K. Day, Miranda G. Green-Barteet, and Amy L. Montz. Burlington, VT: Ashgate, 2014. 17–31.

Gaard, Greta, and Patrick D. Murphy, eds. Introduction. *Ecofeminist Literary Criticism: Theory, Interpretation, Pedagogy.* Champaign: University of Illinois Press, 1998. 1–14.

Garland-Thompson, Rosemarie. "Integrating Disability, Transforming Feminist Theory." *Feminist Disability Studies.* Ed. Kim Q. Hall. Bloomington: Indiana University Press, 2011. 13–47.

Gentry, Amy. "'The Roy G. Biv of Female Experience': A Big Ol' Interview with Libba Bray." *The Oeditrix,* 24 September 2012. theoeditrix.com/2012/09/24/the-roy-g-biv-of-female -experience-a-big-ol-interview-with-libba-bray/. Accessed 11 June 2015.

Gilbert, Sandra, and Susan Gubar. *The Madwoman in the Attic: The Woman Writer and the Nineteenth-Century Literary Imagination.* New Haven: Yale University Press, 1979.

Gill, Rosalind, and Christina Scharff, eds. Introduction. *New Femininities: Postfeminism, Neoliberalism, and Subjectivity.* New York: Palgrave, 2011. 1–20.

Gilmore, Dorina K. Lazo. "Minority Mama: Rejecting the Mainstream Mothering Model." *Mothers in Children's and Young Adult Literature.* Eds. Lisa Rowe Fraustino and Karen Coats. Jackson: University Press of Mississippi, 2016. 96–112.

Gooderham, David. "Children's Fantasy Literature: Toward an Anatomy." *Children's Literature in Education* 26.3 (1995): 171–83.

Goodreads. "Young Adult Fiction with Sex." goodreads.com/list/show/7002.Young_Adult _Fiction_With_Sex. Accessed 16 February 2016.

Gray, Lauren. Class discussion. Illinois State Univ. 8 October 2014.

Greenstone, Daniel. "The Sow in the House: The Unfulfilled Promises of Feminism in Ian Falconer's Olivia Books." *Children's Literature Association Quarterly* 33.1 (2008): 26–40.

Grosz, Elizabeth. *Volatile Bodies: Toward a Corporeal Feminism.* Bloomington, IN: Indiana University Press, 1994.

Gubar, Marah. *Artful Dodgers: Reconceiving the Golden Age of Children's Literature.* New York: Oxford University Press, 2009.

Guerra, Stephanie. "Colonizing Bodies: Corporate Power and Biotechnology in Young Adult Science Fiction." *Children's Literature in Education* 40.4 (2009): 275–95.

Halperin, David M. "The Normalization of Queer Theory." *Journal of Homosexuality* 45.2–4 (2003): 339–43.

Hames-García, Michael. *Identity Complex: Making the Case for Multiplicity.* Minneapolis: University of Minnesota Press, 2011.

Haraway, Donna J. "A Cyborg Manifesto: Science, Technology, and Socialist-Feminism in the Late Twentieth Century." *Simians, Cyborgs, and Women: The Reinvention of Nature.* New York: Routledge, 1991. 149–81.

———. "Otherworldly Conversations, Terran Topics, Local Terms." *Material Feminisms.* Eds. Stacy Alaimo and Susan Hekman. Bloomington: Indiana University Press, 2008. 157–87.

Hartsock, Nancy. "The Feminist Standpoint: Developing the Ground for a Specifically Feminist Historical Materialism." *The Feminist Standpoint Theory Reader.* Ed. Sandra Harding. New York: Routledge, 2004. 35–54.

Harvey, David A. *A Brief History of Neoliberalism.* New York: Oxford University Press, 2005.

Hayles, N. Katherine. *How We Became Posthuman: Virtual Bodies in Cybernetics, Literature, and Informatics*. Chicago: University of Chicago Press, 1999.

Heilbrun, Carolyn. *Toward a Recognition of Androgyny*. New York: Knopf, 1973.

Hekman, Susan. "Constructing the Ballast: An Ontology for Feminism." *Material Feminism*. Eds. Stacy Alaimo and Susan Hekman. Bloomington: Indiana University Press, 2008. 85–119.

———. *Private Selves, Public Identities: Reconsidering Identity Politics*. University Park: Pennsylvania State University Press, 2004.

Held, Virginia. *Feminist Morality: Transforming Culture, Society, and Politics*: Chicago: University of Chicago Press, 1993.

Hennessey, Claire. "'First Times' in YA." Bad Things Happening to Good Sentences. bad thingshappentogoodsentences.tumblr.com/post/74165349614/first-times-in-ya. Accessed 16 February 2016.

Hilton, Mary, and Maria Nikolajeva. *Contemporary Adolescent Literature and Culture: The Emergent Adult*. Burlington, VT: Ashgate, 2012.

Hintz, Carrie, and Ostry, Elaine, eds. *Utopian and Dystopian Writing for Children and Young Adults*. New York: Routledge, 2003.

hooks, bell. *Ain't I a Woman: Black Women and Feminism*. Boston: South End Press, 1981.

Horne, Jackie. "New Adult or Young Adult? Katie McGarry's *Dare You To* and Gayle Forman's *Just One Day*." Romance Novels for Feminists, 2 July 2013. romancenovelsforfemi nists.blogspot.com/2013/07/new-adult-or-young-adult-katie-mcgarrys.html. Accessed 28 December 2016.

———. "Paying It Forward: Heidi Cullinan's *Love Lessons* Series." Romance Novels for Feminists, 29 September 2015. romancenovelsforfeminists.blogspot.com/2015/09/paying-it -forward-heidi-cullinans-love.html. Accessed 28 December 2016.

———. "Romancing Beverly Cleary." Romance Novels for Feminists, 19 April 2016. roman cenovelsforfeminists.blogspot.com/2016/04/romancing-beverly-cleary.html. Accessed 28 December 2016.

———. "Slut Shaming, University Style: Sarina Bowen's *The Shameless Hour*." Romance Novels for Feminists, 12 May 2015. romancenovelsforfeminists.blogspot.com/2015/05/ slut-shaming-university-style-sarina.html. Accessed 28 December 2016.

———. "Surfacing the Sexist Assumptions Behind Revenge Porn: Robin York's *Deeper*." Romance Novels for Feminists, 25 February 2014. romancenovelsforfeminists.blogspot .com/2014/02/surfacing-sexist-assumptions-behind.html. Accessed 28 December 2016.

———. "What Do We Owe Our Exes? Elle Kennedy's *The Score*." Romance Novels for Feminists, 26 January 2016. romancenovelsforfeminists.blogspot.com/2016/01/what-do-we -owe-our-exes-elle-kennedys.html. Accessed 28 December 2016.

Inness, Sherrie. *Woman Warriors and Wonder Women in Popular Culture*. Philadelphia: University of Pennsylvania Press, 1998.

Irigaray, Luce. *Speculum of the Other Woman*. 1974. Trans. Gillian C. Gill. Ithaca, NY: Cornell University Press, 1985.

James, Kathryn. *Death, Gender and Sexuality in Contemporary Adolescent Literature*. New York: Routledge, 2009.

Jensen, Kelly. "Sex in YA Fiction, or 'Fifty Shades for Kids.'" *Book Riot*, 6 August 2013. bookriot.com/2013/08/06/sex-in-ya-fiction-or-fifty-shades-for-kids/. Accessed 16 February 2016.

Kelly, Deirdre M., and Shauna Pomerantz. "Mean, Wild, and Alienated: Girls and the State of Feminism in Popular Culture." *Girlhood Studies: An Interdisciplinary Journal* 2.1 (2009): 1–17.

Kertzer, Adrienne. *My Mother's Voice: Children, Literature, and the Holocaust*. Orchard Park, NY: Broadview, 2002.

Keyser, Elizabeth. *Whispers in the Dark: The Fiction of Louisa May Alcott*. Knoxville: University of Tennessee Press, 1995.

Kidd, Kenneth. "Introduction: Lesbian/Gay Literature for Children and Young Adults." *Children's Literature Association Quarterly* 23.3 (1998): 114–19.

———. *Making American Boys: Boyology and the Feral Tale*. Minneapolis: University of Minnesota Press, 2004.

King, Ynestra. "The Ecology of Feminism and the Feminism of Ecology." *Healing the Wounds: The Promise of Ecofeminism*. Ed. Judith Plant. Philadelphia: New Society, 1989. 18–28.

Kokkola, Lydia. *Fictions of Adolescent Carnality: Sexy Sinners and Delinquent Deviants*. Amsterdam: Benjamins, 2013.

Kristeva, Julia. *Powers of Horror: An Essay on Abjection*. Trans. Leon S. Roudiez. New York: Columbia University Press, 1982.

Kunkel, Benjamin. "Dystopia and the End of Politics." *Dissent*, Fall 2008. dissentmagazine .org/article/dystopia-and-the-end-of-politics. Accessed 7 June 2015.

Lamarque, Peter. *Fictional Points of View*. Ithaca: Cornell University Press, 1996.

Latham, Don. "'Manly-Hearted Women': Gender Variants in Louise Erdrich's Birchbark House Books." *Children's Literature* 40 (2012): 131–50.

———. "Melinda's Closet: Trauma and the Queer Subtext of Laurie Halse Anderson's *Speak*." *Children's Literature Association Quarterly* 31.4 (2006): 369–82.

Lavelle, Moira. "The Fire Last Time: The 1990s Wave of 145 Church Burnings." PRI's The World. pri.org/stories/2015-07-02/fire-last-time-1990s-wave-145-church-burnings-map. Accessed 5 June 2016.

Lehner, Brooklynn. Why Is There a Demon in the House?: Reading and Fetishizing Bad Mothers. Dissertation, Illinois State University, 2013.

Lehr, Susan. *Beauty, Brains, and Brawn: The Construction of Gender in Children's Literature*. New York: Heinemann, 2001.

Lerner, Richard M., and Laurence Steinberg. *Handbook of Adolescent Psychology*, 2nd ed. Hoboken, NJ: Wiley, 2004.

Longhurst, Robyn. "Geography and Gender: A 'Critical Time'?" *Progress in Human Geography* 26.4 (2002): 544–52.

Lynch, Kevin. *The Image of the* City. Cambridge, MA: MIT Press, 1960.

Mackey, Margaret. *One Child Reading: My Auto-Bibliography*. Alberta: University of Alberta Press, 2016.

Mallan, Kerry. *Gender Dilemmas in Children's Fiction*. New York: Palgrave, 2009.

——. "On Secrets, Lies, and Fiction: Girls Learning the Art of Survival." *Girls, Texts, Cultures*. Eds. Clare Bradford and Mavis Reimer. Waterloo: Wilfred Laurier University Press, 2015. 36–52.

——. *Secrets, Lies, and Children's Fiction*. New York: Palgrave, 2013.

Mallon, Ron. "'Race': Normative, Not Metaphysical or Semantic." *Ethics* 116.3 (2006): 525–51.

Marshall, Elizabeth. "Consuming Girlhood: Young Women, Femininities, and American Girl." *Girlhood Studies* 2.1 (2009): 94–111.

——. "Marketing American Girlhood." *Rethinking Schools* 23.2 (2008): 16–19.

——. "Schooling Ophelia: Hysteria, Memory, and Adolescent Femininity." *Gender and Education* 19.6 (2007): 707–28.

——. "Stripping for the Wolf: Rethinking Representations of Gender and Sexuality in Children's Literature." *Reading Research Quarterly* 39.3 (2004): 256–70.

Martin, Michelle H. *Brown Gold: Milestones of African American Children's Picture Books, 1845–2002*. New York: Routledge, 2004.

——. Personal discussion. 9 June 2015. Richmond, VA.

Massey, Doreen. *Space, Place, and Gender*. Minneapolis: University of Minnesota Press, 1994.

McCallum, Robyn. *Ideologies of Identity in Adolescent Fiction: The Dialogic Construction of Subjectivity*. New York: Routledge, 1999.

McCulloch, Fiona. "'No Longer Just Human': The Posthuman Child in Beth Revis's *Across the Universe* Trilogy." *Children's Literature Association Quarterly* 41.1 (2016): 74–92.

McDonald, Brian. "The Final Word on Entertainment: Mimetic and Monstrous Art in *The Hunger Games*." *The Hunger Games and Philosophy: A Critique of Pure Treason*. Eds. George A. Dunn and Nicolas Michaud. Hoboken, NJ: Wiley, 2012. 8–25.

McDowell, Linda. *Gender, Identity, and Place: Understanding Feminist Geographies*. Minneapolis: University of Minnesota Press, 1999.

McGillis, Roderick. *Voices of the Other: Children's Literature and the Postcolonial Context*. New York: Routledge, 2000.

McRobbie, Angela. *The Aftermath of Feminism: Gender, Culture and Social Change*. London: Sage, 2009.

Meeusen, Meghann. "Hungering for the Middle Ground: Binaries of Self in Young Adult Dystopia." *The Politics of Panem*. Ed. Sean P. Connors. Boston: Sense, 2014. 45–61.

Miller, Rose. "Cognitive Perspectives within the Australian EcoGothic." 2nd Cambridge Symposium on Cognitive Approaches to Children's Literature, Cambridge University. 11 March 2016.

Mitchell, Jennifer. "'A Mom-Shaped Hole': Psychoanalysis and the Dystopian Maternal." *Mothers in Children's and Young Adult Literature*. Eds. Lisa Rowe Fraustino and Karen Coats. Jackson: University Press of Mississippi, 2016. 233–49.

Moran, Mary Jeanette. "Making a Difference: Ethical Recognition through Otherness in Madeleine L'Engle's Fiction." *Ethics and Children's Literature*. Ed. Claudia Mills. Burlington, VT: Ashgate, 2014. 75–88.

——. "'The Mother Was the Mother, Even When She Wasn't': Maternal Care Ethics and Children's Fantasy." *Mothers in Children's and Young Adult Literature*. Eds. Lisa Rowe Fraustino and Karen Coats. Jackson: University Press of Mississippi, 2016. 182–97.

————. "'Use Your Head, Judy Girl': Relationships, Writing, and an Ethic of Care in the Judy Bolton Mysteries." *Clues: A Journal of Detection* 27.1 (2009): 22–32.

Moss, Anita. "Feminist Criticism and the Study of Children's Literature." *Children's Literature Association Quarterly* 7.4 (1982): 3–22.

Myers, Mitzi. "Impeccable Governesses, Rational Dames, and Moral Mothers: Mary Wollstonecraft and the Female Tradition in Georgian Children's Books." *Children's Literature* 14 (1986): 31–59.

Nataraj, Lalitha. "Honoring the Feminist Trailblazers Who Inspire Us Today: The 2014 Amelia Bloomer Project." *The Hub: Your Connection to Teen Collections.* American Library Association. yalsa.ala.org/thehub/2014/03/06/honoring-the-feminist-trailblazers-who-inspire-us-today-the-2014-amelia-bloomer-project/. Accessed 28 December 2016.

Nelson, Claudia. *Boys Will Be Girls: The Feminine Ethic and British Children's Fiction, 1857–1917.* Rutgers: Rutgers University Press, 1991.

Nelson, Claudia, and Michelle H. Martin, eds. *Sex Education in Britain, Australia, and America, 1879–2000.* Basingstoke: Palgrave, 2004.

New, Caroline. "Feminism, Critical Realism and the Linguistic Turn." *Critical Realism: The Difference That It Makes.* Ed. Justin Cruickshank. New York: Routledge, 2003.

Nikolajeva, Maria. *Power, Voice, and Subjectivity in Literature for Young Readers.* New York: Routledge, 2009.

Noddings, Nel. *Caring: A Feminine Approach to Ethics and Moral Education,* 2nd ed. Berkeley: University of California Press, 2003.

Nodelman, Perry. "Children's Literature as Women's Writing." *Children's Literature Association Quarterly* 13.1 (1988): 31–34.

Pattee, Amy. *Reading the Adolescent Romance: Sweet Valley High and the Popular Young Adult Romance Novel.* London: Routledge, 2011.

Paul, Lissa. "Enigma Variations: What Feminist Theory Knows about Children's Literature." *Signal* (Sept. 1987): 186–201.

Pearce, Beth. Limitation, Subversion, and Agency: Gendered Spaces in the Works of Margaret Mahy, Cynthia Voigt, and Diana Wynne Jones. Dissertation, Illinois State University, 2014.

Pharr, Mary F., and Leisa A. Clark, eds. *Of Bread, Blood, and The Hunger Games: Critical Essays on the Suzanne Collins Trilogy.* Jefferson, NC: McFarland, 2012.

Pipher, Mary. *Reviving Ophelia: Saving the Selves of Adolescent Girls.* New York: Putnam, 1994.

Pomerantz, Shauna, and Rebecca Raby. "Reading Smart Girls: Post-Nerds in Post-Feminist Popular Culture." *Girls, Texts, Cultures.* Eds. Clare Bradford and Mavis Reimer. Waterloo: Wilfred Laurier University Press, 2015. 287–311.

Pratt, Annis. *Archetypal Patterns in Women's Fiction.* Bloomington: Indiana University Press, 1981.

Pugh, Tison. *Innocence, Heterosexuality, and the Queerness of Children's Literature.* New York: Routledge, 2011.

Rabinowitz, Rebecca. "Messy New Freedoms: Queer Theory and Children's Literature." *New Voices in Children's Literature Criticism.* Ed. Sebastian Chapleau. Litchfield: Pied Piper, 2004. 19–28.

Reynolds, Kimberley. *Girls Only: Gender and Popular Children's Fiction in Britain, 1880–1910.* Philadelphia: Temple University Press, 1990.

———. *Radical Children's Literature: Future Visions and Aesthetic Transformations in Juvenile Fiction.* Houndsmill: Palgrave, 2007.

Rich, Adrienne. *Of Woman Born: Motherhood as Experience and Institution.* New York: Norton, 1976.

Rowell, Rainbow. "Tweet Message." 12 November 2014, 5:38 p.m. Tweet.

Rubenstein, Carin, and Phillip Shaver. *In Search of Intimacy.* New York: Delacorte, 1974.

Sambell, Kay. "Presenting the Case for Social Change: The Creative Dilemma of Dystopian Writing for Children." *Utopian and Dystopian Writing for Young Adults.* Eds. Carrie Hintz and Elaine Ostry. New York: Routledge, 2003. 163–78.

Sawers, Naarah. "Capitalism's New Handmaiden: The Biotechnical World Negotiated through Children's Fiction." *Children's Literature in Education* 40.3 (2009): 169–79.

Sedgwick, Eve Kosofsky. *Between Men: English Literature and Male Homosocial Desire.* New York: Columbia University Press, 1985.

———. *Epistemology of the Closet.* Berkeley: University of California Press, 1990.

Sellers, John A., and Diane Roback. "'Looking for the Next Thing' at Bologna 2012." *Publisher's Weekly*, 22 March 2012. publishersweekly.com/pw/by-topic/childrens/childrens-industry-news/article/51170-looking-for-the-next-thing-at-bologna-2012.html. Accessed 8 July 2015.

Showalter, Elaine. *A Literature of Their Own.* Princeton: Princeton University Press, 1977.

Smith, Vicky. "Unmaking the White Default." *Kirkus*, 4 May 2016. kirkusreviews.com/features/unmaking-white-default/. Accessed 20 December 2016.

Spain, Daphne. *Gendered Spaces.* Chapel Hill, NC: University of North Carolina Press, 1992.

Stein, Katy. "'My Slippery Place': Female Masturbation in Young Adult Literature." *Children's Literature Association Quarterly* 37.4 (2012): 415–28.

Stephens, John. *Language and Ideology in Children's Fiction.* New York: Longman, 1992.

———. *Ways of Being Male: Representing Masculinities in Children's Literature and Film.* New York: Routledge, 2002.

Sutton, Roger. "Reviewing Race." *The Horn Book: Read Roger*, 11 April 2016. hbook.com/2016/04/blogs/read-roger/reviewing-race-2/. Accessed 20 December 2016.

Thiess, Derek. *Embodying Gender and Age in Speculative Fiction.* New York: Routledge, 2015.

Trites, Roberta Seelinger. *Disturbing the Universe: Power and Repression in Adolescent Literature.* Iowa City: University of Iowa Press, 2000.

———. "'Some Walks You Have to Take Alone': Ideology, Intertextuality, and the Fall of the Empire in The Hunger Games Trilogy." *The Politics of Panem.* Ed. Sean P. Connors. Amsterdam: Sense, 2014. 15–28.

———. *Waking Sleeping Beauty: Feminist Voices in Children's Novels.* Iowa City: University of Iowa Press, 1997.

Tuana, Nancy. Introduction. *Engendering Rationalities.* Eds. Nancy Tuana and Sandra Morgen. Albany: State University of New York Press, 2001. 1–20.

———. "Viscous Porosity: Witnessing Katrina." *Material Feminisms.* Eds. Stacy Alaimo and Susan Hekman. Bloomington: Indiana University Press, 2008. 188–213.

Vallone, Lynne. *Disciplines of Virtue: Girls Culture in the Eighteenth and Nineteenth Centuries.* New Haven: Yale University Press, 1995.

Walker, Alice. *In Search of Our Mother's Gardens: Womanist Prose*. New York: Harcourt, 1984.

Walker, Michelle Boulous. *Philosophy and the Maternal Body*. New York: Routledge, 1998.

Wannamaker, Annette. *Boys in Children's Literature and Popular Culture: Masculinity, Abjection, and the Fictional Child*. New York: Routledge, 2008.

Warner, Michael, ed. Introduction. *Fear of a Queer Planet: Queer Politics and Social Theory*. Minneapolis: University of Minnesota Press, 1993. vii–xxxi.

Warren, Karen J., ed. Introduction. *Ecofeminism: Women, Culture, Nature*. Bloomington: Indiana University Press, 1997. xi–xvi.

Watson, Emma. "Gender Equality Is Your Issue, Too." UN Women, 20 September 2014. unwomen.org/en/news/stories/2014/9/emma-watson-gender-equality-is-your-issue-too. Accessed 26 September 2016.

Weldy, Lance, and Thomas Crisp. "From Alice to Alana: Sexualities and Children's Cultures in the Twenty-First Century." *Children's Literature Association Quarterly* 37.4 (2012): 367–73.

Wezner, Kelley. "'Perhaps I Am Watching You Now': Panem's Panopticons." *Of Bread, Blood, and The Hunger Games*. Eds. Mary F. Pharr and Leisa A. Clark. Jefferson, NC: McFarland, 2012. 148–57.

Wickens, Corrine M. "Codes, Silences, and Homophobia: Challenging Normative Assumptions About Gender and Sexuality in Contemporary LGBTQ Young Adult Literature." *Children's Literature in Education* 42.2 (2011): 148–64.

Wiegman, Robyn. *American Anatomies: Theorizing Race and Gender*. Durham, NC: Duke University Press, 1995.

Wilkie-Stibbs, Christine. *The Féminine Subject in Children's Literature*. New York: Routledge, 2002.

Willits, Sally Miller Gearhart. "My Trip to Queer." *Journal of Homosexuality* 45.2–4 (2003): xxix–xxxviii.

Wood, Eleanor. "Pushing the Envelope: Exploring Sexuality in Teen Literature." *The Journal of Research on Libraries and Young Adults: The Official Research Journal of YALSA*, 2 November 2010. yalsa.ala.org/jrlya/2010/11/pushing-the-envelope-exploring-sexuality-in-teen-literature/. Accessed 16 February 2016.

Zipes, Jack. *Don't Bet on the Prince: Contemporary Feminist Fairy Tales in North America and England*. New York: Routledge, 1987.

———. "Foreword: Utopia, Dystopia, and the Quest for Hope." *Utopian and Dystopian Writing for Children and Young Adults*. Eds. Carrie Hintz and Elaine Ostry. New York: Routledge, 2003. ix–xi.

# INDEX

Abate, Michelle Ann, xv, 123, 141, 142, 190n

ability, xii, xxiii, 17, 25, 32, 33, 44, 57, 77, 161, 162–66, 169. *See also* disability

ableism, 43, 161

*Accidents of Nature*, 161. *See also* Johnson, Harriet McBryde

adolescence, as concept, xvi, xviii, 4, 5, 10, 14, 29, 32, 62, 71, 74, 83, 92–93, 123, 130, 132, 140, 147, 170–80, 189n; definition of, 187n. *See also* preadolescence

adolescent literature, 23, 31, 82–83, 97, 101, 121, 136, 140, 189n; definition of, 187n; scholarship of, xii–xvi, xvii, xxiii–xxiv, 7, 12, 15, 29–30, 57, 60–61, 72, 83, 85, 95, 120–24, 130–32, 136, 144, 155, 159–60, 167–69, 179, 181, 184–86, 189n, 190n. *See also* young adult (YA) literature

adolescents, xxii, 32, 34, 35, 74, 100, 119, 127, 132, 189n

*Adventures of Huckleberry Finn*, 56, 109, 188n. *See also* Twain, Mark

aetonormativity, 32, 35, 45–46, 49, 57

African Americans, 21, 31, 34, 36, 40, 44, 45, 47, 49, 51, 54–55, 56, 66, 73–74, 78, 189n; children's literature, xv; feminism, xiii. *See also* blackness

age, xii, xxiii, 32, 35, 38, 39–40, 42, 44–46, 49–50, 52, 53, 57, 60, 63, 71, 77, 100, 107, 120–21, 127, 132, 138, 140, 183

agency, xix, xx, xxv, 11, 12, 18, 20–26, 41, 47, 59, 62, 63, 66, 68, 71, 72, 76, 80, 83, 84, 86, 99, 100, 103, 108, 118, 119, 165, 176, 182, 188n, 189n

agender, xvi, 5, 100

agential realism, 12, 26

Alaimo, Stacy, xviii, 5, 156, 187n

Alcoff, Linda, 6, 10

Alcott, Louisa May, xiii

Althusser, Louis, 18, 188n

Altmann, Anna E., xiii

American Library Association (ALA), 190n

*Anatomy of a Boyfriend*, 131. *See also* Snadowsky, Daria

Anderson, Elizabeth, 15–16

Anderson, M. T., 61

apocalyptic fiction, 62, 83, 84, 87, 93, 96–99. *See also* post-apocalyptic fiction

Aristotle, 86

Asch, Adrienne, xxi

Asian Americans, 111–12, 113. *See also* Korean Americans

Attebery, Brian, xiv

Barad, Karen, 7, 8–12, 17, 21, 22, 24, 29, 33, 40, 59, 108, 156, 185, 188n, 189n

Barclay, Bridgitte, 17, 188n

Barrie, J. M., 168

Basu, Balaka, xvi

*Beauty Queens*, 5, 17–29, 34, 188n. *See also* Bray, Libba

Beauvoir, Simone de, 10

*becoming*, 5, 11, 17–25, 27, 35, 41, 43, 53–58, 66, 67, 70, 77, 113, 132–33, 136, 137, 139, 142–43, 145, 165, 166, 188n; definition of, 12–13, 29, 30

*Becoming Naomi León*, 35, 39–44, 57. *See also* Ryan, Pam Muñoz